The Great Land

The Great Land

by BOOTON HERNDON

Weybright and Talley
New York

THE GREAT LAND

LIBRARY OF CONGRESS CATALOG CARD NUMBER: 70-131567

MANUFACTURED IN THE UNITED STATES OF AMERICA

VAN REES PRESS • NEW YORK

Sun, moon and stars give answer; shall we
    not staunchly stand,
Even as now, forever, wards of the wilder   20
    strand,
Sentinels of the stillness, lords of the
    last, lone land?

"The Pines"
Robert W. Service
1905

To those sentinels of the stillness, the Alaskans—Aleut, Eskimo and Indian, pioneer and Cheechako—with the firm belief that in sharing the bounties of their beloved state with their fellow men they will eternally conserve vast areas of its wild beauty for all species.

The Great Land

Chapter I

ONE hazy-blue day in late summer, after the first frost had turned the vivid colors of the Arctic tundra to a soft heather, a big gray grizzly came shambling along the braided channels of the Sagavanirktok River, shoulders rolling and hips swinging. Though the eight-foot monster, biggest carnivore in the Western Hemisphere, appeared to be out for a stroll, he was actually hard at work, prospecting. Suddenly, his myopic eyes registered a quick movement on the blurred landscape. Now he could call on his acuter senses. As he moved swiftly but quietly to the small hummock, his sensitive ears caught the rustle of escaping feet. The superb equipment of his long nostrils augmented his hopes: the scent was fresh. Somewhere inside that surface structure was his daily bread—a plump, tasty ground squirrel.

The bear put his heavy equipment into operation; clawed paws at the end of heavy muscles started excavating. From time to time he stopped, sniffed, and resumed digging. And then he found his reward. The big fellow chomped, wiped his jaws, and sat down.

Such an event happens every day in the pleasant Arctic summer. This one, however, had a large audience composed of men engaged in the same basic complex of operations. For not a hundred yards away, on a gravel platform, stood a drilling rig. Its location on that precise spot had come about through much the same series of processes the grizzly had used, though where one bear had spent only a matter of an hour or so in a nearsighted search for a surface mound, many men had devoted decades to seeking a similar structure thousands of feet be-

1

neath the thin layer of vegetation covering the permanently frozen substrata. Geologists, in many ways as myopic as the bear, had covered the area by canoe in the summer, helicopter in the winter, looking for indications that further investigation might be warranted. Then had come the seismic crews, listening with electronic ears to the sound waves penetrating down through the sedimentary layers from small explosions set near the surface. From their maps and records and a background of accumulated knowledge had come the decision to put a million dollars' worth of muscle and equipment to work drilling a hole in the ground. Now a diamond-studded bit was grinding away through solid rock. From time to time the men on the surface would stop drilling, sniff and snuff in their own arcane ways, then resume.

The bear had been after a small quivering creature trapped in his own burrow; the men were after oil, trapped in its own sand. If they hit it, the impact of their discovery would add to that already making waves throughout the economy and the power politics of the world. The rig was located on the North Slope of Alaska, near a small indentation on the Arctic Coast called Prudhoe Bay . . .

Late that night, to get away from the smoky heated air of the bunkhouse, I opened up the refrigerator-type door, designed to keep the cold air out, not in, passed through the insulated air space to the heavy outer door, opened it, and walked out onto the gravel platform, eight feet thick, on which the rig complex was built. In just a few steps I was down on the squishy tundra —too thick to swim in, too thin to walk on, as a driller from the sand hills of Texas had described it. I stopped before the muck came over my boots. Though the ice was creeping inexorably out from the lake shores and a light sprinkling of snow dusted the peaks to the south, it was a pleasant night for September in the Arctic, windless and only a few degrees below freezing. I pushed back the hood of my parka and looked up at the stars. They flashed and coruscated in the thin, cold, unpolluted Arctic air; I had to look almost straight up to see the North Star, and the sword and belt of Orion were spraddled out on the southern horizon.

Though the diesel engines throbbed behind me, rotating the bit through rock formations thousands of feet beneath, the night seemed strangely still; by now the round-the-clock sounds of the rig had become so much a part of life that I'd have heard them only if they quit. The grizzly had either wandered off or was tucked in for the night. The men were busy on the rig, or whiling away the idle time in the airtight, almost soundproof bunkhouses. I was all alone, under the North Star.

In this tiny portion of the vast Arctic wilderness no one cared about the stars in the heavens or one man—or one bear—on the surface of the tundra. What counted was underground, one mile, two miles, three miles down. Where I stood, some 200 million years ago there had been a warm and heavily populated sea. Little creatures, more of them than the stars in the sky, lived, died, and decayed in the balmy waters, each bequeathing, as sole proof of its existence, a tiny droplet of oil to a species yet unborn, man. Sediment drifted down over the eons, forming layers hundreds of feet thick totaling thousands of feet in all, and creating a sandstone crypt for all the little creatures that had lived there and all the oil they had left behind. To the north, to the east, to the west, and even behind me to the foothills in the south, stretched limitless strata of oil-bearing sands. Now the little droplets were measured by the barrel and by the billion, billions of barrels of crude petroleum. The whole Arctic basin was full of the stuff.

This seemingly worthless acreage, slush under the pale Arctic sun, concrete-hard under the winter nights when high noon is twilight, was now the center of attention in the worlds of finance, fuel, transportation, and the fast buck. "This is the biggest thing that's happened here in forty years!" an expert in petroleum securities had told me, and the *here* he had indicated with a sweeping wave of his hand was not the tundra but the financial district of New York; we had been sitting in his Wall

Street office at the time. His period of 40 years dated back to the last great American oil discovery, the East Texas Field in 1930.

In Houston and Dallas, Tulsa and Denver, New York and London, Montreal and Calgary, the oil people were counting up the billions already spent and scraping up the billions yet to be put into exploration for, and production and transportation of, the black gold. Managers of the big funds and investment trusts were buying thousands of shares of oil companies and related industries, and multimillionaires in New York townhouses and two-bit investors in small towns were adding up their paper profits.

The massive ice-breaking tanker *Manhattan* was crunching a trail in the Arctic ice in the first meaningful voyage through the Northwest Passage—a trip of as yet unrealized potential to the industrial complex of the Northern Hemisphere. Residents of Alaska were dreaming of private planes and heated pools— some had already become millionaires before the first barrel of oil had left the state. People were streaming in, with and without grubstakes, to look the situation over and take what was not already nailed down or pull the nails of what was. Even the natives, whose land had been turned over by one handful of white men to another, were awakening to the value of the birthright they had never knowingly relinquished in this desolate land of unique loveliness, that northernmost, westernmost, ignored-the-most area of fantastic beauty, of incomputable riches from sea and earth, the area its original inhabitants aptly called Alyeska, the Great Land.

The geographical limits of Alaska are in themselves hard to imagine. I once heard an Alaskan good-naturedly tell a Texan newcomer whose mouth was a little larger than his manners, "Listen, if you don't lay off Alaska we'll cut ourselves in two and then you'll only be the *third* largest state." And this is true; Alaska is indeed twice as big as Texas, with Arkansas left over. Most of us from the Lower 48 have no idea of the size of

Alaska; I think it's because map-makers have to reduce its scale to get it on one page of the Atlas.

Visualize a map of the United States. Superimpose the northern coastline of Alaska on the Minnesota Canadian border. The main hulk of Alaska will extend southward to Arkansas, taking in parts of the Dakotas and almost all of Nebraska and Kansas on the west, all of Minnesota, Iowa, and Missouri in the center, and Michigan and Illinois on the east. Its southeastern panhandle will run down to Florida and the Alaskan peninsula will cut a swath through Oklahoma and Texas, then swing through New Mexico and Arizona and all the way up to San Francisco.

People who make telephone calls between Alaska and New York usually say there's five hours' difference, and they're right in a way; from Alaska, to reach anybody on the East Coast before he goes to lunch at noon you've got to put in a call before 7 A.M.; from New York, if you want to catch someone when he first gets in his office at 9 in the morning you've got to cool your heels until 2 in the afternoon. But it is five hours only if you're calling one broad strip in central Alaska that contains its two main cities, Anchorage and Fairbanks, and extends northward to the area of oil exploration on the Arctic Ocean. Alaska actually encompasses four time zones. It really should include five, and two days, but the international dateline has been bent to avoid that much confusion. Even so, reaching over the 180th parallel, Alaska contains both the westernmost and the easternmost parts of the United States.

It's hard for the people in the rest of the United States, or the world for that matter, to visualize life in Alaska. Its two major chroniclers, Robert W. Service and Jack London, emphasized the harsh winters, rugged landscape, dogsleds, and the aurora borealis, which, contrary to legend, does not go snap, crackle, and pop. I never heard it make a sound, and, according to the meteorologists who have studied it, neither has anybody else.

"The Cremation of Sam McGee" and *The Call of the Wild* notwithstanding, all of Alaska is not always cold; it has several climates. In the barren north, the weather is cold and dry; in the southeast, once the most populous area, where Juneau and the original capital, Sitka, are located, it's mild and wet. It rains almost daily—over 100 inches a year—and it's hard to stand up when the wind is blowing, as it usually is. Two more Alaska climates and two-thirds of the total population of Alaska —and a much larger percentage of the non-native people—lie along the north-south strip of the state's only railroad. It runs from Seward on the central southern coast, through Anchorage, which began as a tent city for railroad construction workers, and then through the Alaska Range to Fairbanks, 470 miles in all.

Anchorage, with a population approaching 50,000 in a trad-ing area of 125,000, is the largest city by far in Alaska, and a crossroad city of the world. It's the halfway refueling point between Europe, New York, and Tokyo. Most of the big inter-national airlines stop there; Japan Airlines alone has 45 flights a month. No other point in the world has non-stop flights to the world's three largest cities, New York, London, and Tokyo. It's the only airport I know of where you can legally hunt moose with a bow and arrow; one day in January, 1970, a BOAC 707 on the London-Tokyo route had to circle the airport for an hour until the people below could shoo a moose off the runway.

Warmed by the Japan current, Anchorage is misty and com-paratively mild. The city was barely saved from embarrassing situations on three occasions in the winter of 1969–1970; be-lated snowfalls just did make possible a white Christmas and cover for the big snowmobile and dogsled races.

Some 350 miles north of Anchorage across the Alaska Range is Fairbanks, Alaska's second largest city with 15,000 people in a borough of 46,000. (Juneau, the bypassed state capital, has a population of less than 7000 and is unreachable by land from anywhere. You either take a boat or hope that the wind dies down long enough for the pilot to land your plane.) Fairbanks, like Anchorage, is booming; the two cities are connected by nine jet flights daily. They're also connected by the Alaska Railroad, but for passenger travel the route is more picturesque than functional. The one train a day stops to pick up any hunter or cabin dweller who waves it down, and also to blow its horn at moose on the tracks. The moose frequently stands his ground and bellows right back, which makes for an interesting sonic duel but a lousy schedule.

The Alaska Range contains several towering peaks, including 20,320-foot Mt. McKinley, the highest mountain in North America. On a clear day you can see it from both Anchorage and Fairbanks. "The mountain's out," people say. The Alaska Range is a massive bulwark that holds back the moist air from the sea to the south, the dry air from the polar regions to the north. In summer you can walk out to your plane in Fairbanks in bright sunlight with the temperature in the 80s, cross over the range into clouds, and land at Anchorage in temperatures 20 degrees cooler. In winter you can take off from Anchorage at the mean temperature of 11 degrees, say, cross the Alaska Range, and land in Fairbanks an hour later in temperatures anywhere down to minus 60.

For all practical purposes these two cities mark the extremes in Alaska. They are different in many other respects, because Fairbanks is actually the frontier town that people in Anchorage would sometimes like you to think it is.

"Wild and wide are my borders," English poet Robert W. Service had the Great Land say. Those borders, which include a coastline longer than that of the entire continental United States, contain some of the earth's most spectacular scenery, and wildlife to feed and clothe its hunters and fishermen as well as to sate the most enthusiastic nature lovers. In all this space live 300,000 people, roughly the same number as the population of Akron, El Paso, Jersey City, or Miami, and more than half of them are clustered around Anchorage and Fairbanks. I have flown over this vast land for hours without seeing one sign of human habitation beneath; truly it is America's last frontier.

Nowhere in Alaska is the last frontier more demanding, more

challenging, than that area known as the North Slope, which
stretches northward from the sinister brown peaks of the Brooks
Range to the Arctic Ocean. Though it comprises only a tenth
of the state, all far above the Arctic Circle, the Slope is larger
than any state east of the Mississippi. In all this area, when the
1970s began, the only town worthy of the name was the Eskimo
village of Barrow. There was no road longer than a dozen miles
or so, and not one mile of paved highway.

During its short summer the North Slope is a desert swamp
containing uncounted thousands of lakes and ponds; there's
little precipitation but what moisture does fall cannot soak into
the permanently frozen ground beneath and it just sits there.
In the winter it doesn't snow as much on the North Slope as it
does in Virginia, and yet you'd think you were in an almost con-
stant blizzard. The gales moving down from the polar region
pick up the light snowflakes, moistureless in the subzero air,
and move them from here to there and back again. One oil
drum will cause a drift 500 yards long, and so tightly packed
you can drive a tractor over it. The temperature drops down to
the minus 50s and 60s, and the almost ceaseless winds double
the discomfort and danger from the cold. Climatologists call it
the chill factor. At 40 below, a temperature man can normally
live with, a comparatively mild North Slope wind of 20 miles an
hour produces an effective equivalent of 95 below. Exposed
flesh freezes in 15 seconds, for the harder the wind is blowing,
the more cold air goes past the tip of your nose. If you don't
want to lose it you'd better cover it up. The North Slope is a
good place to quit smoking. Your nose runs so much it puts out
your cigarette.

Surely this inhospitable land would be one place on the surface of the globe that industrial man could leave alone in its
own strange and untouched beauty. It has not been uninhabited;
for several thousand years a strong and self-sufficient but cheer-
fully gregarious people have lived in delicate harmony with
the harsh but bounteous environment. They have made their
homes in sod huts, in tents of caribou hide, or even in igloos

made of ice, warmed by fires of seal oil and the finger-thick branches of the squat bushes called willows. They eat the rich blubber of the seal and walrus, fish from the streams and ocean, and meat from the vast herds of caribou that still roam the tundra as once bison roamed the Great Plains. They have killed for food, not for fun, and haven't wasted a sinew. They clothe themselves in double thickness of hides, fur turned both inside and outside, and sole their caribou leggings with sealskin, softened in urine, cut to shape, and crimped with bites from the strong jaws of the women. They have governed themselves well, and between hunting expeditions far out on the ice, for seal, walrus, whale, and even polar bear, these cheerful and gregarious people enjoy each other's company.

This is no place for the white man. He isn't geared to it. Things don't work right. In the strange phenomenon called a whiteout—white sky, white fog, white snow combined—you have no point of reference and you don't know which way you're going. Your compass points east. In this upside down world you get sunburned when there is no sun, and from below rather than from above, for the ultraviolet waves bounce off the snow. Yet, driving and aggressive, we not only go there but keep working even when conditions become abnormal. Eskimos, who don't go out when the temperature is 50 below, or if caught on the trail build a windbreak of packed snow and wait it out, see us stumble around in weather too cold for polar bears and think we're nuts. We're products of the age of steel, but in these extreme temperatures our finest alloys shatter under stress like a sheet of thin pond ice. Can you imagine a derrickman, a hundred feet up on the monkey board of a drilling rig, swaddled in cumbersome down coveralls, parka, hood, mask, and mittens that turn his hands to clubs, leaning out over nothing and attempting to fasten the jaws of the elevator around the top of a 90-foot length of drill pipe? Instead of the Eskimo's steaming igloo, all he has to back into is a three-sided shelter with a tiny heater known appropriately as a hot ass.

So what the hell was I doing there? Well, going to places and

finding out things that you and I are curious about is my business. I do it. Getting there wasn't easy. In the period after the
big strike, operations on the North Slope were surrounded not
only with snow but with secrecy. Journalists were not invited.

I began the campaign for permission in New York, with two
friends named Charles B. Eddy, Jr., and Neal Allen, both vice
presidents of the Chemical Bank, which has special interest in
oil investments. They became intrigued by my efforts to get
into the forbidden land. After some high-level operating, Neal
arranged for me to see the associate general counsel of Atlantic
Richfield Company, Thomas W. diZerega.

Though based in New York, diZerega's activities cover Alaska
and transcend legal affairs. Even with the Chemical's introduc-
tion, I was scared to death when I picked up the phone in my
home in Charlottesville, Virginia, to ask such an important
executive for an appointment. We'd been talking only a moment when he used the word "house" in some context or other.
Not many people pronounce it the way he did, and I do.

"My God, where are you from?" I asked.

"Ah'm from Aldie," he said. I was talking to another small-
town boy from Virginia.

Tom turned out to be young, pleasant, cooperative, and ex-
tremely knowledgeable about Alaska. We arranged to meet
there. In the meantime an old friend whom I met while writing
a book on the U.S. Jaycees, Senator Mike Gravel of Alaska, invited me to use his office in Anchorage, complete with Adelaide.
That's really the only name she needs, as everybody knows
Adelaide; she's the gateway to Alaska. In private life, however,
she is the wife of Charles Blomfield, a prominent Anchorage
architect from New Orleans via Notre Dame and Texas, and
the mother of his eight children. (They like to go out for breakfast en famille on Sunday morning: $40.)

Tom diZerega introduced me around the Anchorage Arco
office. Lee Wilson, production and drilling superintendent, made
the arrangements for me to go to the North Slope. I would be
headquartered at the Prudhoe Bay base camp and visit a well,

Nora Federal No. 1, Arco was drilling with Home Oil Company of Canada. We were meticulous in setting up the ground rules. Nora was on tight-hole status, and I was to ask no questions about the well and honor-bound to forget anything I heard. But if through ignorance I did ask a sensitive question, I was to be gently informed to that effect, not thrown to the wolves. This was passed along in advance all down the line through the scrambler telephone connection Lee had with the Slope operations. (The one man who didn't get the word was the Home engineer, Ray Paschke, who is built like a big oil drum. Fortunately when he challenged me he was sitting on a top bunk with a tray of pastry on his lap, and I could talk faster than he could move.)

I made no deal in exchange for Arco's cooperation, which was great, but they don't have to worry. I just don't know anything bad to say about the company's operations in Alaska, and that goes for the other major companies, particularly British Petroleum and Humble, whose representatives I worked with there. From the top down, the oil people I talked to considered themselves lucky to be in the Great Land and wanted to help it get rich but stay beautiful.

The Eskimo has difficulty transporting his kill of caribou or walrus back home by snowmobile, dogsled, or hide-covered boat. Industrial man must ship thousands of tons of metal and other necessities over the surface. He has tried it in every conceivable way. In the 1940s a Government expedition used pack horses. Some got away. Years later an Eskimo was telling a visitor about a strange shaggy creature he had shot. The hide was serviceable, he said, and the meat tough but edible, but the remarkable thing was that the beast had metal feet.

In the 1950s and 1960s, hauling goods in over the frozen tundra from Fairbanks, across the ice of the Yukon and through the one negotiable pass in the Brooks Range, required two weeks of round-the-clock driving. The Cat train, as it's called, carries more fuel for the Caterpillar that pulls it and food and housing for the men who drive it than the payload itself. For heavy trucks roads were built of the obvious and ubiquitous material, snow, and rivers bridged with reinforced layers of ice. But these roads are serviceable only in winter. To come in by sea, whether from the west through the Bering Strait and around Point Barrow or from the east down the Mackenzie River in Canada, is a multimillion-dollar gamble against the unpredictable ice floes that move in from the north like a thousand-mile-long bulldozer.

That leaves the air. Long before there was any interest in the North Slope, Alaska was the flyingest place in the world. Over most of the state the stages of transportation skipped directly from dogsled to airplane; there are many areas the wheel still hasn't reached, for the bush pilots use skis in winter, pontoons in summer. In most of Alaska, remember, roads just don't exist. But although flying has won complete acceptance, it's not because airplanes are the safest way to travel; it's because they are the only way. Flying conditions are even more treacherous than other conditions in this unfathomable state. You fly with death in Alaska. You put it out of your mind, but it's there.

"Everybody in Alaska, everybody I know," a young woman whose husband flies his own small plane told me, "could name several good friends who've been killed in air accidents. But what do you expect us to do, walk?" She abruptly changed the subject.

Nevertheless I've never seen a man hesitate to step into a plane in Alaska, no matter what type it was, who was flying it, the destination, or weather conditions—and I've seen and flown in some beat-up looking planes in some atrocious weather.

What brings the white man to the land of the Eskimo, where the wind-driven snow obliterates the runways and strange atmospheric disturbances cut off all radio contact, where metal snaps like pine twigs and man becomes so fragile that even breathing can be dangerous, lest it freeze the lungs? The answer, of course, is oil, oil in such inestimable quantities that even the most enthusiastic optimist may someday be proved guilty of understatement.

Even figures based on proved reservoirs mean nothing today, because announcements of bigger finds may be released tomorrow. The first big strike, however, by Atlantic Richfield Company, followed almost immediately by British Petroleum, produced a flow of oil of such magnitude from an underground reservoir of such dimensions that the experts estimated the quantity in this one structure at Prudhoe Bay to be between five and ten billion barrels. Based on the lower figure, this is the largest field ever discovered in North America, and it is but one in a vast area whose limits will not be determined for years to come.

From the purely selfish domestic standpoint, the North Slope discovery guarantees another decade of oil consumption as we know it in the United States today. Some say there's a century's worth of oil up there. This news may make little impression on the average consumer, who assumes that the service attendant will fill his tank, his fuel oil distributor will make regular deliveries, his plane will take off with sufficient fuel to get him where he is going, and his country's tanks, war planes, rockets, and ships will continue to run, fly, or proceed. Others, who hope or believe that the internal combustion engine with its pollutant-laden flatulence is on its last wheels, couldn't care less about the scarcity of its fuel. The petroleum analysts, however, plotting the curve of increased energy consumption in the years to come, have been less complacent. Before the North Slope discovery, they saw rapidly decreasing reserves of crude petroleum —oil in the ground—in the United States. Natural gas was in even shorter supply. In short, the nation was running out. But with the Alaskan reserves, for a period running well into the 80s, perhaps into the next century, the United States and Canada will have oil and gas to burn. Furthermore the oil is "sweet"—low in sulphur.

Petroleum products comprise the largest part of the total energy market. Many electric power companies have switched from high-sulphur coal to oil or gas. Water power is not available everywhere, and atomic energy has a long way to go before it can provide even half of our power requirements economically and without danger of pollution. (Sometimes I wonder, incidentally, just where the people touting the electric car think its power is coming from. We already have sporadic brownouts in sections of the country where people want more electricity than is available. What would happen in the middle of July, say, when electric companies are already taxed to the utmost providing current for air conditioners, if a million owners of electric automobiles all plugged in their battery chargers at the same time?)

Petroleum furnishes much more than power. The petrochemical industry has grown remarkably since World War II. You don't only burn gasoline in your automobile engine; you also grip a petroleum-plastic steering wheel, sit on a petroleum-vinyl seat, put the petroleum-derived sole of your shoe on the accelerator, and the tires made from petroleum start rolling over the asphalt road. Most plastics are made from petroleum, and plastic encases your telephone, your television, and a good portion of everything you eat—which was probably grown with petroleum fertilizer. We wear clothes made of petroleum-derived fibers woven in petroleum-powered factories, shipped in petroleum-burning vehicles, sold in petroleum-heated or -cooled stores, and when we get them dirty, we wash them in a petroleum-derived detergent in a plastic encased washing machine.

Unless you walk, you can't get to a conservation club meeting to protest air pollution without petroleum; you can't even write me a letter accusing me of being a captive of the oil lobby without using paper from trees felled by power saws and treated with petroleum-derived chemicals, and if this gives you a headache, take an aspirin—it's petroleum, too. Some 2000 products are made from petroleum. Each of us in the United States uses 20 barrels a year.

Walter J. Levy, the world's leading petroleum economist, has stated that the enormous North Slope discovery has shifted the petroleum center of gravity from the Middle East to the Arctic. Those 300 billion barrels of petroleum reserves in the Middle East have caused nothing but trouble: the North African campaigns of World War II, the Suez crises, the Russian shipments of arms to the U.A.R., the French attempts to woo Libya with Mirage jet fighters in 1970, and American and British meddling in general, for example. There was an atmosphere of reserved elation in London following the BP strike in Alaska. "Now we can tell the bloody sheiks to go to hell," an oil executive said smugly over his whisky and soda, pronouncing the word "shakes," of course.

The course of action, or lack of it, in gunboat diplomacy in the Middle East is still conjecture, but events of comparable nature in the financial world have already happened; they're history. Alaskan oil has brought about the demise of one major American oil company, Sinclair, in the largest corporate acquisition in petroleum, has enabled British Petroleum to take over Standard of Ohio without firing a shot or putting up a farthing, and set the stage for the biggest auction in history.

On September 10, 1969, I sat in an auditorium in Anchorage and listened to responsible people bid a total of $1,400,000,000 for a few isolated chunks of the most worthless-looking land I ever saw. As the offers had to be accompanied by a 20 percent down payment in certified checks, there I was in a room with a quarter of a billion bucks. This money didn't buy title to or even rent the land; all the successful bidders got was the obligation to lease the oil rights for additional money, to spend more millions drilling holes in the land they did not own in the hopes of finding something underneath it, and to pay at least a 16 percent royalty if they did find anything and could get it to market. The world's biggest real estate deal involved land not even Eskimos would live on, and the successful bidders didn't purchase a square inch of it. This is high finance?

Most Alaskans, used to being caught up in history like a fishing boat in a williwaw, an Aleutian storm in which the wind blows straight up, take the newest boom in stride. Remnants of bonanza towns of Gold Rush days are still scattered around, some with inhabitants. In one of these on the lower Yukon, a bush pilot told me, live a total of five old sourdoughs. One was the madam of one of the largest whorehouses in Alaska. Trade slackened off many years ago, but she just likes to stay where once the action was.

During World War II Alaska was the scene of the only land battle fought in North America; the Japanese, aware of the strategic location of the Aleutian chain, occupied several islands before being chased out by wet and shivering GIs. In 1964, the strongest earthquake ever measured in North America wiped out several villages on the southern coast and almost wrecked Anchorage. The city rests on a platform of blue clay, and whole areas of it shook like jelly until it slid off its rock base into Cook Inlet. More than 130 people were killed throughout the shock area, many of them drowned by gigantic waves.

"It was a tragic event," an Alaskan woman told me, "But it did have one beneficial effect. All the pictures and newsreels showed that we do have a city here, not a cluster of igloos. We're defensive about that."

The Great Land is primarily a man's land. It's an area of promise and challenge for anyone willing to work, and paradise for those who like hunting, fishing, and the great outdoors.

"Alaska is like a beautiful woman," H. A. "Red" Boucher, the mayor of Fairbanks, said. Red, who put in 20 years in the Navy including service in the Pacific from Pearl Harbor to Okinawa, is not normally given to poetry. But we were reminiscing in his office late one night. "She has so many personalities, it's a tremendous challenge to be in love with her. Man, she'll give you the beautiful summers and sunsets, when just being alive with her is a joy and you can go out and fish some wild and lovely stream and *whap*, you got a strike, just like that. Then just when you think you've got her, all warm and pliant and cuddly, she'll drive the temperature down to sixty below and freeze your ass off. Oh, she's a bitch. She constantly tests you, to see if you really love her. Back in 1967, when we began taking those warm glorious days of sunshine around the clock for granted, she pulled the plug and sent a torrent of mud and water down on us. She'll shake the ground under you and knock your house down on your head. She's a real, living thing, she makes us identify with her. She's got so much to give, but you've got to love her, otherwise she'll chase you out of here."

Though it may be the husband's desire for the great open spaces and the challenge of opportunity that brings a family to Alaska, my wife, Bonnie—who says I never take her anywhere so I took her to Alaska—was told over and over again, in gracious homes and shoddy trailer camps, in small groups at lunch and large groups at meetings, and, of course, in beauty parlors and shops, that it is the wife who determines whether or not the family will stay. In the mobile society of America today, most wives adjust to a new community without too much difficulty. In Alaska the adjustment is harder. It's farther from home, living costs are higher, it's almost impossible to buy a home, much less hire somebody to help with the housework, the kids track in mud from the unpaved streets at break-up time in the spring, and not every woman thinks of the cold in terms of skiing and ice skating. Just about every family we talked to knew of men excited with existing or potentially meaningful careers who had been dragged back Outside by an unhappy wife.

Though it may be unfair to the more urbane community of Anchorage, the winter life of a Fairbanks housewife points up some of the difficulties of Alaskan living.

In Fairbanks Bonnie and I moved in with State Senator Edward A. Merdes, a dear friend from way back, and his wife, Norma, and their six children. Their winter morning ritual was intriguing. Ten or 15 minutes before Ed goes off to work and the kids go off to school, he starts the car to let it warm up. Heated garages are almost imperative in Fairbanks. Those who don't have them plug their cars into special receptacles. You'll notice a short length of electric cord hanging out of the hood over the front bumper. Plugged in, it provides current to one heater in the radiator, another under the battery, and a third inside the car. This last is not for comfort, but to protect the vinyl seat covering, which cracks at severe temperatures. When the car sits for a while, the tires flatten out and you bump for blocks.

While the car is warming up, Ed and Norma bundle up the children into layers of expensive clothing. Those under school age have to come along; they can't be left alone. Children who walk to school must be admonished not to run, lest they breathe too deeply and get ice in their lungs, but at the same time to keep moving, don't stop. Schools never close in Alaska, by the way. Snow and ice may snarl up traffic and keep the school buses from running in the Lower 48. For thousands of years in Alaska, however, far from impeding transportation, snow and ice have *provided* transportation. This is the only way dogsleds, and now snowmobiles, can get around. In the towns, snow smooths out the bumpy streets and at subzero temperatures you get excellent traction.

When the car is warm and the children are clothed, Norma, in down-filled parka, down-filled pants, and mukluks, goes to the garage door and opens it when Ed gives the signal. He backs out, she closes the door, and jumps into the car. They drive slowly, squinting through the ice fog, dropping off the children at school and Ed at the office. If Norma stops at the supermarket on her way home, she has to leave the engine running. For a long stop she has to find a car plug.

In the extreme cold mothers of small children practically imprison themselves. Just to go next door for a cup of coffee requires so much bother clothing the children for the weather that many women don't do it. The excitement of the holiday season keeps women going until January, but then the letdown sets in. Most suicides in Alaska occur between January and March. Some women turn to the bottle, others go Outside dragging their husbands with them. Most women get jobs as soon as the children are in school, both to augment the family income and to have something to do.

One morning I was chatting with the chambermaid, a pleasant woman in her 50s, in our small but $38 room in the Anchorage Westward. She commented that Anchorage was not ultra-fashionable. Curious why a woman who tossed around two-syllable Latin prefixes was cleaning bathrooms, I learned that the groceries for the dinner she cooked for her husband and two high school children averaged $12 a night.

To accommodate the working housewives, the supermarkets stay open until midnight during the week, 10 P.M. on Sundays.

Everything is expensive in Alaska. A house that costs $23,-000 in Seattle—and Seattle prices aren't cheap—costs $45,000 in Anchorage and $60,000 in Fairbanks. In an effort to beat the high cost, many men build their own; you see bank presidents hammering away on Sundays. Money is expensive, too. To get a $30,000 mortgage in 1970 you had to pay a service charge of about six percent, making the total borrowed $36,000, and the interest rate would be ten percent—if you could find someone to lend you the money in the first place.

And then there's heat. Ed Merdes was paying 31 cents a gallon for fuel oil in the winter of 1969–1970, exactly double what it cost me, with the January bill running close to $200. The preceding summer the first frost hit July 7, damaging some of Ed's 12-foot sunflowers; the furnace gets no vacation in Fairbanks. As water must run constantly through the city mains to keep from freezing, elaborate plumbing is required in each house, and water is expensive. So is electricity.

Winter clothing can cost $200 or $300 even for children. Food is out of sight. And a bottle of ordinary bourbon that cost $3.89 in Washington, D.C., cost $5.69 in Fairbanks—on sale.

With prices already high, some Alaskans see no boon in the oil boom. It can't help but raise them further. "These oil executives come in here acting like they're doing us a big favor," a man in Anchorage said. "As far as I'm concerned they can all go back where they came from and leave the oil in the ground.

Our schools are already on double shifts and they're bringing in more kids. We're gonna have to pay to educate them. These new people don't care about prices. Do you realize that they get hardship pay for living here? The big companies pay their executives forty-five percent extra on the first thousand dollars of salary, twenty-five percent after that. Take a guy with a base pay of twenty-five or thirty thousand dollars—figure it out yourself. He couldn't care less if my grocery bill goes up."

Skilled labor can make as much as a thousand a week on the Slope, and they come in from all over. I met Swiss, Norwegians, Germans, Poles, and Texans, Texans, Texans. One night in a bunkhouse I heard someone singing a song that sounded strangely familiar. The singer turned out to be a young Dutch geologist born in Bandung, educated in Utrecht, trained in London— and playing an Italian-made guitar and singing "Guantanamera" in Spanish.

A year after the big strike the pattern of growth was already obvious. Fairbanks was emerging as the transportation and service center for the North Slope; Anchorage was developing as the professional center with big office buildings springing up. Oil is one of the most sophisticated industries, requiring many forms of expertise, many ancillary operations. Even as a visitor I saw both cities changing, expanding, as new businesses moved in. In Anchorage my cab drivers were always getting lost taking me to new offices on new streets. In Fairbanks the *News-Miner* devoted a full centerfold of its weekly oil section to a map of the area around the airport. In addition to the big airlines and oil companies you'd expect to find there, there were also a dozen flying services, freight services, drilling companies, tool companies, mud companies, and geophysical companies. A friend of mine named Ed Parsons put all his savings into a couple of lots near the airport years ago when only a handful of people were sniffing around on the Slope; by the end of 1969 he was pulling in a total of $5000 a month rent from eight companies, most of them operating out of trailers.

Alaska has a sad history as a looted land. It began back in the eighteenth century with the Russians taking fur-bearing animals almost to the point of extinction; it continued as the Americans exploited salmon, lumber, gold, and copper. Today the looting is still being attempted, but in more subtle ways. The money men from the Lower 48 come in with attaché cases filled with prospectuses for financial deals. They'll buy practically any-thing—and they expect to make a profit on it.

The new riches of Alaska have coincided with, and given impetus to, a twentieth-century-style native uprising. The people who have lived in Alaska longer than anyone else have decided to legalize their original occupation of it. The Alaskan natives began pressing claims for land and money. Their action re-sulted in a freeze on the leasing of potential oil lands and de-layed the biggest private capital construction job ever planned, the Trans-Alaska Pipeline. It gave some hope to all the Indian population of America, and stimulated sympathy in those non-natives in all the states who know their ancestors gave the noble red man the shaft. What an easy way to atone for our forefathers' attempted genocide—give Alaska back to the Indians.

It's a wonder there are any natives left there to take it. The Russians began the slaughter in the Aleutian Islands about 300 years ago. Some Aleut conservationists, objecting to the Russian depletion of just about everything in fur, killed about 50 trap-pers and traders. The Russians retaliated by cutting down the Aleutian population from some 25,000 to about 4000.

The Alaskan natives had never bothered to claim their own land. In 1867 a handful of Russian soldiers officially handed it over to a handful of American soldiers. The natives weren't con-sulted. ("Maybe we should sell Siberia to America," an Eskimo said. "We don't own it, either.") The Americans extended the attempted Russian extermination of the Aleuts to all the Alaskan natives, the three separate ethnic groups of Aleuts, Eskimos, and Indians, though with more sophisticated means, chemical and germ warfare. The deadly chemical was alcohol; in southeast Alaska it was known as Hoochenoo. Smallpox and measles were the most efficient killers among the Tlingits and Haidas in the southeast. In the Eskimo country, along the western and northern coast, New England whalers borrowed girls from the villages, copulated with them in shifts around the clock, and sent those who survived back to their villages laden with gifts of bastards, syphilis, and respiratory diseases. By 1950 it was estimated that 95 percent of Eskimo children were infected with tuberculosis by the time they were 14. Emil Notti, a former president of the Alaska Federation of Natives, says he had an uncle who had 11 children, 10 of whom died of tuberculosis.

The missionaries came in and attempted to educate these nomadic hunters according to the principles of Western civilization. The Bureau of Indian Affairs attempted to suppress the native languages. I once asked a State Senator, a sharp young Eskimo named William T. Hensley who is one of the less than one percent of the entire native population who has a college degree, what his Eskimo name was. Apparently no one had ever asked him such an intimate question before, because he had to write it several times before he was satisfied. It came out Ighga-ghruk. "There is no written Eskimo language," he said. I later became friends with a young Eskimo from Greenland, however, who said that he had learned to read and write both his native tongue and Danish in his village school.

Native children go to one-room elementary schools in the villages. Hensley told me with great affection of his grade school teacher; she was a Negro woman from one of the southern states who inspired in him the will to learn through praise when it was deserved and a smack on the hand with a ruler when it was not.

The village child who wants more than a grade school education must leave home to get it. The Bureau of Indian Affairs provides an education for these children of the north in schools in southeast Alaska, Oregon, and, believe it or not, Oklahoma. It is heartbreaking to watch a group of 13- and 14-year-old children being herded out to their plane for a school year in the

Lower 48. (They may dream of a white Christmas but they sure won't be home for it.) You ought to hear Red Boucher, Fairbanks's tough, redheaded mayor, sound off on the subject of sending Alaskan children to Oklahoma. His voice breaks into a falsetto when he gets excited. "This is out of the *trees!*" he screams.

The Alaskan native, Aleut, Eskimo, or Indian, is lucky to live until he's 35, and that life is a disease-ridden, meager existence in a garbage-strewn ghetto in the middle of nowhere. Some come to the big city, Anchorage, but most of those I've seen there were either getting thrown out of, or were scratching to get back into, the bars around 4th and C. I don't know the Aleut and the Indian too well, as most of my travels in Alaska were in the oil country to the north, but the Eskimos I've known are friendly people with marvelous traits. Anyone who goes out into the Arctic Seas in boats made of walrus hide and brings back seal, whale, walrus, or even polar bear, has got to be both brave and dexterous. A BP geologist who has worked with native populations in the Middle East, Nigeria, Australia, and Papua was most impressed with the Eskimos, particularly their hand and eye coordination.

They are also consummate politicians and have in recent years begun to use the transportation and education furnished by the white man to unite against him. The result is the Alaska Federation of Natives. Its demands, for millions of acres of land, millions in cash, and a royalty on Alaskan oil in perpetuity, have caused turmoil in Alaska.

The great majority of non-native Alaskans today recognize that the natives have been ill used, and as hunters and fishermen themselves, they respect the native knowhow in doing their own thing. I found only a handful of Alaskans who did not put education for every child in the state at the top of the list of priorities for the future. They realize that this is a race in transition, changing from the primitive life of the hunter to the bill-paying life of the affluent society, and the transition is going to be tough.

But as the natives increased their demands I witnessed less empathy, more animosity in the bargaining. Getting legal help from the Outside put more willows on the fire. Nevertheless it seemed clear that if the price of getting those billions of gallons of oil out of Alaska was to treat an aborigine fairly for the first time in the history of mankind, then that price would be paid. In the 1970s, oil rules the world.

Oil has brought to Alaska over $900 million in one day's action and interest of more than $185,000 per day on that amount alone, and will bring incalculable royalties extending over an incalculable period of time. Applying the lesson of the Gold Rush, when the real dough was made by the services and suppliers, oil money may be only a portion of the whole. Alaska has got it made.

For millions of people throughout the world, the real question is not the financial condition of a comparatively small number of entrepreneurs but what happens when money meets one of the last great wilderness areas.

The Alaskan oil rush coincides exactly with an explosive concern over man's pollution of his own environment. The 1970s have been referred to as the ecological decade; one sociologist has predicted that it is the beginning of the period of the ethology ethic. Others, more pessimistic, say that it is the beginning of the end; we have inadvertently begun the inexorable process of ecocide, the murder of the environment. It's a little awesome to realize that one of the great conflicts in the history of mankind—the hunger for money and oil versus the world's need for land, water, and air—is taking place here.

It's fitting that the battlefield is the Great Land, for its very immensity provides the perfect setting for such a battle. To the victor will go the spoils, and that's the proper word. Will the prize be the preservation of a land of haunting beauty, of delicate fragility, of fascinating wildlife, or the generation of just another man-ravaged natural slum?

The damage potential extends far beyond Alaska. To take

one horripilating example, should a titantic tanker of the future split itself open on an iceberg and disgorge its oil on the Arctic, the heat absorption of the large dark surface could, within the realm of climatological conjecture, lead to the melting of a substantial portion of the Arctic ice cap and thereby raise the level of the oceans. Goodbye New York City.

I'm not usually shy about getting into fights, but before jumping into the controversy over Alaskan ecology, I happened to recall the words of one of America's homespun philosophers, Josh Billings, who said, "It is better to know nothing than to know what ain't so." I have some views of my own on ecology; I've coughed in the smog of the cities and stood choked with rage and frustration on my favorite river as the dead fish came floating by. But I also like the comfort and convenience made possible by the industrial utilization of natural resources. I've discussed the problem with scores of people considered knowledgeable in the field and have waded through piles of books and papers pertaining to the subject. From the quantity of misinformation, extravagant statements and contradictions, and ranting hostility, I've come up with the conclusion that a lot of the authorities writing with positive vehemence seem to know what ain't so. I don't want to join their company. The many interpretations of what should be basic scientific facts are confusing enough; the independent Alaskan attitude compounds them.

Alaskan nerves are rubbed raw by Outside criticism, and Alaskans sound off. Thomas E. Kelly, Commissioner of Natural Resources and a man of enormous power, could have been speaking for most of his fellows when he remarked, "I get damned sick of people who have never been to the North Slope prejudging everything." The Anchorage *Times*, by far the state's largest and most influential newspaper, made the following comment on his remarks:

"With a bit of reverence, despite his perhaps undiplomatic language, we say Amen.

"In the last year or so Alaska has had a bucketful of advice on how it should manage its affairs, most of it unsolicited and most of it from would-be experts who have never seen the country.

"We've been told everything from how to manage our wildlife to how to lease our land, and in the process lectured to as though we have never looked around to see the beauty of nature in the State in which we live.

"Mr. Kelly isn't the only one of us who is sick of the sermons from those who have failed elsewhere to manage their own affairs and now seek to pawn off their views on Alaska.

"Good for him."

If I went back to Alaska carrying the banner of the Wilderness Society or the Sierra Club, two of the groups most vociferous about the Alaskan ecology, I think I'd take an armed guard. Just to classify yourself as a conservationist raises the hackles of the Alaskans you meet. But I like to think that I can get along with people, and in long conversations on planes droning over the huge state, in bunkhouses on the North Slope and walks over the tundra, in bars, restaurants, and homes in Anchorage and Fairbanks, in offices in Alaska and in the Lower 48, I received some pretty clear, if conflicting, impressions of just what is going on up there. I have buttressed them with my own personal observations of the terrain itself and the operations thereon.

First of all, there is absolutely no question that during the first 30-odd years of exploration for oil on the North Slope terrible damage has been done to portions of the land. That's a fact that the most ardent advocate of exploiting the state's resources will not deny—if you approach him right. I was talking once with a man who has spent a quarter of a century as a consultant on the Slope and who knows it intimately and loves it. His bread and butter come from the big companies that hire him, and conservationist propaganda from the Outside irritates him. But we'd gotten to know and trust one another—which is why I'm not identifying him by name—and in the middle of a tirade against the Outside preservationists, he shot me a quick glance, grinned, lowered his voice, and said, "Of course, if it weren't for them we'd still be shitting in our own nests up there."

The conservationists, though often strident and in some cases misinformed, have caused many about-faces in the methods of operation on the Slope. Many changes, too, have been initiated by the operators themselves, some because of the watchdogs looking over their shoulders, and some because they can see the results of chewing up the countryside as well as anyone else. Just because a man is paid by an oil company doesn't mean that he wants to destroy his own country. Many oil corporation executives and Alaska state officials are conservation conscious and enforce with increasing rigor the practice of what they preach. The individual Alaskan, although he has become prejudiced against the epithet, is himself an ardent conservationist. He loves his land. He is grateful to it for providing him with the opportunity to hunt and fish, and the flesh of the caribou and the moose, the salmon and the rainbow, is a succulent dividend. With the prices of beef in Alaska, it's nice to have a few hundred pounds of moose in the freezer. Although he might gripe about the stringent game laws, if pressed he admits they are just in principle. He's dead serious about preserving game for his sons to hunt.

Two friends of mine went off on a three-day moose hunt. They made elaborate and expensive preparations and were flown in by a bush pilot to a remote lake. As soon as the pilot took off two bull moose appeared from different directions. Two shots, and each man had his moose. That's the limit: one hunter, one moose. They spent the three days until the plane came back watching the moose stroll by unharmed.

What I'm trying to say is that Alaskans in general—there are some greedy guts even in the Great Land, of course—have respect for the laws and reverence for the land. Many came from areas in the Lower 48 that have been ruined by exploitation and pollution. They want to keep what they came to find. They also know they couldn't sit on all that oil even if they wanted to.

The 1970s mark a new period in the exploitation of natural resources in Alaska, and the pressures are great. The effectiveness of conservation practices can be judged only by the generations to come, but I believe that they will still see vast areas of wild beauty in the Great Land.

One crisp, cold day I happened to notice the state flag waving in the wind. The golden stars that form the Big Dipper and Polaris on its royal blue background were dancing. Anything in that dipper was sure spilling out, I thought—and then a couplet from good old Service hit me. Says "The Law of the Yukon"—

> Of cities leaping to stature, of fame like
> a flag unfurled,
> As I pour the tide of my riches in the eager
> lap of the world.

Well, I don't think the Great Land is going to empty out all its goodies, and that's fine. It is not certain at this point in time that what does spill out will be of complete benefit to mankind. Maybe we'd exist a little longer on the earth we're wearing out if that oil stayed in the ground. But the people of Alaska are entitled to some of their immense wealth and what it will buy. Alaska has more to offer the world than just mineral wealth. It has the opportunity to profit from the mistakes of the past and to lead the way into the future.

Alaskans are making determined, sophisticated efforts to better their own living through modern technology while at the same time conserving their land, water, sky, and wildlife for the generations to come. Maybe they'll be successful, and maybe a world hell-bent for ecocide can learn from them before it's too late. Thanks to the Great Land, then, there may yet be meaning to the words of the prayer—World without end, Amen.

Chapter II

MANY ROADS TO PRUDHOE

As we were driving the four-door pickup over the rough gravel road along the beach at Prudhoe Bay, Leon Stokesbury, an Atlantic Richfield Company superintendent, waved his hand toward the sea and said, "You know, I've heard that the Arctic Ocean isn't salty."

I thought about that a minute. "Well hell," I said, "let's find out."

Leon stopped the truck. We solemnly got out, two men in parkas, plaid shirts, whipcord pants and boots, walked over the charcoal-gray beach to the calm green water, squatted, and dipped up a double handful of Arctic Ocean. Compared to the thick saline solution of the Gulf of Mexico on the Texas beaches, it tasted only a little bit salty.

"Wonder why that is," I said.

"Beats the hell out of me," Leon said. Having completed the experiment, we went back to the pickup. Low on the horizon behind it was the Arco complex of new buildings with a rig sticking up in the air. How did all this get to Prudhoe? Let me count the ways.

I myself had tried several of the ways to get to Prudhoe: by Fat Albert, the 737 jet that makes the run regularly, by a Twin Otter, the flying taxicab of the North Slope, piloted by a young Finn known as the Red Baron, by a couple of smaller planes and a brace of helicopters, by truck, and, finally, there was the day I'd come swooshing across the tundra in a Hovercraft, yaw-

ing and sliding at 50 miles an hour, to take the eight-foot embankment of the gravel airstrip at full speed.

Eskimos, early explorers, and the first wave of geologists had
come in over the sea ice and the frozen tundra by foot, dogsled,
the tracked military vehicle called the Weasel, and by Cat train—
one or more Caterpillar tractors pulling a string of huts on
runners called wanigans. They'd come in during the short summer by kayak, walrus boat, tug, and barge. They'd paddled in
collapsible canvas boats down the Sagavanirktok River, tossed
in the white waves of the rapids—Sagavanirktok means rushing
waters—then scraping bottom in the shallow channels as the
blue water made braids through the oyster-white rocks.

But all these were only the physical means of transportation
to this remote little bay on the Arctic coastline. What about the
missions of the men who had come here? The Eskimos had
come through in migrations eastward and on hunting and fishing expeditions. The early explorers had been seeking the Northwest Passage, or just what was where. The geologist had come
with picks and pocket transits and then with sophisticated ap-
paratus for divining oil.

More men had brought in hundreds of thousands of tons of
drilling equipment and the supplies to keep it and the crews
going. Behind them were the decision makers, executives who'd
put up millions in a crap-shoot gamble based on the recommendations of men who knew the odds.

The cautious and the faint-hearted had quit their exploration
on the North Slope years before. The confident and the brave
had persevered. And even then only a set of peculiar circum-
stances had come together to make Prudhoe possible. The whole
thing had almost never happened . . .

THE EARLY EXPLORERS

Parameters is a word geologists like to use when they're talking about extreme limits. It's a word that could be applied to
geologists themselves, because they're so wildly different, as

this persistently curious journalist who busted freshman geology found out.

One day I was talking with John A. Sweet, who is in charge of all Atlantic Richfield's Alaska explorations, in the rubble-strewn—rock samples, maps, reports—room he calls his office. Sweet wears wild bushy sideburns and is a Republican delegate to the state Assembly. I was trying to find out about the early search for oil on the North Slope, but Sweet made it plain he had no interest in past history.

About that time another geologist dropped in, handed Sweet something, and left. He was short and stocky, and he looked like a welterweight whose head had been beaten into his shoulders.

"That's Marvin Mangus," Sweet said. "He's been up here a long time. He might remember."

Later that day I called Mangus and learned that Sweet had just given him two hours to get his stuff together and get out. This doesn't happen to a man every day, not even to a geologist, but once I got to see him he forgot his current activities in his nostalgia for those early days on the Slope. His wife made coffee and the three of us talked for hours.

Mangus had graduated from Penn State and come to Alaska with the United States Geological Survey in 1947. By that time it was known that all of Northern Alaska, from the Brooks Range to the Arctic Ocean, a distance varying from 60 to 120 miles, and from Cape Lisburne on the west coast to the Canadian border, some 650 miles, was a great sedimentary basin. A few areas had been worked over, but most of the great expanse sloping down from the mountains to the sea remained a topographic mystery. Nobody really knew what was on the surface, much less what was underneath. Survey parties were sent out to map the area above ground and beneath.

Ah, those were the days. "You know the worst thing that happened to the Arctic?" Mangus said. "The alcohol thermometer. We had mercury thermometers. Mercury freezes at forty-two degrees below zero so we never knew how much colder it was. We just kept going, even when the Eskimos holed up. I remember we had a plastic bucket and one day the thing just turned to dust. Must have been minus sixty. And the wind. There was always wind. That made it even colder than it was."

Because the snow obscured the outcroppings of rock, the actual survey work was done during the short summer. But in the winter they had to get ready. Marvin was with several survey parties over the years whose mission it was to explore the rivers that started in the Brooks Range and flowed to the coast. As the three or four men in the party couldn't carry all the supplies needed for the duration of the trip, they had to cache them along the way. First they'd scout the route in a small plane, an old Cub or Bellanca, and find an expanse of ice long enough to land on—sometimes on a river but usually on a lake near the river. Landing on ice was no problem to the bush pilots. It was only a question of a place where the snow had blown clear.

From headquarters at Umiat—about the east-west center of the Slope and midway between the mountains and the ocean— Mangus would fly in with the pilot, low under the drifting fog in the twilight hours of the middle of the day. They'd land, unload supplies, lug them up on the frozen banks, mark the spot and return to the plane. Sometimes, when they couldn't get the plane close to shore, its skis would freeze to the ice before the men got back.

"Then we'd tie a rope to the tail of the plane. The pilot would pull back on the throttle, easy, and I'd stand back there jerking the rope on one side, then the other, trying to break it loose. When it broke loose I'd drop the rope and start running after the plane. I was mighty fast in those days."

If it took longer than a few minutes to cache the supplies they'd have to drain the oil to keep it from freezing in the engine. The minute it hit the ice it would freeze so hard they could walk on it. To get the plane started again they'd put smudge pots under the engine and cover the whole thing with canvas to keep the heat in. Bush pilots had been practicing that since the first planes were brought to Alaska in the 1920s; Lord knows how many of the old canvas jobs were burned up.

The supplies flown into the caches had to be carefully packed. For containers they used 55-gallon oil drums, so common on the Slope that they are known as Alaska State Flowers. The packing crews cut the tops off with torches, packed them up again, then put on clincher tops. This was the most important part of the process, because the drums had to be protected against the cleverest thieves in Alaska, the bears.

A bear is nature's greatest locksmith; he can open anything. On one occasion when the crimping tools wouldn't work, the mechanics secured the tops with nuts and bolts. The bears opened every drum. A lot of the food inside was in cans, but the bears were equipped with their own can openers, strong jaws and sharp teeth. Each can was mashed steamroller flat, but the teeth marks told what had happened to the contents.

Bears would save themselves a lot of trouble if they'd only learn to read labels; they'll go to just as much trouble with cylindrical objects like flashlights or cooking stoves as they will with a can of peaches. The only thing that seems to be safe from them is dried fruit. One time a family of bears got into a 700-pound cache and disposed of everything, including opening and draining the Coke bottles, but didn't touch a nice big package of dried apples.

In late May or June, with spring break-up, the bush pilots would take Mangus and his party as far up into the Brooks Range as they could find a gravel bar to land on. Then the men were on their own, but the living was easy. The caribou were starting to come back through the mountains, and Dall sheep would actually wander through the camp, or halfway through. I have yet to find an Alaskan who doesn't like to sink his teeth into a Dall sheep mutton chop.

The work was difficult but fun. Geologists are natural born rock chippers. They like to shinny up mountainsides, looking for different rock strata and chipping samples for the boys back in the laboratories. They hoped to establish a pattern. At Umiat, green oil with a reddish tinge dripped out of sands dating back as recently as 50 million years. In the Brooks Range, however, a massive upheaval had tipped the entire basin upward, exposing strata that extended right down to the basement, dating back 600 million years. Any oil in these strata had long since been squeezed out and disappeared. But that didn't matter. They were not looking for oil but for the types of rock that could contain oil, and the sequence in which they were laid down.

In the Brooks Range the whole awesome story of the earth is laid bare before your eyes, and if mystery fills you with dread, this is a fitting place to look for it. For these are the ugliest, most threatening mountains I have ever seen. The barren jagged peaks look as though a race of giants sprayed them carelessly with brown lacquer eons ago; rusty brown streaks of it remain. There is really no danger in the Brooks Range; I know that I'm a lot safer there than wading a trout stream in the beautiful Blue Ridge in company with the copperheads. Unless you're crazy enough to sting a grizzly with a bullet, corner a wolverine, or get in the way of a bull moose, the only dangerous animal in the Arctic is the pretty white fox. If one comes at you, slavering, look out. He's got rabies.

The brown crags of the Brooks Range give me the uncomfortable feeling that they're moving in on me, but to a geologist they're beautiful. They show the world as it once was, a mass of heavy, iron-laden rock. Pressure from the sides forced this entire region downward into what geologists call a geosyncline, which is simply one hell of a big depression. Then, the layers tell you, the rivers began pouring their sediments into the basin. Seas washed over it, receded, and returned. There were eras in which the seas were as warm as the Caribbean and filled with long-extinct tiny creatures, the manufacturers of petroleum. Why was this now-frozen part of the world once a sunny paradise? Who knows. Maybe it was once located in a tropic zone, and drifted here. Maybe the world was turned sideways then; the magnetic pole was once, after all, located near Hawaii. Geologists put forth these theories, but they don't all agree with one another.

As the seas receded, the trees began to grow. There were maples and sycamores. And finally, within comparatively recent times, another great upheaval came, forming the Brooks Range and upending all these layers so that geologists can get a good look at them. The glaciers, moving rivers of ice, scraped the mountainsides and gorges, and pushed big boulders and little pebbles out across the Slope. The rivers still follow the glaciers' channels. Though the region is dry, with precipitation falling as snow and mist, in the early summer the melting ice fills the channels with rushing water, and provides transportation for man from the mountains to the sea.

In their trek into the mountains, survey parties carried collapsible boats that folded up into back packs. When the time came they opened up their packs, assembled their boats, and took off on a wild and hairy ride through the rapids, skirting massive boulders, shooting down long chutes, paddling furiously to avoid being tipped over into the icy water. The rivers carried them out of the shadow of the mountains into summer on the tundra.

Suddenly in June, the brown vegetation of the tundra explodes into a thousand colors. As though they know their lives will be short and they must live each multicolored moment, flowers bloom with a blazing intensity. Herds of caribou materialize, munching on beauty. The fat little ground squirrels the Eskimos call Sik-Sik, because of their whistle-like calls, pop out of their burrows. The tiny lemmings, following their strange biological cycle, appear, multiply, then disappear. The wolves gobble them up in the fat years, but seem to exist equally well in the lean. The birds, over a hundred species of them, come in to nest. One species commutes all the way to the Antarctic. The noisy bluejays and big ravens like to hang around camp.

When the flowers awaken, so do the mosquitoes and the gnats. They come in swarms, like black snowstorms. Today the workers on the Slope go through bottles of insect repellent as though it were whisky. In earlier days the only protection was a head net. The mosquitoes would pile up so thick on the net, trying to get at you, that you couldn't see out. Some little devils always managed to get through, and when you ate, they ate with you and on you. Some people swell up terribly. Others seem to develop an immunity. The survey parties always sought a gravel bar between two channels; the mosquitoes usually found them, but at least they had to work a little harder. Birds learned to follow the parties, and feasted on the mosquitoes trying to get in the tents. Sometimes the geologists would hear a moose let out a bellow of anguish and see him go charging into a lake. A cloud of mosquitoes would arise from the splash and buzz around impatiently until their meal emerged again.

On their downstream junket the parties stopped at bluffs to check the exposed layers of rock. When they came to their caches they would splash across the melted tundra to replenish their supplies. At intervals they would make their way still farther back from the rivers, exploring, checking. Later the Air Force flew over the Slope and mapped the region by means of aerial photographs.

The men were constantly on the lookout for oil seepages, of course, but more common was escaping gas. They could see bubbles breaking on the surface of the lake. Each party carried a supply of empty bottles and funnels. They would paddle out to the bubble, place the funnel and bottle over it, then cork it and take it back to headquarters for testing. Often the gas would test out to be methane. Strike a match to it, and it would give a little puff.

"We looked for gas seepages from the air, too," Mangus said. "You could see big ones in lakes. One was clearly visible from two thousand feet up. One geologist claimed that he had ignited it. We went out in a float plane and took a sample. It turned out to be pure nitrogen. He must have had a mighty powerful match. Another time I was flying over a lake when I saw what seemed to be a tremendous bubble. I had the pilot fly a circle around it and I kept my eyes glued to the spot. All of a sudden there was a splash, and a big loon came up and flew away. First time I saw a bubble fly."

It was getting late. Mangus had an early morning appointment with a new client. (It was to form his independent consulting firm that he had given notice to Arco; in that time of tight security the company wanted the break to be immediate.)

"Oh, that was a romantic period in Alaska," he mused. "In my life, too. But it's gone now, gone forever, like the days of Daniel Boone and Davy Crockett. All I can say now is that it was fun while it lasted."

Oil exploration, like oil formation, occurs in layers, and the earliest phases have disappeared back into mystery. We know that petroleum products have been used or abused for thousands of years. Pitch was used in the building of Babylon. When the snows of Mt. Ararat in the Taunus Mountains melted and flooded the plains, ingenious boatwrights used pitch to make their vessels watertight; one of them was named Noah. The natives of Alaska have also long used the pitch from oil seepages to waterproof their kayaks. They burned tar. But when did they, or any other race of man, first put petroleum products to work? Nobody knows.

Nor does anyone really know how petroleum itself first got started, or how it collected in convenient reservoirs. There are generally accepted theories, of course, but some geologists are still not convinced that oil is organic in origin. The migration of oil—how it moves about under the ground, in which direction, and how far—is another question geologists squabble over.

In spite of the lack of complete accord, let's assume that oil comes from creatures who lived in comfy conditions during different periods of time dating back hundreds of millions of years. About man's search for it underground we can be more positive; the time span is little more than a century. In Alaska it's less than that.

Forty years went by after the first well was dug in Pennsylvania in 1859, before a few oil entrepreneurs began drilling in Alaska. That first oil boom has been pretty well forgotten today, as it was the Gold Rush that produced the headlines—and $700,000,000. Churning around in the mud caused by some 150 inches of rainfall per year, prospectors drilled more than 30 shallow wells in the Katalla area on the south coast, and actually hit enough oil to justify a small refinery. On early maps, Katalla is shown in big letters while Anchorage, 200 miles to the west, does not appear at all. The refinery was turning out about 15 barrels of gasoline a day for the fishing boats in the area when it burned in 1933. That was the end of Katalla. Like many of the Gold Rush towns, when the pay dirt payed out, the town was abandoned.

Almost forgotten, along with the 154,000 barrels of oil produced by Katalla wells, has been the fact that they, along with the immense wealth in gold, salmon, and lumber, came within a whisper of winding up in the hands of the Russians. At 4 A.M. on March 30, 1867, Secretary of State William H. Seward signed a treaty agreeing to purchase Alaska for $7,200,000. The deal was prompted by gratitude; Russia, unlike Britain and France, had remained loyal to the Federal Government during the Civil War and the purchase of this unwanted territory was in the nature of a gift. The Senate was adjourning that day and it ratified the treaty with just one more vote than was necessary. Five months later, in an impressive ceremony witnessed by the entire Russian garrison of 100 troops and some 300 Americans there for the occasion, Alaska was turned over to the United States. It was a buy-now, pay-later transaction. The following year Congress was called upon to get up the money for the territory the United States had already taken possession of, and public, press, and Congressmen screamed that they were being robbed. Alaska was called Seward's Folly, an icehouse, a worthless desert, a land of savages in a climate unfit for civilized men. One Congressman said that anybody who would seek a home in those regions of perpetual snow would be insane, and another that the barren, unproductive region covered with ice and snow would never be populated by an enterprising people. The major factor in the eventual appropriation of the money was that America would embarrass its good friend, Russia, if it gave the icehouse back.

For years after the purchase Alaska just sat there. Until the discovery of gold in 1895, there were only about 300 white people in the entire territory, and nearly all of them were in Sitka. The Gold Rush changed that. Strikes were made all across Alaska, and men went where the gold was. (Women went where the men were.) As a boy, reading about the Gold Rush days, I gathered that it was all pretty hairy, but you really have to see Alaska to realize what man will do for gold. Going into the Klondike area from southern Alaska, the first barrier was the mountain range. If you made it over the pass—and many didn't—you could probably make the cross-country hike to the headwaters of the Yukon River in Canada without much difficulty. There you built a boat that would probably crack up and drown you in the vicious rapids above White Horse. If it didn't, you still had hundreds of miles to go across the lonely wilderness. If you wanted to take the easier but longer route, you could go by ship around the Alaska Peninsula to the west coast of Alaska, and then up the Yukon by riverboat or dogsled. Either way the main road was the Yukon, a twisting, many-channeled crescent that flows 1900 miles from its source near southeast Alaska up through Canada, across the state north of Fairbanks, then down south into the Bering Sea. Of all the poor miserable bastards who went to all this trouble and danger for the privilege of working like a dog to separate gold from rock, the one I empathize with is a fellow who landed on the beach at Nome, said the hell with going any farther, and started panning right there. Laziness can be rewarding; the gray sand was rich with gold.

While thousands of men were breaking their backs looking for gold, a few dozen were engaged in even more arduous activity just to map and measure the place. The ordeals of the recent explorers of the North Slope, like Marvin Mangus, are unpleasant enough; the hardships of their predecessors were fantastic. Some went into the jumbled mountains of the Brooks

Range in winter by dogsled, waited for spring break-up, then left the dogs behind and, in flimsy native canoes, rode the icy swollen rivers down through the boulder-strewn channels of long-departed glaciers. Others paddled up rivers on one side of the Range as far as they could go, then packed their food and canoes on their backs through the long steep passes to come down on the other side. All they brought out with them was information, for they were members of the U.S. Geological Survey, then as now an efficient and dedicated organization. "If all your country's governmental agencies were like the USGS," a British Petroleum executive told me, "you'd have no problems in America today. Come to think of it, I guess I could say the same thing for Britain."

Though geologists rarely get rich working for the Government, at least one left behind a legacy worth millions when converted. I met his stepson one night, a young fellow named Cliff Burglin who was pointed out to me as the sharpest and most trustworthy lease broker in Alaska. I had a couple of drinks with him, then later dropped around for a long talk. He has a messy office in one of the dreariest buildings in Fairbanks. When pushed, he admitted that well, yes, he was a millionaire, several times over, but that he didn't intend to let it interfere with his business. He'd really been lucky, he said, his stepfather had been a geologist . . .

"Who is he?" I asked politely.

"His name was Foran."

"Do you mean *William T. Foran?*" I asked, and he nodded proudly.

Foran's name is not widely known even in Alaska—he isn't even mentioned in the history written by Ernest Gruening, former Governor and Senator—but in the history of oil in Alaska he ranks number one. Just before World War I three areas, Elk Hills and Buena Vista Hills in California and Teapot Dome in Wyoming were set aside as naval petroleum reserves for the fleets of the future. Primarily because oil seepages had been reported, and no doubt because there was no other use for it anyway, in 1923 a chunk of northwest Alaska the size of Indiana was set aside and designated Naval Petroleum Reserve No. 4. Everybody in Alaska calls it Pet 4.

In the early 1920s, Foran led two survey parties into this area. On the second junket he surveyed a strip of the marshy coast south of Point Barrow, then proceeded up the meandering Kaolak River by canoe, waded through the mushy tundra exploring the numerous unnamed streams feeding into the Kaolak, then portaged south to the Utukok. Still carrying the canoe, he crossed through the broad stretch of the western portion of the Brooks Range near Thunder Mountain to the headwaters of the Noatak. From there it was all downhill, dodging the boulders to Kotzebue. Even his fellow geologists, used to slushing through clouds of mosquitoes and climbing mountains with canoes on their backs, paid him special tribute.

Twenty years later during World War II, the Joint Chiefs of Staff, afraid that the war might continue on for decades, began looking around for more domestic sources. Foran was placed in charge of oil exploration in Alaska and given two years to back a comprehensive report with recommendations. He had more than 20 geologists under him and he not only collated their data but went out into the field himself. One of his parties was led by an Eskimo guide to some oil seepages on the Colville River never before seen by a white man. Foran had to see it himself. One of Alaska's famous bush pilots, Sigurd Wien, took him there in a single-engine plane.

To you or me what Foran saw would just be a funny looking hill. To him it was an anticline. An anticline, which literally means against gravity, is a geological term for an underground hill, or structure. Imagine a bed with several heavy blankets on it. Compress the bottom layer to make a ridge, as nature once did, and if you look sharp you'll see the general outline on the counterpane. Known as surface geology, this is the simplest form of oil exploration. I know a wildcatter in Texas who has made millions of dollars out of the ability to see a raised place on the ground.

From the oil seepages throughout the entire area, Foran knew that he was in a sedimentary basin. From the oil dripping out of a cutaway bluff and polluting the Colville River, he knew that there were oil-bearing sands right at that spot. With thousands of feet of sedimentary layers pushing down from miles around, the oil in the sands would be pushed up into the anticline, and trapped there. Look on your map of Alaska about 80 miles up the Colville River, and you'll see the name Umiat. Foran put it there.

Six months ahead of schedule Foran returned to Washington and made his report to Secretary of the Navy James E. Forrestal and a bunch of top brass. He dramatically unrolled a huge cylinder of oilcloth on which potential petroleum areas in Alaska were outlined. He recommended that other more accessible regions be exploited immediately and that Pet 4 should be explored for the long war. President Roosevelt personally approved further exploration in Pet 4, and Foran was commissioned a Navy lieutenant and placed in charge. Setting up a permanent camp for a detachment of Seabees, geologists, and drillers at Barrow, northernmost point in the United States, required several months of logistics.

Meanwhile Foran had further geological studies to make at Umiat. The exposed bluff gave a good picture of the rock layers that were valuable to an understanding of the entire North Slope.

Foran's recommendations led to drilling operations at Umiat and a dozen other locations over Pet 4. By this time, naturally, the operation had grown too big for a mere lieutenant, and layer after layer of higher ranking officers were piled on top of him like geological periods. When the war ended the entire operation was turned over to a private contractor and Foran returned to civilian life as a geology professor. But the drilling went on. A total of 36 test wells were drilled, 11 at Umiat, and this was the only field that positively produced oil. A friend of mine who was with the contracting company still has some Umiat oil in vials sitting around his house. He uncapped one and handed it to me as though it were a 1945 Lafite Rothschild. It looked, felt, and smelled like plain old oil to me, but my friend said it was very unusual. "You can run a diesel engine with this just as it comes out of the ground," he said. "The wells are only about 1500 feet deep. You can stomp 'em in with high-heeled boots."

Estimates of the Umiat reservoir were placed from 70 to 100 million barrels. I'd like to have it in my backyard, but at Umiat in the 1940s that amount wasn't even worth stomping for.

Across the river from Umiat, Foran had determined the existence of another anticline, called Gubik. This field contains gas, up to 300 billion cubic feet of it. Inasmuch as the population of the area is composed mainly of lemmings, there wasn't much market for it then. Today the need for it is increasing.

Another promising-looking structure was found at Barrow, but as at Gubik, nothing came out of the holes but gas. A geologist familiar with Barrow told me that he is convinced that it was once an oil trap. "I think a meteor hit right on top of it and the oil escaped," he said, "but don't use my name. No point in both of us getting laughed out of town."

The only useful production of fossil fuel in the whole area was from the Barrow field. Its natural gas today heats the town and the modern laboratories of the Naval Arctic Research Institute. Barrow, one of the largest native towns in Alaska with over a thousand inhabitants, is pretty in winter when the snow is on the ground, but in summer it's a squalid nest of tarpaper shacks. Every few feet, along the dirt streets, you see a 55-gallon oil drum cut in half with slots cut in the sides. These support the one-inch pipe that delivers gas to the houses. Thanks to the $12 million spent on Pet 4, Barrow has the warmest Eskimos in the world.

THE BUSH PILOTS

When the Pet 4 exploration began in 1943, Barrow was one of a few small coastal villages served once a year by the Government ship *North Star*. In the summer one of the Wien brothers might fly a little Bellanca in from Fairbanks or Nome, but any connection with the world to the south was sporadic at best.

Alaskans love to throw statistics at you and in aviation the figures are particularly impressive. One out of every 20 Alaskans has a pilot's license, for example, and a fifth of all the float planes in the world are moored on Lake Hood at Anchorage. It could well be more, for there's a three-year waiting list. Alaskans revere their heroes, too, and many of them are fliers. Rarely in peacetime have so few men been of such direct service to so many.

Late one night, in his comfortable trailer near the airport at Fairbanks, I was talking with Ed Parsons, who is known throughout the native villages in the northern half of Alaska as the Great White Father. The sobriquet has two meanings. Ed is a tall skinny man in his late 60s, has white hair, and always wears a white shirt. He is also responsible for putting in a communications network and all-weather landing fields at villages throughout the north. Typical of the Arctic fliers, he never asked questions when asked to perform some vital service for the natives.

Ed and I had been talking about the dangers and hardships of flying in the Arctic, and I asked what kept him going. What was he trying to prove?

He grinned. "Well, for a long period there, I probably came as near enjoying a kingdom status as any man ever does," he said. "Not everybody with a lot of ego—and I've got plenty—gets to satisfy it. I did."

This proud and successful man, the Great White Father, had arrived in Alaska on the edge of a nervous breakdown. His expertise was really more in communications than in aviation. He had made the mistake, back home in Astoria, Oregon, of inventing cable television too soon. He had a working model serving television sets in his neighborhood on Thanksgiving Day, 1948, but he couldn't sell its practical application. He couldn't even patent it. After three years of frustration, he cracked, got in his plane, and started flying north. He wound up at Circle Hot Springs northeast of Fairbanks. Lolling in the soothing waters just below the Arctic Circle, Ed decided to make a completely new life for himself in Alaska.

His timing was perfect. Arctic aviation was ready for him. One airline, with a half-dozen small planes and a handful of bush pilots, covered the entire northern half of the state. But its landing fields were lakes and rivers, serviceable only when they were frozen hard or not frozen at all, and as for communications, most of the time they just didn't exist. Parsons, refreshed and invigorated, took on the challenge of the Arctic. He went to work for Wien Airlines.

The name Wien, particularly in the northern part of the state, is legendary. Noel Wien, the first of the four Minnesota farm boys to make flying history in the north, arrived in Fairbanks in 1924. He had an old World War I training plane known as a JN-1, or Jenny. One of his first trips was also the first across the Arctic Circle. On the way back he met a wind stronger than Jenny and landed out of gas on a sandbar 40 miles from the nearest village. It was in the spring right after break-up. He waded through the mush, built rafts to cross the swollen rivers, and took three days to make the 40 miles.

The Aviation, as it was called in those days, alleviated some of the hardship of the prospectors and trappers out in the bush, as well as helping the villagers. Most natives saw their first plane with awe. Joseph Lincoln, the Toksook Bay correspondent of the Fairbanks daily *News-Miner*, reported one incident. The *News-Miner* prints the dispatches of its native correspondents as it receives them, and this is the way it appeared:

> There was an old storie that I used to hear when I was a kid, when the air plane's started to apper. Well anyway at this certain village which I don't know there were men in the kasgik a place where men used to gather during the day time hours and while they were there telling stories some one hallord from outside airplane and sure enough every one came out running to see the plane.
>
> And there was one certain man that was so amazed that he

kept looking up and when that plane turned this man kept looking and started to walk and while he was walking he disappeared all of a sudden and sure enough he had fallen in the ditch and he came out of that ditch walking and still looking at the plane so finelay the plane landid and left after. And after it lefted one of the men askid this man if he had known what had happen'd to him at that time and he said no. So this man told hom that he had fallen in the ditch at the time of the plane and this man did not know that he had fallen. So I guess that's about all I can say for this month.

Flying in the Lower 48 in the days before navigational aids was complicated enough. Pilots flew contact, which mean they followed railroads and highways, rivers and known terrain features, from town to town. In Wien's territory there were no highways, no railroads, and only scattered villages. The rivers meander aimlessly, and there were no maps. Yet pilots, if they lived long enough, learned to find their way around. They spotted significant differences in each of the thousands of lakes and found ways of getting through the jumbled masses of mountains even when the clouds were lying right on top. I don't see how they were able to pick their way through the narrow canyons in their underpowered, overloaded little planes. It's still a hazardous operation.

Flying south through Windy Pass in the Alaska Range in a small plane, for example, we were bucking winds that had swept up unbroken from the Equator to pour through this one shallow break in the great mountain bulwark. The purpose of the flight was to inspect the terrain, and we had to fly low. The pass turns and twists, and other gorges feed into it. Sidewinds came at us from different angles and velocities, and we were caught in one vortex after another. The pilot knew the pass so well that I could see his knuckles tighten on the wheel even before we got knocked sideways by a cross current; he knew the precise second it would hit us. I wondered what it had been like for the early pilots snaking their way in old canvas World War I planes through the uncharted peaks of the Brooks Range.

Noel Wien learned his landmarks and brought his brothers, Ralph, Fritz, and Sigurd, up to join him and form Wien Alaska Airlines. Ralph was killed in a crash, Fritz remained a mechanic, Noel gave up commercial flying and sold his interest to Sig, and that left Sig Wien the king of the Arctic pilots. It was a good thing he was available for the exploration of Pet 4. Bill Foran gave Wien personal credit for saving months of time; aviation in general probably saved years. When the advance group first went in, for example, in three Navy DC-3s, Wien led the way in his little Bellanca. The big planes couldn't land on what passed for a runway at Barrow, but Wien scouted the ice floe off the coast and found a level place on the sea ice for them to set down. It was June, and the ice might move out at any moment; Wien flew almost around the clock for three days, ferrying men and equipment to shore. He had just finished his last load when the ice moved out.

When Foran went to inspect the Umiat anticline, Wien flew his party there. The only sandbar on the Colville suitable for landing was seven miles from the anticline. He circled the area again, and though it was late in the spring, he found a patch of snow on the north slope of a hill, right where Foran wanted to be. It took some delicate maneuvering to land on the incline, but Wien did it, and made six more trips before the snow wore out.

During the Pet 4 exploration years, Wien and his pilots developed the techniques of petroleum aviation. A constant frustration was the problem of radio communication. One minute a pilot would be talking with a ground station, the next moment everything would go dead. Radio waves don't behave properly in the Arctic, thanks in large part to the aurora borealis. The aurora is caused by sun spots, which go through major cycles of 11 years, minor cycles of 28 days. Scientists tracking guided missiles lose them in the aurora. Airlines lose track of their pilots. Pilots lose themselves. Sometimes peculiar activities within the earth's ionosphere just wipe out everything. Radio operators call this an outage, and consider it an outrage.

Before the Pet 4 exploration, pilots respected the meteorological and communications problems of Arctic flying and simply did not go up when conditions weren't right. But with hundreds of men working on Pet 4, there was always somebody breaking a leg, burning down a bunkhouse, or wanting a letter from home, and putting pressure on Wien to get a plane in. Ed Parsons came out of Circle Hot Springs, all recharged and ready to go, and set out to whip the radio waves into line.

Ed never came up with a solution to the entire problem. Sun spots are a formidable opponent and even the most sophisticated electronic gear often does not emit a peep during an outage on the Slope. But he was able to minimize many of the problems. He established over 100 radio stations throughout northern Alaska where none had been before, and won a successful battle with bureaucracy to increase the power of the key stations. Some of his early tricks were frowned upon by the authorities. During one outage, when long-range communications were impossible, a man was seriously injured at Barrow and needed immediate assistance. Several planes happened to be in the air at the time, and were close enough to each other so that the SOS could be relayed from one pilot to another in a line-of-sight, zigzag course back to Fairbanks.

By 1954 Wien Airlines had the only communications network in the Arctic. Scandanavian Airlines was interested in an over-the-pole flight from Europe to the Orient; the route would save thousands of miles. With the comparatively short-range piston planes of the period, however, and with no communications in the polar region, SAS had to proceed carefully. As no American airlines were interested in the polar route, the Federal Aviation Authority disclaimed any responsibility for establishing communications. The Scandanavians had a station on Spitsbergen Island on the other side of the pole, but it's a long way from there to Anchorage, the planned refueling point.

A special study group spent a year with Wien studying Arctic flying. Parsons, on behalf of Wien, improved the station at

Barrow and trained a group of Eskimo girls to operate it. For years this privately operated station handled all communications for all trans-polar flights; the Eskimo girls became known as the Angels of the Arctic.

The trans-polar airlines also studied the survival kit Parsons had developed and equipped their planes with kits just like it. Bush pilots had been carrying survival kits for years, but each one represented the individuality of its owner. Every pilot had a sleeping bag and emergency rations, but hardly any two agreed on a heat supply. Some carried stoves made from five-gallon oil cans.

Ed designed a small gasoline stove that would burn leaded gas taken from the airplane fuel tanks. He also designed a heater weighing less than two pounds that would warm the airplane engine. The ultimate test of his gadgets occurred one day when Noel Wien, the founder of the airline, made a dead stick landing on a frozen stream north of Fairbanks. In the crazy Arctic atmosphere his distress signal jumped over Fairbanks and was picked up in Juneau, more than 600 miles to the south. Word was sent back to Fairbanks, where Ed, with his special heater, was able to get his plane in the air within minutes. That same day Wien was back home, snug and warm.

With communications problems minimized, if not licked, Parsons set about finding a solution to another Arctic problem. With the hazardous flying conditions and strong winds, small planes were frequently running out of gas. Every pilot carried extra gas in the cockpit, but it was necessary to land to fill the tanks. A network of airstrips would not only make emergency landings easier, but if built near native villages would provide year-round air service to their inhabitants. But how could he get bulldozers in to build them? Parsons worked out a standard procedure. He would scout out a suitable landing place on a frozen river or lake, land, and mark it with panels made of plywood. Back in Fairbanks a crew would disassemble a bulldozer and load it on a twin-engine cargo plane, usually a C-46.

Though the last C-46 was built in 1943, the 30-year-old plane is the workhorse of Alaska. It has huge wheels that enable it to land on a rough surface, and has a comparatively large carrying capacity.

The plane would land on the area Ed had marked, and the villagers would come running out to help unload it. A Wien mechanic would show the villagers how to put the bulldozer back together again, and how to operate it. They'd start it up and run it off the ice onto dry ground near a gravel bar. One thing there's plenty of in Alaska is gravel. When the ground thawed, the newly taught native bulldozer operators would start at the source of gravel and extend the strip out from it. A strip adequate for twin-engine planes could be built in a few days. The bulldozers were war surplus, picked up cheap, and the one that built the airstrip would be left there to maintain it. Many a World War II bulldozer is still in operation in Alaska today, keeping the airstrip smooth.

Villagers were no longer dependent on dogsleds for supplies —Ed was present at the last run of the last dogsled mail route in Alaska—and the people were grateful. The Great White Father basked in their appreciation; once it saved his life.

One of the most dangerous Arctic hazards is known as blowing snow condition. Though the skies may be perfectly clear, the strong wind picks up the snow so that at ground level, you think you are in a blizzard. Inexperienced fliers look down, see the landmarks, and set down with a feeling of security that turns out to be utterly false. For in the blowing snow horizontal visibility turns out to be zero; you come down into a white blur. Ed, running low on gas one day, found a village with no difficulty, but he could tell that the blowing snow would obliterate the runway. He buzzed the town. The villagers, recognizing both the situation and the plane of the Great White Father, hastily got everybody out, including the children in the one-room school. They all formed a line on either side of the runway. Ed could see them from the air, pointed the nose of his plane directly between the two lines, and made a routine landing.

THE BULLDOG BRITISH

In a state filled with natural wonders and almost supernatural characters, one man stands out like a human Mt. McKinley at sunset. He gave me an excellent description of himself. I had asked him if he had ever had any trouble with tough guys in the bush. "Well, no," he said in his soft Irish accent. "It's never too difficult when you're six feet two with orange hair."

F. G. "Geoff" Larminie is an Irishman with a French Huguenot name who left a position as professor of zoology in Australia to be sent by British Petroleum in London to hunt for oil in Alaska. When he arrived in 1959, he was 32, with just two years of geological experience under his russet tweed jacket. To anyone familiar with the history of BP, the reason he was sent to Alaska is self-explanatory. A company official, flying over the Brooks Range, had looked down and remarked, "Why, they look just like the Zagros Mountains." It was north of the Zagros, in Iran, that the first BP geologists, working in temperatures that started at one hundred degrees at dawn and climbed steadily during the day, had spent seven years in a stubborn search before finally hitting oil in 1908. That strike started British Petroleum on its way to becoming the third largest company in the world outside the United States, and established a pattern of aggressive exploration unequaled by any other oil company. Larminie brought with him to Alaska the traditional, plodding methodology of The Company, a 70-year-old procedure new to America.

"Our Company has always had field geologists, few in number but second to none," Larminie said proudly. (All the BP people I've met have a note of pride in their voices when they talk about The Company.) "We've always gone out in the field and done this form of work. Not done it in the office, not done it from photographs, not theorized over it, but gone out and mapped the thing. This is the classic mode of geological exploration and it's difficulty to decry it, because it works. There's a tendency among our American colleagues to feel that if they are not settled behind a desk with lots of people to do their work for them by the time they've reached their thirties they've somehow failed. Instead of dragging their feet around the curious places of the world, they fear that if they get out of the corporate womb and take off for these nasty places they're forgotten. This doesn't apply to the people who have contributed more than anybody else to the knowledge of this country, the United States Geological Survey geologists. They're cast in the mold we recognize. We have a most happy relationship with them."

BP has always been an exploration-minded company, for there is precious little crude in the British Isles. It already had an enormous share in the major fields in the Middle East, but the expulsion of The Company by Iran in 1951 stimulated even greater exploration efforts in other, more stable, parts of the world. Alaska was a natural place to look. It was known to have several sedimentary basins, and, of course, the Brooks Range looked like the Zagros Mountains. "We have a tendency toward the homologous rather than the analogous," Geoff explained, and I nodded wisely.

The USGS activity and the Pet 4 exploration had resulted in much information on the geology of the North Slope, but the difficulties in moving around in the summer when outcroppings were not obscured by snow had limited their operation. The Navy experimented with helicopters, but gave them up as too hazardous. Just north of Anaktuvuk Pass is Shainan Lake, a pretty blue monument to both the helicopter pilot who drowned in it and the end of American helicopter operations on the Slope.

Then BP came along. It had been using helicopters in all parts of the world, and had perfected the technique. In the winter Larminie explored the Slope in fixed-wing planes to find suitable campsites. Supplies, the bulk of which was fuel for the helicopter, were then flown in by C-46s, landing on frozen lakes. In late June, the geological party, consisting of a dozen

men, would fly in by float plane, and the helicopter would follow.

"We worked out a plan based on the range of the workhorse
of surface operations, the Bell G3B," Geoff said. "It has a range
of about thirty miles carrying a pilot and two men, or a pilot
and five hundred pounds of rock samples, depending on how
you split up the load. We'd take two men out in the morning,
dump them off, come back, take two more out, and so on. We
worked in overlapping circles of thirty-mile radius. We'd wander around in the mountains and get chased by bears. I shouldn't
say that, really. Nobody ever came to any harm.

"We had firearms in the camp, but we didn't carry them
with us. I found that most geologists didn't know what to do
with a gun anyway. At the beginning of the season I'd hand
a new man a .45 or a .357 Magnum and ask him to hit a gasoline can about twenty paces away. Bullets would go everywhere but into the target. That was usually enough to persuade
a man that there were better ways of handling bears. They have
three physical characteristics—very good hearing, very good
smell, and bloody awful eyesight. If the wind is wrong and the
bear can't smell you, he gets curious and comes trundling up to
see what on earth this blur is that's wandering around. At this
point he's only curious. But if he gets struck in the bung by a
.357 Magnum slug, he suddenly becomes a very committed
bear. It's wiser to get upwind where he can smell you, or, even
better, make a loud noise. Bang on something, shout. They
hate to be hollered at. We had no problems. On the rare occasions when man and bear did encounter each other suddenly,
each took off in different directions at high speed in mutual
terror."

A geologist, according to Larminie, has the rare opportunity
to acquire an intimate knowledge of his fellow men at their best
and their worst. Usually none of the members of the party,
frequently University of Alaska students, knew each other when
they started off to live together in the remote wilderness for
three or four months. Soon the helicopter pilots took an interest

in geology, and the geologists all became expert helicopter pilots.

"We never held a stick or anything, but we learned enough about instruments and things like manifold pressure to worry ourselves silly.

"Helicopter mechanics were the most unusual breed of all. They were always capable of working at this enormous pace for long periods, then, like dormice, they could sleep for astonishing periods of time. They can sleep better than anybody I've ever come across.

"Cooks are interesting, too. They are stuck around the camp all day, of course, and busy themselves with all sorts of things. One cook we had was a voracious reader of classical literature, another was a poet. They hunt or study animals, and frequently tidy up the camp. They hate messy camps. They also hate helicopter pilots. That's a known fact—a helicopter pilot is to a cook as a red rag is to a bull, and vice versa."

One spring the cook Geoff had signed on got sick at the last moment and Geoff had to hire a replacement. The new man had just retired from the Army as a staff sergeant after 20 years of service. He had excellent references and impressed Geoff with his organizational ability. Normally the cook makes up his own list of supplies, but as time was short and Geoff knew what would be needed, he prepared the list in detail. After several days in the field it was necessary to make up a new list but the cook kept postponing it; finally Geoff realized that he couldn't read or write. He had absolutely no interest in the countryside; he was a completely urban animal. He became increasingly neurotic. Being a cook, he blamed the helicopter pilot for the whole thing.

One morning Geoff was awakened by shouts coming from the mess camp several yards away. He climbed out of his sleeping bag, grabbed his rifle—"I had no idea what I intended to do with it"—and ran to the mess camp. The cook was brandishing his longest and sharpest knife, preparatory to carving up the pilot. Geoff and the rifle changed his mind. In his neurotic state his mood changed abruptly and he began apologizing profusely to everyone, even the pilot.

"Forget it," Geoff said. "You're going home." Promised that he was leaving as soon as a plane could arrive, the cook smiled softly, walked to the top of a hill behind the camp, and stood there motionless, facing north, for six hours until the plane came in.

To Geoff the geology of the region was even more interesting than the people. It was a detective story. On the Slope, between the foothills and the ocean, there are no outcroppings. He could stand in the mountains and see them disappear to the north, then rise again at Barrow. Rocks from the Jurassic period —some 180 million years ago—were only 100 feet beneath the surface at Barrow—but where were they halfway between?

This may have been a detective story to Larminie, but not to me. Detective stories have people, and the people usually have identifiable names. Larminie's whodunit, or rather whereisit, deals with rock layers with family names like Mesozoic and Paleozoic, representing eras; given names like Cretaceous, Jurassic, and Triassic, representing time periods within the eras, and still further identifications like Sadlerochit and Lisburne. These periods date back more than 600 million years. Who can imagine 600 million years?

"It really doesn't matter what you call a rock," Larminie said. "You pick out a rock unit and you recognize it as rock A. As long as you're always talking about rock A, you're all right. Out in the field even geologists tend to talk somewhat sloppily about age groups of rocks. Final identification is made back in the laboratory. You can make thin sections of it to examine its mineralogical composition. You can extract the fossil material from it. Then you can put a label on it."

To the lab technician, fossils are like fingerprints. We all know, for example, that dinosaurs aren't around any more. They disappeared mysteriously, during the Cretaceous period about 60 million years ago. You won't find many dinosaur bones in a chunk of rock chipped off an outcropping, but a paleontologist

might well find the remains of a tiny shellfish called ammonite
that gave up the ghost at the same time as the dinosaurs. So
when a paleontologist sees an ammonite fossil in a sliver of
rock, he can positively identify it as being at least 60 million
years old. By identifying other fossils that lived at different
periods, he can narrow the period down still further. From these
identifications geologists can make a map that, according to
Geoff, is the basis for everything.

Now come the seismic crews. They bore a hole in the ground
and put in an explosive charge. Lines are put out with sensitive
listening devices called geophones, or more commonly, jugs.
The charge is set off and each jug records the length of time it
takes the sound to travel to each layer of rock and back again.
When BP first contracted with the independent seismic companies, the shots were set off in the summer. Back came some
peculiar echoes. "We got dud results that summer," Larminie
said. "It was a complete waste of time. We deduced that the
strange noises resulted from melting layers beneath the surface.
We went back in the winter, shot the area over again using the
same lines, and received beautiful results."

Every time the sound penetrated a different layer of rock it
sent a different reflection back to the jugs, which recorded them
in the form of a squiggle on a revolving drum. BP geologists
put all those squiggles together, matched them up with the layers
already identified from outcroppings and the voluminous Pet 4
records, and constructed a cross-section map of the earth's surface all the way down to the basement rock. From this and information gained by other sophisticated means, they could make
a decision whether to drill and where.

The point selected for BP's first Alaskan well was called Shale
Wall, located in a lemming pasture 40 miles east of Umiat.
That began one of the most dramatic odysseys in the Arctic.

Drilling rigs are heavy things. So is the fuel it takes to run
them. Men have to operate the rigs, and they need warm places
to sleep and food to eat. How to get these tons of bulky equip-
men to the drill site?

Pet 4 operators had brought their equipment by ship to Barrow, then towed it with tracked vehicles across the sea ice to the Colville River and up the river to Umiat. BP considered this method but knew that the advance and retreat of the sea ice in the Bering Strait during the short summer was completely unpredictable. The odds were better that there would be open water along the northern coast between the Colville River and the Canadian border.

As there is considerable oil activity around Calgary and Edmonton, supplies were available there. But from Edmonton to the Arctic Ocean—it's called the Beaufort Sea at that point— is 2200 miles; the last lap is the 1500-mile Mackenzie River. For this junket equipment was loaded on 600-ton barges at the busy port of Hay River, population 1000, on Great Slave Lake, the source of the Mackenzie.

The river, in summer, resembles the Mississippi. At some points it is 1000 feet across, at others five miles. At its delta it splits up into a half-dozen channels. The tug and its string of barges made the trip down the river in ten days. That's the same length of time it took Alexander Mackenzie to paddle his canoe down it in 1789 in the vain hope of reaching the Pacific.

Though it's hard to picture a tugboat and a string of barges racing against time, there was a sense of desperation on board as the tug started the 400-mile journey along the northern coast to the Colville. When the ice floes come in, they come in fast. They gouge the sand up into walls along the beaches, and they would have carried the tug and its barges right up to those walls. But the early calculations held, and the tug made its stolid way through the open sea unperturbed.

At Beechey Point on the Colville delta the cargo was loaded onto smaller lighters that took it up the twisting, many-channeled, island-studded Colville to the point where one of the strange features of the Arctic flatlands, an ice formation the Eskimos call pingo, sticks up like a finger. The gravel bar on which the cargo was off-loaded is now known officially as Pingo Beach. Men and equipment waited there for winter and the

tundra to freeze. Then, in the bitter cold that made the trip possible, the convoy started out overland for the drilling site. The
way you move 130-foot rigs across open country is crazy. One
end was hoisted onto the bed of a huge Kenworth truck, the
other on the bed of a similar truck; one of those trucks had to
be driven backwards the entire twisting route.

The rig was set up; drilling began. Shale Wall was a dry hole.

British Petroleum drilled six more wells in the central area
of the North Slope. Sinclair was a partner in the first few ven-
tures, but it couldn't stand the expense, and got out. Other companies came and went on the Slope during those years; Shell
drilled one well and quit.

The expense in drilling on the North Slope is not merely
double or triple what it costs in, say, Texas; it can well be multi-
plied by a factor of ten. The rest of the oil world watched in
amazement as British Petroleum kept pouring pounds into the
frozen Alaskan earth. One of the reasons for BP's perseverance
was the chairman of the board, Sir Maurice Bridgeman. Sir
Maurice, who has since retired, was a geologist himself. Another was the BP tradition of aggressiveness; it hangs in there.

As the bits punched out one dry hole after another, Geoff
Larminie reviewed the entire operation. It had been natural to
gravitate toward the area of the known reservoir at Umiat, since
the whole geological area was known to be a sedimentary basin,
there were outcroppings to study, and a structure with oil in it.
But Geoff suspected now that the Umiat field was atypical of the
area. From the age of the deepest rocks penetrated, he could
see that they were only scratching the surface.

The knowledge obtained from the wells was, of course, valuable. With all the tools at the petroleum industry's command,
from the sore feet of the geologist to the most sophisticated
geophysical gear, only the drill can produce definite results.
And the drill indicated that BP was near the center of the basin.

A sedimentary basin, like a washbasin, is usually deepest
in the center. At this point, too, occurs the greatest thickness of
sediments. These sediments usually comprise a high percentage

of potential source rock, but the weight of the thick layers above compress the fine grains and express the hydrocarbons upward toward the margins. That's where they should have looked; the Umiat structure doesn't belong where it is.

To the south was the complex, smashed-up region of the Brooks Range. That left the north, so BP moved up the Colville, and drilled two more wells. In one, Colville, there was a layer of good hydrocarbon shale. It would have been worth developing in the middle of England, but on the North Slope it was not considered commercial.

Nine wells BP had dug, and had participated to some extent in others. Now even the BP bulldogs were becoming discouraged. Geoff Larminie had been taken away from Alaska for a two-year duty in the Middle East. He was sent back with orders to make a definite recommendation either to expand or curtail the Alaska operations. "Inasmuch as the total scope of the operations were composed of me and my secretary, it would have been difficult to curtail them." And so BP's venture in the new world hung on one man.

Geoff liked the looks of another structure to the east of Colville at Prudhoe Bay, where BP shared acreage with Atlantic Richfield. He could not recommend that operations be ended with that structure still unexplored. But there was another course of action: a holding operation. "Well, we thought," Geoff said, "we'll just sit back. We've made all the running on the Slope from 1962. Let somebody else have a go. If they find oil it's only a matter of prestige. From a hard economic point of view it makes no difference who finds it first."

BP, and Geoff Larminie, stayed on to see what would happen at Prudhoe.

THE GOVERNOR AND THE CONSULTANT

During the years when BP was carrying the ball on the North Slope, a few hopeful Alaskans were becoming increasingly impatient with the reluctance of the rest of the industry to get in there and drill. One of them was Walter J. Hickel, a whip-cracking, big-time operator who, when impatient, can be placed at several degrees below impossible.

He'd come to Alaska when he was 19, a tough Kansas farm kid with just 37 cents. I asked him why he'd left Kansas. "What the hell was there for me to do there?" he barked back. He was a bouncer in a barroom, worked on the railroad, and built a house and sold it. He built two more and sold them, too. He became a millionaire, then governor of Alaska, running as a Republican in a traditionally Democratic state, then Secretary of the Interior.

When I first encountered him in the summer of 1969, during a period of feverish activity on the Slope, he was en route to the National Governors' Conference with two department executives in attendance. He was impatient. My wife and I were the only other passengers in the forward compartment, and perhaps because the stewardess had been lavish with the wine, I thought Hickel might like to chat about the big things happening in his state. I introduced myself, mentioning some mutual friends with oil companies active on the Slope.

It was the wrong approach. To an entrepreneur like Wally Hickel, the petroleum industry was as slow as crude oil on the North Slope in January. He was used to moving both swiftly and boldly. Almost immediately after America's worst earthquake had destroyed a large section of Anchorage, Wally had announced plans for a ten-story luxury hotel five blocks from one of the demolished areas. He built it, too. (A couple of geologists have told me that the Captain Cook sits right on top of a fault line, but the customers don't seem to care. You'd better make your reservations well in advance.)

He gave me a sharp lecture on how the big companies had been hesitant about coming in. "We knew there was oil up there all along," he barked. "We couldn't interest anybody. Finally we threatened to drill ourselves. Then they got busy."

"Who's *we*?" I asked.

"The state of Alaska!" he said. "I was governor."

I was aware of that fact, and also of the cost of exploration on the North Slope. "But where would you get the money?"

"Hell, we had it," he said. "Look, you go see Jim Dalton in Fairbanks. He's got the whole story. *Then* you come talk to me."

In Fairbanks, Jim Dalton was as hard to find as oil. "He goes out in the bush and stays for weeks," a friend of his said. "His own wife doesn't know where he is."

While I was wildcatting for the elusive Jim Dalton, my wife, Bonnie, was happily scurrying around learning about life in Alaska. She left a message that she had met a reporter named Mike something-or-other who had invited us to dinner. Getting plastered with some newspaper guy was not on my agenda, but I hadn't been left much choice. When Bonnie's friend came by to pick us up, Mike proved to be a she, and a good-looking, buxom blonde she at that. I missed her last name.

That morning Mike had walked 12 miles with her daughter as practice for a marathon coming up. Then had come an emergency assignment; vandals had broken into the elementary school at North Pole, on the other side of Fairbanks, and had busted up everything in the building except the television sets. She'd covered the story, taken photographs, and picked us up on the way home. I wondered ruefully what kind of dinner we were going to have.

Mike and her husband live four or five miles outside of Fairbanks—so far, she commented, that in the wintertime nobody comes to see them. That kind of trip requires emergency gear— sleeping bag, heating unit, rations—to avoid freezing to death if you have car trouble or run off the narrow gravel road.

Mike, active and energetic, had come to Alaska as a girl; her father was on a World War II construction job. She'd married a mining engineer and lived for several years at Barrow in a quonset hut. During the winter, to avoid cabin fever, she liked to visit Eskimo whaling camps out on the sea ice. She carefully followed the trails made by the Eskimos; the ice looked all the same to her, but she knew the Eskimos must have good reason for the detours in the otherwise straight trail. She learned to make a windbreak out of ice when she stopped for lunch, and to dress in layers, the way the Eskimos do. There's a fine distinction between being warm and being too warm: perspiring feet eventually become frostbitten.

Once Mike hitched a ride in a bush plane taking supplies to a whaling camp 20 miles offshore. The pilot promised to come back for her, but he never showed. Mike spent the night in a sleeping bag on the ice. Next day she walked back home.

The house Mike drove us to was one of those handsome Alaskan structures made of logs, high on a hill overlooking birches and poplars pale gold in the fall which blended into the faraway blue wall of the Alaska Range with its big white apostrophes of snow-covered peaks. Her husband, a man in a red and black plaid shirt, with blue eyes crow-footed from squinting on northland trails, came out to meet us.

"This is Jim Dalton," Mike said proudly, and there went another Alaska legend. Jim Dalton's own wife did know where he was. He was right there shaking hands with me.

James W. Dalton is an up-dated version of a Jack London sourdough. His father, John, had arrived in Sitka in 1882 under armed guard and had been promptly thrown in jail; the ship he'd been on had been poaching fur seal. The captain took the rap, and the loss of two years' accumulation of skins, and the members of the crew were released. John Dalton went north to Haines, crossed the Alaska Range, and set up a trading post. Honesty was more than a virtue in those days, it was a matter of survival. The Indians combated inflation by tying a profiteer's head to his heels and throwing him out in the woods to die.

Then came the Gold Rush and Dalton made his own strike; he drove cattle over the Chilkoot Pass, floated them down the Yukon, and sold them in Dawson for a dollar a pound on the hoof. When a better route into the interior was pioneered, up the Copper River, he built a pier at its mouth and the boom town of Cordoba grew up around it. A young woman came in on a cruise ship and he sweet-talked her into jumping ship and marrying him. When Jim was due, she insisted that he be born in the United States, not a territory, and went to Seattle for the event. She returned to the states again when her husband died, but Jim had to get back to Alaska. He traveled steerage class from Seattle for $30, and rode a freight car to Fairbanks and the University of Alaska. Today the modern, handsome university hums with sophisticated studies, but in the Thirties Jim lived in a wooden dorm and there were only two or three other students in his engineering classes. "It was like having a private tutor," he said.

When the Navy contracted Pet 4 exploration to a private concern, Arctic Contractors, Jim went in as foreman and wound up as general superintendent. He was involved not only in the actual search for oil, but in the supporting phases—logistics, transportation, construction. Nothing was known about any of them in this land of paradox. The right way to do something anywhere else was often the wrong way on the North Slope, and you paid for mistakes in money, failure, and life itself.

Even the experts ran into trouble. Scouting out the route for the first overland haul to Umiat, the Weasels broke down in the harsh weather and rough terrain and two men named Bagby and Curtin were sent out with dogsleds. Bagby had to return to base for supplies. When he got back to the trail camp he found Curtin's equipment and heavy clothing, but the man was missing. He hasn't been found yet. And Curtin was no cheechako; he was a corporal in the Eskimo scouts.

Sometime later an experienced bush pilot, flying a Stinson Norseman proved on many Arctic flights, was lost with a passenger somewhere east of Barrow. Neither the plane nor the men have ever been found. Another plane went down with four men aboard; it took six days to locate it, and by that time there were no survivors.

In summer, when the marshy tundra thawed out, overland travel was almost impossible, even for vehicles equipped with huge tires. Tractors settled into the bog; some disappeared for good. In winter, travel by wheeled vehicles was too difficult to be worthwhile. A new means had to be invented. Frames for large sleds with drill pipe for runners were welded together in the crude machine shop at Barrow. Wanigans—wooden huts for sleeping and eating—were fabricated and fixed to the sled frame. On the first trip over the tundra, two tractors started out pulling ten sleds. They couldn't do it. Two sleds had to be left behind and another tractor brought up. Of the eight sleds, only four carried payloads; the other four were wanigans. Eventually the tractor trains, now called Cat trains after the wondrous Caterpillar tractor, were arranged so that one lead tractor broke trail and pulled the comparatively light wanigans; two more pulled the heavier payload.

Someone got the idea of equipping the lead tractor with a bulldozer blade, so that it could smooth out the route as it proceeded, knocking the tops off hummocks and cutting through the banks of streams. It worked fine, but then came summer. The extreme fragility of this peculiar terrain became devastatingly apparent.

The tundra, though rock hard in winter, is nothing more than a thin layer of vegetation over the permafrost. (It can be six inches or many feet; no dimension is standard on the Slope.) Permafrost is anything that remains at a temperature below freezing the year around; it may be gravel, sand, silt, rock, or ice. It may extend down a thousand feet or more. When you knock its insulating cover off with a bulldozer blade or churn it up with a tractor, heat from the summer sun penetrates into the permafrost, and it thaws. On the slightest grade, the water runs off, carrying silt with it and exposing more permafrost. Erosion takes place quicker than the slow-growing vegetation can cover it. Flying low over the North Slope today, you can see Cat tracks made 20 years ago. Your descendants will see them a thousand years from now. Some have become deep gulches that are growing ever wider, ever deeper.

"On toward the end there," Jim Dalton told me, "when we saw what we were doing, I'd tell a new bulldozer operator, 'drop your blade just once and you're fired.' "

Another problem was erecting buildings and rigs on this

treacherous, unstable stuff. Anybody knows that a concrete slab makes a strong foundation, so the Navy Seabees who built the first camp leveled a section of tundra, poured concrete on top of it, then erected a building. Over a period of months, the slab began to buckle. The heat within the building was enough to penetrate through the concrete into the frozen tundra. The area where the stove was located sank the fastest. After a year they figured it had settled all it was going to, and evened it up by pouring more concrete. It just kept on sinking. Other concrete slab foundations, following the non-pattern of the North, rose. This happens when water collects beneath the surface in summer, freezes, and heaves in winter. The phenomenon produced disconcerting results in the Barrow graveyard, when bodies began emerging from the surface.

One method of licking the foundation problem was to scrape up gravel from the river beds and build a pad five to ten feet thick. This often worked. Another, and more ingenious, method was to use what nature provided. As Dalton says, in the Arctic you always work with nature, never against her. Wood does not rot in the Arctic; an untreated piling will stay there practically forever. But pilings of treated steel crumble like soda straws when driven into permafrost; logs splinter. Holes had to be prepared, either by boring them with augurs or thawing them out with steam. Spruce logs brought up from below the tree line were inserted, and secured with nature's help.

Lakes freeze only to a depth of six feet or so; find one deeper than that, augur out a hole, insert a pump hose, and you've got water. (But you've got to work fast, or it will freeze solid in the hose.) The tanks in which it is transported back to camp must be heated and insulated. Now all you have to do is pour the water in the hole, and it will freeze solid around the log. Where else in the world do you go to all this trouble to keep water from freezing, only to freeze it again? But it's worth the effort, for the buildings constructed on these pilings, provided sufficient space was left between the floor and the tundra for the air to circulate, are still there today. Some are a little battered, for investigative bears have broken in during periods of vacancy and bears don't always use doors and windows, but the pilings are as good as new.

Drilling for oil in permafrost caused unimagined difficulties and frustrations. Take one earthy phase of the drilling operation —mud. As the bit rotates in rock, with the controlled weight of from 30 feet to five miles of drill pipe on top of it, it grinds out cuttings whose size and shape is determined by the many types of rock encountered and the many types of bits designed for each. You don't want the bit to get hot, of course, nor do you want the cuttings to just lie there, and that's where mud comes in. It's a dirty-looking solution of water thickened with an expanding clay called bentonite that is pumped down the pipe under pressure and squirts out through holes in the bit. The fluid rises to the surface in the space between the outside of the pipe and the circumference of the hole, with cuttings suspended in it like beans in chili.

There are about a hundred other substances you can put in mud. If you're going through a porous layer of rock or sand, for instance, and all your mud is leaking out, you can throw in stuff like ground-up pecan shells or sugar cane to close the pores. But one thing that doesn't mix with mud is this largely unknown substance called permafrost. If it's a frozen mixture of water and sand, silt, or gravel, the mud melts the stuff and the hole caves in. It binds the drill pipe, which may snap off. Then you have to open up the hole and send down special tools to fish for the pipe and pull it up.

Drill operators have tried all sorts of tricks to get through the permafrost. They have chilled the mud, adding salt to keep it from freezing, or have used chilled diesel fuel or compressed air. On Pet 4 they ran into so many problems with conventional drilling rigs that they even tried the old cable tool method used in Pennsylvania a hundred years ago, and in Persia and Katalla in the early 1900s. In this system the tool, a heavy chunk of serrated metal called a spud, is attached to the end of a cable, winched up and let drop with a thump, again and again. (A well was officially begun when the spud was dropped for the first time; thus "spud in" today means to begin a well.) After it has pulverized whatever it's banging into, a basket is sent down to clean out the bottom of the hole and then the thumping begins again. Shallow wells were dug on Pet 4 by this archaic method.

A total of 36 wells and 44 core tests—narrow holes drilled to find out what's down there—were begun on Pet 4. On many attempts all that was accomplished was to bury, permanently, a lot of broken-off drill pipe.

Eight million dollars were poured into Pet 4 between 1945, when full-scale operations got underway, and 1953, when they ended. Some oil and gas were located, but the most practical product of those years was experience. The operators learned how to do things—and how not to do things. One of the interesting by-products was the establishment of the Arctic Research Laboratory under Dr. Max Brewer, which has carried on America's most comprehensive study of the whole spectrum of the Arctic.

Ten years went by. During those years several companies made passes at the Slope, spending an estimated total of $55 million. Their work increased the knowledge of the area, both above and below ground, but produced no oil of commercial value. In some respects oil exploration on the North Slope was a microcosm of oil exploration over the world in general. In 1959 through 1966, for example, the oil industry spent $6.5 billion drilling dry holes. Eight out of nine wildcats—wells drilled in new exploration areas—are dry. Despite improvements in exploration and drilling technology, the cost of the average well increased during that period from $43,000 to more than $56,000. North Slope wildcats, of course, as do offshore wells, cost in the millions.

As a result of the increasing cost of battling the odds, the annual number of exploratory wells dropped 40 percent, from 14,707 in 1957 to 8,879 in 1968, according to the American Petroleum Institute. The Institute viewed these figures with alarm, for while the search for oil was decreasing, the demand for oil was increasing. By the end of the 1960s, petroleum was furnishing 75 percent of the total energy in the United States. By 1980, according to Department of the Interior estimates, the annual petroleum demand will have risen by 50 percent, and by the year 2000 we will be using twice as much oil and gas as we are today. In the meantime the reserves in the traditional oil-producing states—Texas, Louisiana, California, Oklahoma, and Kansas—will dwindle. As it is the 573,000 American wells average only about fifteen 42-gallon barrels of oil per well per day. Though there's some skullduggery involved, with production held back in rich wells to keep costs up, still two-thirds of all the country's wells produce only about four barrels a day. Whether you or I agree with the restriction on imported oil is beside the point for this discussion; it may be a golden fancy to the consumer or a black nightmare to the oil industry and its stockholders, but unlimited importation of cheap oil is a dream. Oil from shale and coal is an eventuality, but an expensive one.

In 1966, Jim Dalton completed an extensive reappraisal of the Pet 4 exploration. The North Slope, he wrote, "is probably the largest and most promising relatively unexplored area remaining in the United States." He went on from there to discuss, in a 62-page report plus appendixes, the results of the Pet 4 and subsequent explorations, and to set forth a complete program for further exploration based on the knowledge already accrued. He concluded that a three-stage program, involving a seismological survey, a test well, and four exploration wells, including everything down to hand tools, could be carried out for $4,827,020.

I didn't happen to have $4,827,020 in 1966, so my observation may be qualified, but the re-appraisal looked pretty good to me when Jim shyly poked it at me three years later. I asked him what its effect was. He is, unfortunately for dramatic impact, too honest an individual for his own good.

"Not a damn thing as far as I know," he said.

It's a long way from Jim Dalton's cluttered little office in a dingy building in a sorry section of ugly downtown Fairbanks to the one-man auditorium of the Secretary of the Interior of the United States. And there's a big difference between weather-beaten Jim Dalton in his plaid shirt and scuffed moccasin-toed high tops to Walter J. Hickel, rosy-pink from his personal sauna and exuding confidence and ego. I told him I had done what he had told me to do. I'd seen Jim Dalton, I'd studied his report, and now I wanted to know more about what he meant when he said, "Hell, we had the money."

"Well, basically I said this, Boo," he said. "I was talking to one of my assistants and I wondered whether we could get the right people interested in the opening of the Arctic and Prudhoe Bay. I mentioned the fact that if we couldn't make it success-fully that the state of Alaska would go ahead and drill it itself. And my executive assistant said, 'Governor, that's socialism.' I said, 'Bull, it's not that, it's oil.' "

"Well, there was a hell of a lot of money involved here," I said, "The state of Alaska didn't have that much money."

"It wouldn't have taken much to drill Prudhoe Bay," Hickel said. "Two or three million dollars would have done it because the state owned the land. You wouldn't be involved in buying leases or any of that sort of thing. All you'd be involved in was developing. It didn't happen—but it was our method of saying we were going to make it happen."

"In other words," I said, "you didn't think you were going to do it."

Wally sat there behind his huge desk and looked at me di-rectly for several seconds. His lips moved in a small, conspira-torial smile. "It was an option," he explained gently.

One of the sure characteristics of people who play for big stakes is that they don't show their cards when they bluff you out of a pot. They just smile a little bit and pull in the chips. Because there may be a next time.

I didn't push Wally any more as to how he could conceivably

have gotten away with spending state money drilling for oil at Prudhoe Bay. The point is, somebody *did* drill for oil at Prudhoe Bay. That somebody was Atlantic Richfield.

One day in 1957, a laconic geologist for Richfield Oil Company named William C. Bishop kicked a tree in the moose country on the Kenai Peninsula south of Anchorage and said, "Drill here." They drilled there and brought in the Swanson River field. Later tests showed that if Bishop had kicked a tree 500 feet away he'd have missed the structure, and the well would have been dry. But when you hit oil nobody cares how close you came to missing it.

The decision on where to drill is actually based on many factors involving many people, and Bishop assured me that he was only one member of the team. But his was the boot that kicked the tree, and the Anchorage Chamber of Commerce appropriated it and plated it with gold.

The Swanson River field is one of several in the Cook Inlet area just out of Anchorage; you can see the flares from the platforms coming in to the airport. It's a long, long way from the civilization of Anchorage to the North Slope, and in the 1950s it was a lot longer. Further, the trip was hardly necessary. Northern Alaska was composed entirely of Federally owned land and for obvious reasons during the Cold War years it was closed to exploration. How could the Government defend it?

Geologists are a curious breed, however, and Bishop did make one junket into the area. He flew into Umiat in a Grumman Widgeon, having first told all his friends just exactly where he was going; if he got lost he wanted them to know where to start looking. As it was, the trip was hardly eventful. Umiat at that time was occupied by a small Army installation. A captain met the plane, chewed Bishop and his pilot out, and restricted them to the base.

"He did invite us to lunch," Bishop recalled, "and charged exactly 36 cents for it. The price was reasonable, but that's a long way to go to save money on meals."

The area north of the Yukon and Porcupine rivers was opened up by executive order in 1958, and Richfield moved in. The decision of this comparatively small West Coast company to get into the action was based on another of those coincidences in which Alaska is so rich; the history of the state could be written in coincidences. In 1949 the Navy had invited oil company executives and geologists up to see what was going on—and, hopefully, to give suggestions on how to do it better. But a trip to the Arctic coast of Alaska in 1949 was not quite the same as a cruise to the Bahamas, and not every major company officer jumped at the chance.

One who did was Richfield's chief geologist, Rollin Eckis. He looked at the oil seeps, saw enormous structures, and came to the quiet conclusion that this was a tremendous basin. "The whole thing looked like a dream," he told me. By 1958 Eckis was in a position to explore that dream; he was president of Richfield. He sent Bishop to the Slope on a field survey that summer.

Bishop inadvertently timed his arrival with that of the mosquitoes. "They weren't big, but they sure were hungry." The party mapped surface structures, checking the elevation with pocket transits, looked at outcroppings—"they were there, all right—" and saw rocks favorable to the generation of petroleum. The party spent three months on the Slope, at a cost of about $100,000. That was like putting up a nickel to get in a no-limit game. Each year the stakes got bigger. After geological field mapping in order to evaluate the basin, the company made an air magnetic survey to get a general idea of what lay beneath the surface, then sent in seismic crews for more detailed information. Richfield, which was neither rich nor big as far as oil companies go, had to go to Humble Oil and Refining Company, which was both, for $3 million to keep going. Humble ran more tests. Then came the moment of truth. Early in 1965 the decision was made to drill on a site near the Sagavanirktok River, about midway between the Brooks Range and the Beaufort Sea.

Humble went along. The well would be called Susie after a nearby benchmark.

Now the company had to get a drilling rig in there. Pet 4 and British Petroleum had brought rigs and supplies by water to the Arctic coast, then over the frozen tundra to the rig site. But was there a better way? Richfield sent one of its top drilling superintendents, Benjamin T. Loudermilk, then working out of Calgary, to Alaska to look the situation over.

Bennie, who wears suspenders and looks like a country store-keeper, had had some experience with Cat trains on the Macken-zie, and he first investigated the possibility of transporting a rig overland, from Fairbanks across the Brooks Range. He and John "Tennessee" Miller, head of Frontier Rock and Sand, Inc., got together to discuss it. Frontier was taking the first Cat train from Fairbanks to the Slope and Bennie hitched a ride.

Frontier built its own sleds for the trip, using steel six-inch runners. The wanigans were plywood covered with canvas. A casual South Dakotan named Leroy Dennis headed the train; his navigational equipment consisted of one compass and one Indian guide. The surface of the interior of Alaska is composed of bogs called muskeg, lakes, rivers, and forests of small, slender birches and spruce. As nothing but dogsleds had ever passed that way before, the lead Caterpillar had to break trail. In the intense cold the trees snapped like matches. There was plenty of ice on the Yukon, and the train started on across it. The lead Cat had almost reached the far bank when the ice suddenly gave way. Momentum carried the Cat forward, and Dennis found himself sitting in the cab looking up at a solid chunk of ice over his head. He was in an air space between river and ice. The water drowned out the engine but wasn't deep enough to flood the cab.

The other Cats found solid ice upstream and made the cross-ing safely. One of the operators made a U-turn, came back to the bank, dropped his blade for an anchor, and tried to winch Dennis out. The unbroken ice between the Cat and shore was too thick, and the Cat wouldn't budge. The ice had to be broken up with dynamite. On shore, the engine and hydraulic system were drained to get the silty river water out, then filled with new oil and hydraulic fluid. Dennis pushed the starter button and the engine started up as though nothing had happened.

But in the meantime they'd lost their Indian guide. He'd had enough of this white man's foolishness and started out on foot for a native village a few miles downstream. Loss of the guide didn't bother Leroy Dennis at all; he still had his compass. He took the train to the mountains, through Anaktuvuk Pass, and down through the foothills onto the Slope.

This is not the most pleasant way to see northern Alaska. The wanigan-bunkhouses are tiny, crowded, stuffy, and messy. Wet mukluks and gloves hang from the ceiling. The men sleep in their clothes. There's little point in washing or shaving, for the settlements along the route are hardly fun cities. At Livengood a hand-lettered sign on the door of the log trading post run by the one white inhabitant boasted ICE COLD BEER; the temperature was 20 below. The only other major point on the route—or anywhere in northern Alaska—was the cluster of Eskimo huts at Anaktuvuk Pass, each with caribou hides drying on the roof. Sled dogs were curled up in the shelter of their windbreaks. Anaktuvuk Pass has one advantage in winter. The caribou droppings left behind twice a year by the migrating herd, and which give the place its scatological Eskimo name as well as its distinctive atmosphere, are frozen solid and covered with snow.

Thirty-one days after the train had started out, in the middle of nowhere with no terrain marks that anyone could see, Dennis stopped and dropped his blade. "This is it," he said. He was less than a mile from the point on the map that was his destination.

With all credit to Leroy Dennis, Bennie Loudermilk could see that this was no way to get a 22-ton rig, with its massive machinery, stacks of drill pipe, and thousands of barrels of fuel oil, to the drill site. He said so in a report to the home office, and went back to Canada.

That summer, on his vacation, Bennie went back to the North Slope, moved in with a seismic crew, and waded around in the tundra. He saw the ruts, three feet deep, left by the tracked vehicles. He had the seismic crew drill a hole, and saw it fill full of water immediately. He put in a piece of piling, and it floated right up to the top. He quickly learned what the Pet 4 operators had learned years before; summer is no time to put in a rig on the North Slope.

The Richfield people discussed other ways of getting a rig in to the Slope. One wild idea thrown out on the table was airlift. The two largest planes in use on the Slope at that time were the C-119, known as the flying boxcar, and its old forerunner, the C-82. To break a rig down sufficiently to pack the pieces into either of these planes, however, seemed an insuperable task.

It was just at that time that Lockheed Aircraft Corporation was seriously considering making its C-130 Hercules available for civilian use. More than 700 C-130s were in military service, but one, just one, might be available; it was a company demonstrator. Alaska Airlines, itching to get its corporate hands on one of the planes, suggested that it lease the demonstrator and airlift the rig. The proposal went up to Rollin Eckis. He thought the idea was mad, but as he began to study the specifications of the Hercules the project seemed more reasonable. It was truly a formidable piece of machinery. It would carry a payload of 25 tons; the cargo compartment was 10 feet wide, 9 feet high, and 41 feet long. That meant you could put a bunkhouse, a Caterpillar, or a pile of 31-foot lengths of drill pipe in it. As for the rig, it might just be possible to cut it up into sections and reassemble it on the job. Eckis was assured that flying to the North Slope would be no problem; the monsters were designed for short, rough runways, and had been used in the Antarctic. Further, although at first glance the airlift concept seemed expensive, other considerations, such as standby time for the period the rig and supplies would be plowing along through the ocean in barges, might balance out the total cost. With airlift it might be possible to rig up and get going in a period of weeks.

Eckis gave the authorization to investigate the airlift idea further, and if it looked okay, to go ahead with it. It was an informal discussion, just a few men sitting around in an office, but that's the way they did things at Richfield.

The more Eckis's people and Alaska Airlines studied the possibility, the better it looked. Then came a letdown as big as the plane. Lockheed let it be known that it was not about to entrust its only demonstrator to Alaska Airlines to haul a drilling rig around in the Arctic. There are always methods of getting around such difficulties, however; Charles S. Jones, chairman of the board of Richfield, and Daniel J. Haughton, chairman of Lockheed, were friends. Eckis suggested to Jones that he suggest to Haughton that he sure would like Alaska Airlines to have that plane. They got it.

The airlift was a two-stage operation. The drill site was 17 miles west of an airstrip known as Sagwon on the Sagavanirktok River. It was only a mile or so of gravel smoothed out by a bulldozer brought in piecemeal by a C-46, but it would do for the sturdy Herc. On one of its first flights the big Herc came in during a snowstorm and bumped to a stop on the rough gravel. Two mechanics were out in the snow assembling a Caterpillar delivered in pieces by a C-46. They watched as the Herc's rear door, 8 feet by 9, let down to form a ramp. The floor of the high-wing plane sits only 40 inches off the ground. A roar started up inside, and out of the plane, down the ramp, came a DC-8 Caterpillar, all 48,000 pounds of it, under its own power. The men stood there motionless and speechless in the snow.

"Holy mackerel," one of then finally said. "That one's ready made. We won't have to put it together."

From Sagwon the Herc-delivered Cats built the road to the drill site. In the meantime a drilling rig had to be procured and prepared for airlift. Few oil companies own their own rigs; drilling is usually a lease operation. Loffland Brothers happened to have an excellent rig, No. 162, in Alaska and idle at the time.

It was already winterized. Through no fault of its own, in its eight-year history No. 162's batting average was zero. It had been brought to Alaska in 1957 to participate in an exploration disaster on the Alaskan Peninsula, another godforsaken spot. Punching a 14,000-foot hole in that barren, volcanic, wind-swept region took a year and a half and as much money as had been spent for the whole state of Alaska 90 years before. The company stuck with the fiasco, Cities Service, didn't go back to Alaska for years.

The rig then drilled two more dry holes in southern Alaska for other companies. With that kind of record, its next job was a natural. It was barged out to Amchitka Island in the Aleutian chain to drill a deliberate duster for the Atomic Energy Com-mission: it put a four-foot hole down a half a mile, so that the AEC could explode a bomb in it. With not a drop of oil to show for four attempts, the rig was brought back to Anchorage and sent up the railroad to Fairbanks. There a Richfield crew cut its 145-foot length into Herc-sized pieces. In preparation for the arrival of the world's biggest plane the Frontier Cats at the drill site prepared a mile-long runway. Material used: snow. Frontier's Tennessee Miller had discovered that by simply push-ing the icy crystals around they lock themselves together with-out packing, and provide an excellent surface for even 130,000 pounds of plane and payload.

The airlift of No. 162 began in January, 1966, and in 21 days it was all over. The plane flew 72 round trips, delivering 1,649 tons of rig, pipe, fuel, trucks, mud, and all the miscel-laneous supplies necessary for drilling. The most exciting thing about flying a complete drilling operation 330 miles across the Arctic Circle and over the Brooks Range to a field made of snow on the barren North Slope was that absolutely nothing happened. The Herc flew in snowstorms, in temperatures of 70 below zero, in nights more than 20 hours long, and during pe-riods when sun spot activity knocked out communications. Many of its round trips, including unloading time, were made in three hours, thanks to the carefully planned assembly of the loads.

A load would not consist just of a huge truck, for example, but of a huge truck packed tight with smaller items. Drill pipe was stacked on aluminum skids, which could be winched off in a few minutes.

As the supplies continued to come in, men were on the job assembling the rig. Within a month after the first flight the rig was up, mounted on pilings, and ready to go.

Bennie Loudermilk had arrived at Susie right after New Year's. He was greeted by a snowstorm and a temperature of minus 63 degrees. He immediately began putting in a foundation of pilings, stuck 18 feet in the frozen ground. He dug the holes with a seismic rig drill, using air to blow out the cuttings. Then he inserted the pilings, and added water, a little at a time. "We did it by feel," he said.

The most difficult problem was obtaining the water. The nearest lake of sufficient depth not to freeze solid was 16 miles away. The driver of the Cat pulling the water tank left camp at six o'clock every morning, and usually returned about six at night. He'd take a thermos jug of coffee and some good thick sandwiches with him. If he didn't get back by six, somebody would go out to look for him.

With the pilings frozen firmly in place, the crew erected the rig. Though no rig had ever been cut up for airlift before, it had been done so skillfully that the pieces fit together like a simple jigsaw puzzle. The drill floor sat 14 feet off the ground; with that much air space the heat from the big diesel engines that powered the rig and the burners warming the drill floor would not thaw out the permafrost.

But the mud did. The bit was hardly two pipe lengths deep when the hole started caving in. Bennie set lengths of 30-inch conductor pipe in it. The mud gushed up on the outside of the conductor pipe, pouring out all over the tundra. Bennie tried to cement the pipe in place, but the wet cement simply thawed the hole out bigger. Three times he reamed out the hole and started all over, but it wouldn't work. He pulled up the 30-inch conductor pipe, and drilled down to 157 feet, letting the mud run. Then

he set in 20-inch casing, and began the cementing operations
again. The cement thawed cavities in the permafrost, worked
its way up to the surface, and began bursting out of holes under
the rig. The frozen ground around some of the pilings began to
thaw, and they got loose and wobbly. Bennie kept right on
pumping in the cement. If more pilings thawed out, the entire
145-foot derrick would topple. But it was 50 below, and Bennie
took the chance that the cement had to set sometime. It did.
From then on, as far as the bit drilling away beneath the surface was concerned, the operation was just like any other anywhere else in the world.

On the rig, however, it was a different ballgame. "I thought
I'd experienced cold weather in Canada," Bennie told me, "but
I'd never seen anything like that. The wind made the difference.
The cold penetrated right into the machinery."

The rig had been described as being winterized, in that the
drill floor was protected by aluminum sections. But what had
been adequate on the Peninsula, the Aleutians, and southern
Alaska might as well have been chicken wire in the howling
winds of the Slope. The rig had two heaters, also adequate for
the balmy Peninsula, but running them together did not produce
enough steam to protect the drill floor. The mud lines froze,
and had to be thawed with butane torches. Bennie set smudge
pots all over the floor; everybody on the rig was black with soot.
The steam froze before it got to the hot ass for the derrickman
100 feet up on his monkey board. He was one cold and miserable son of a bitch.

The drill crew was composed primarily of tough, mature men
from Montana and Wyoming—you see few men under 35 on
rigs on the North Slope—and they could take the cold as well as
anyone. They were dressed for it, in down underwear and coveralls. But on days when the temperature fell into the minus 50s
and the wind blew at 30 and 40 miles an hour, even the tough-
est roughneck felt it in his bones. The wind blew the light ice
snow horizontally, so that even in the pale light of noon bunkhouse and rigs were obscured from each other. The changing

shifts shuffled back and forth along guide ropes. But the drilling continued. Only on one occasion, when the wind was blowing at 70 miles an hour, did Bennie shut down. To continue meant stacking several 90-foot lengths of pipe vertically in the rack. Bennie was afraid that if he gave the wind a stand of pipe to push against, it would rotate the rig off its base.

Drilling a hole in the ground is a science, and watching the teamwork of a crew is sheer entertainment, even in the bitter cold of the Slope. A good crew works together as precisely as a professional football team, each man executing his assignment with exquisite timing.

The best part of the performance occurs when the crew is carrying out what's known as making a trip. As the bit grinds through the rock beneath the surface, it gets dull, and there's no quick way to change it. Figure one out and you'll make a fortune. The only thing to do is to pull up the entire string of pipe, take off the old bit, put on the new one, then run the whole string back down again; that's making a trip. As the well reaches down to 10,000 feet, say, this operation may take 12 hours or more.

Each man performs several activities with different tools in the space of several seconds. The driller, who is the chief of the crew, operates the winch that pulls three lengths of 30-foot pipe—a stand—out of the hole. The roughnecks, the skilled members using specialized equipment plus timing and muscle, unscrew the 90-foot stand. The driller hoists it, and the derrickman, high on the monkey board, leans out, throws a coil of rope around it, and guides it back to the vertical stack. The whole procedure is repeated again, and again, and again, until the bit comes up. Then they change it, and start all over again, in reverse, lowering the string 90 feet at a time until it reaches the bottom of the hole.

When the crew is making a trip, the rig is not making hole; it's not drilling. In a particularly hard strata of rock a bit may become dull in a few hours, which means in essence that many hours are wasted in order to drill for a few more. There are other reasons, too, for pulling the string out; a lot of things can go wrong.

A drill crew is composed of a couple of roustabouts, the common labor of the rig; the roughnecks, the derrickman, and the driller. On the Slope their tour (pronounced tower) of duty is 12 hours on, 12 hours off, 7 days a week. The schedule varies from company to company, but a typical one is 20 days on the site, 10 days off. The company furnishes transportation to Fairbanks or Anchorage.

In overall charge of the drilling operation is the tool pusher. He is responsible for everything that goes on 24 hours a day; the operation never stops. He usually works seven days on, seven days off.

All these men are employees of a drilling company, such as Loffland. The oil company, like Richfield, has its representative on the job. He's the drilling superintendent or drilling engineer, and he is in complete charge of the entire drill site. He usually works seven days on, seven days off, as does the geologist, who examines the cuttings brought up by the mud. Frequently two companies go in together on a well, as at Susie with Humble and Richfield. One is the official operator, but each keeps an engineer and a geologist on the job.

The mud company that has the contract on the well also has a representative on the site. A trucking company, like Frontier, furnishes vehicles and drivers. There is also a radio operator-meteorologist, and there may be guards, furnished either by the oil company or by a private company. There may be mechanics, welders, electricians. Finally, there are the cooks, who work for still another independent company. The head cook is responsible for all meals, although his assistant usually prepares at least one, and does all the baking. The bull cooks help out in the kitchen, wash dishes, and do the housekeeping in the bunkhouses.

In addition to working different hours and different schedules for different employers, the men on the rig draw different wages. A roustabout can make $20,000 a year, a driller $30,000. A tractor operator on a Cat train can make more than $1000 a week. How much money a North Slope worker has at the end of the year depends on how much he spends with women and bartenders in Fairbanks and Anchorage. They are skilled operators, too.

But money is not all these men are looking for. Most of them are from oil areas in the Lower 48, and they grew up with oil in their blood. They want to be where the action is. One driller, coming off tour after making a trip and dripping with mud, told me that he was there because he just couldn't bear the thought that sometime in the future he would not be able to look back on all this and realize that he was a part of it. A roughneck coming by heard him and said, "Yeah, you're here for the challenge and you can hardly wait to get back south again and spend that challenge."

Life on Susie was primitive, uncomfortable, and dull. The bunkhouses were old aluminum-sided buildings previously used by a seismic company. They were heated by oil stoves; if the flame went out the fuel turned solid.

One of the miseries was the lack of water, hot *or* cold, for washing and plumbing. There were no showers, only three washbasins, and rigs are filthy places to work. The toilet was a one-holer set over the tundra, slightly warmed by an exhaust pipe from one of the diesel engines passing through. It didn't heat the air under the hole, however, and most of the men got a bucket, lined it with plastic and squatted over it in the bunkhouse. The contents would freeze solid in a minute outdoors, and be easy to dump.

"We never bothered to go to the toilet just to take a leak," Bennie told me. "Just go outside, turn your back to the wind, and piss on the snow. That is, if you could find anything to piss with in that cold."

They melted snow to make coffee in the bunkhouses. It tasted awful. In off hours, most of the men simply hung around the bunkhouse. A couple tried running a trap line, and caught a white fox or two, but it was difficult to get around on the tundra, and they didn't keep at it long. Some read, and somebody was always playing hillbilly music on a portable phonograph. Poker went on almost around the clock, but the stakes were held to a quarter limit and three raises, to protect the suckers from losing their shirts to the cardsharps and to prevent trouble. As it happened, there was no trouble.

"We lived like a big family," Bennie said. "You could leave anything anywhere, it would never be stolen. We cracked jokes and kidded, sure, but we all looked after each other. I never knew anybody who'd refuse to do anything. If we needed an electrician or a mechanic, and he was asleep, all we had to do was tell him and he'd get up and get the job done. Whether the plane came in at noon or the middle of the night, the forklift operator was out there to unload it."

The big reason for morale—or lack of it—in any remote site is food. The better the men eat, the harder they work and the less they bitch. Though life at Susie was primitive and dirty, there was always plenty to eat. To accommodate both tours, which worked from twelve to twelve, four meals were served a day, one at midnight. The allotment was $9 per man per day. "Give 'em steak, steak, steak," Bennie told the cook. "Give 'em all they want of it." The baker worked hours every night, turning out pies, cakes, doughnuts, pastries. "I want to see pastry all over this camp," the catering service boss told the cook, and there was, day and night. Of course, Bennie pointed out, flour's a hell of a lot cheaper than meat but he didn't care as long as the men were satisfied. Once he thought a watermelon would be a nice touch, and one was flown in. It got smashed up in the plane, and he ordered another. Eight watermelons were shipped in before they received one fit to eat.

Susie kept drilling ahead until June, when the tundra turned into a bog. It started up again in the fall, this time with a new heater that forced steam all the way up to the derrickman and improved winterization. By January Susie was down to 13,500 feet. At that depth the rock is usually hard, the bits wear out faster, and a round trip can use up two days. It's expensive drilling at that depth anywhere; in the Arctic it's even more so. At that point Susie had eaten up $4.5 million. That was enough. Susie was abandoned. The crew went off and left No. 162 standing there, forlorn and deserted in the icy winds of the North Slope.

THE MOUNTAIN MAN

Before dry Susie brought on a bad trip the mood in the company offices back in Anchorage had been euphoric. Other factors, far from Anchorage, had contributed to the groovy feeling. Three years before, the somnolent Atlantic Refining Company, with headquarters in Philadelphia, had acquired a small New Mexico company. Its president, Robert O. Anderson, at 45 a self-made multimillionaire and America's largest individual landowner (more than a million acres in cattle spreads), came along as part of the deal. He received $36.7 million in Atlantic stock, but Atlantic got *him*. Two years later he took over as chairman of the board. A man straight out of the Renaissance, Anderson had many interests—business, finance, art, outdoor sports, literature, philosophy, philanthropy, conversation, conservation—and he performed them all superbly. Running the $900 million company from Roswell, New Mexico, he poured new energy into it, woke it up, changed its direction, and increased its net income 26 percent in his first year.

Richfield was a typical Anderson operation. The West Coast company had gone broke in the 1930s and Sinclair and Cities Service had gained control. Now the anti-trust division ordered them to divest themselves of their interest. Richfield's chairman, Charles S. Jones, wanted to sell out and retire. Other major companies approached him in a cautious, orthodox corporate manner. Anderson, instead, invited himself to Jones's Utah ranch. They went trout fishing together; Anderson can lay a dry fly on the water under a bush without making a ripple. Between casts, and over meals of fresh-caught rainbow, Anderson and Jones worked out a simple, uncomplicated merger. In little more than a year Atlantic Richfield Company's production had gone up 12 percent, earnings had increased from $90 million to $130 million, 500 new stations were opened up, and the supply of crude oil—Atlantic had always been crude-poor—increased to 70 percent of its needs. Dillard Spriggs of Baker Weeks and Company, Wall Street's premier oil analyst who had kept up with Anderson since he first became a mere director of Atlantic, was telling his clients that AFI, Atlantic's ticker-tape symbol, was one of the best investments in the petroleum industry. "The day Anderson became chairman of the board I put my mother-in-law in Atlantic," he told me. That's confidence.

In the Alaska office, the new corporate spirit only enhanced the enthusiasm; the staff there was already hooked. Years before in Wyoming, John M. Sweet's boss used to tell him, "Boy, I'm going to send you to Alaska," and Sweet would say, "When do I leave?" One day in 1962 the orders finally came through: "Okay, you can get out your long underwear now." He became Arco's chief explorationist in Alaska.

"Sometimes I regret not having lived back in the early 1800s," Sweet said. "I'd have been one of the mountain men, one of the early explorers of the west. Oil exploration in Alaska is the closest thing to it. This is where the action is in this company. The other areas have run out of exploratory opportunity, but here we're full of it. Atlantic has been active in Alaska since 1958. We didn't make a lot of noise, but we were here, out in the field, looking, studying. When we merged with Richfield we got their work, acreage, and enthusiasm. The other companies used to say 'you guys are crazy.' Well, maybe we were, but we had something to be crazy about."

Atlantic had started in the Umiat area and had worked north and east toward Prudhoe Bay. It was Sweet's job to coordinate the activities of the geologists and the geophysicists, to study their reports and recommendations, and to make the final recommendation to the producing division, headed by executive vice president Louis F. Davis in Dallas. From the work done in the field Sweet knew that a large anomaly, or anticline, existed beneath the surface on the margin of the North Slope's sedimentary basin at Prudhoe Bay. He was not completely convinced that the structure contained oil in commercial quantities; no geologist can ever be completely convinced of anything.

But they would never know unless they tried, and Sweet was all for trying. It was the last gasp.

"We almost didn't take that gasp," Sweet said. "Richfield had already taken Humble on for $6 million. We didn't want to go it alone, but we couldn't get anybody else. We tried to farm large blocks out but got no takers. We went to everybody —the major companies, foreign companies, the large independents. We noised it around that we were wide open. Nobody would touch it, nobody."

Suddenly Sweet hit the arm of his chair so hard it must have hurt his hand, and let out one of the strangest expletives I have ever heard from a would-be mountain man. "*Gracious*! If only people know how we had to fight to get the company to drill on the Slope, how close we came to never drilling. Do you know what tipped the balance? It was Susie, that rig standing there over a dry hole."

When Susie shut down, there was not one well being drilled on the Slope. Every company had quit. Millions had been poured into that Arctic wasteland, and nobody had anything of value to show for it.

"We all just felt kind of sick after Susie," Lee Wilson, the Alaska production and drilling superintendent, told me. Like Sweet, Wilson was a gung-ho oil man. His father was a drilling contractor and when Lee was four years old his father let him detonate the explosive charge in a well he had just drilled to start the oil flowing. "I tell people I shot my first hole back in '29." His future was determined: he became a petroleum engineer and rose swiftly in the company. He was in Libya when he got the chance to go to Alaska, and he jumped at it. Then came $4.5 million worth of dry Susie.

"John Sweet came to me with an idea," Lee said. "He said we had one last chance to hit a big field on the Slope. I've heard geologists talk before, and I take their dreams with a grain of salt. I guess I'm a pessimist. But all he wanted me to do was back him up with some facts and figures. I had them, and I went along. We went to Dallas. Marvin Mangus came too. John made a two-hour presentation to Louis Davis and his staff. He gave it all he had. I told you I was a pessimist, but before he got through I was rarin' to go."

"I guess my main function, in the final analysis, is selling," Sweet told me. "My job is to push right up to the point where if I push one more time I'll get a knot on my head. I would be derelict in my duty if I didn't go to that point."

This time Sweet had a secret weapon, and Wilson to provide the ammunition for him. The Loffland rig was on the Slope. It had cost $900,000 to get it there—$200,000 more than it was worth. Atlantic couldn't leave it there; the company was obligated to get it back to Anchorage. Though the load would be lighter, for the tons of fuel oil, mud, and watermelons had been used up, still the return trip would cost a half million dollars with nothing to show for it. Prudhoe Bay was only 70 miles to the north. The rig could be moved overland in winter. Let's try one more time.

Davis authorized the move. Humble came in; Arco would be the operator on the well. A Cat train moved up from Fairbanks and took No. 162 to the new site two miles from the beach. In retrospect, the move was a penny-wise operation. "It took a whole month, running twenty-four hours a day," Bennie Loudermilk said. "Tied up a rig, must have cost three hundred thousand dollars. It was a fifteen-minute flight for a Herc and I bet it wouldn't have cost as much."

In spite of Bennie's grumping, moving the rig, setting it up, and getting underway all proceeded fairly smoothly for an Arctic operation. Prudhoe Bay State No. 1 was spudded in on April 26, 1967.

The rig closed down in June with the spring thaw, and started up again in October when the tundra was frozen solid. It was the only well drilling north of Cook Inlet. That was a bad year in Alaska; the manic-depressive state was at the bottom of the cycle.

One day in the late fall a plane from Prudhoe landed at Fairbanks. In an hour the news was all over town—the plane was covered with oil. There could be only one speculation: Arco had hit a gusher up on the Slope, and it must have been one hell of an eruption to reach the plane on the airstrip.

But no word came from the Slope, and the doldrums set back in again. There was good reason for the silence. That was no gusher, that was a goof. With modern techniques of drilling, the days of the gusher are long gone. The mud man on the well site can double the weight of his mud by adding baroid, which is four times the weight of water. At 8210 feet of hole, that's enough to hold anything down. The bit had indeed encountered a show of gas in a 40-foot strata at that level. The geologist on the well wanted a core cut out of the formation for examination. Something went wrong down there, and the tools got stuck. The drilling engineer eased up on the mud pressure. It was like removing the cork from a well-shaken bottle of hot champagne. A distillate of the consistency of carbonated salad oil exploded out of the hole and splattered everybody and everything for hundreds of yards. The pipe remained stuck in the hole.

In the Richfield merger Atlantic had acquired a combination troublemaker/troubleshooter named Bill Congdon, a huge, rough Californian who looks like he could dig a well with his bare paws. Congdon had bulled his way up the ladder from roustabout to become Bennie Loudermilk's most trusted lieutenant. "You're the ugliest son of a bitch in the world," Bennie told him one time when Bill called in to report he had accomplished a particularly difficult mission, "but if you was here right now I'd kiss you."

To straighten out the mess at Prudhoe Bay State No. 1, Loudermilk called on Congdon. He went, but under protest. The Alaska Chamber of Commerce ought to build a wall around Congdon; he is the state's worst advertisement. He hates cold weather. He wouldn't be caught dead in anything but skin-tight blue jeans, and he can't get them on over the goose-down long-johns necessary on the Slope. One time, making emergency re-pairs, he was nailing a loose board back in place. He had trouble hammering the nails with his thick gloves, and stuck a couple in his mouth. It was 50 below zero. You could hear him holler in Fairbanks.

"If Bennie Loudermilk hadn't asked me personally," Congdon told me, "I'd never have come within a thousand miles of this fucking place." But he did come, and this burly, tough-talking man performed his unique artistry a mile and a half below the surface at Prudhoe Bay State No. 1. He brought the well under control, maneuvered the pipe around the mass of metal aban-doned at the bottom, and continued drilling. He stayed on the job week in, week out.

One day Loudermilk got word to him that he was getting a raise. "Keep your goddamn raise and hire somebody who knows something to come up here and help me," Congdon said.

At 11,800 feet, the geologists ordered an electric log run to see what they had. A sonde was lowered, and pulled up at a con-stant speed. The electronic impulses sent up to the surface gave a good indication of what was down there, and at what level. The little squiggles on the roll of paper produced elation back in Sweet's office, and now the official testing began. "The first test brought up water," Congdon said. "It was an ugly yellow color and it smelled like dinosaur piss."

The next test, from another level, showed 22.5 million cubic feet of pressure from gas. "All the company VIPs were there," Congdon said. "They told me to let it go. We ran pipe eight hundred yards out from the well to a flare pit. When we let it go it built up to a pressure of forty-two million cubic feet. It burned for four hours before we put it out. Pilots a hundred miles back over the Brooks Range said they could see the flare. A cloud of black smoke just lay there. Sand flew all the way back to the rig, I thought it was going to cut it to pieces. When we shut it down there was a hole there big enough to put a building in."

But then the oil came up, and from three separate levels. Sweet, low-sulphur oil of fine quality and copious quantities. Number 162, plus the combined efforts of thousands of men and millions of dollars and the efforts of a half-century, had finally hit it big.

One well does not a reservoir make. Before the official test, John Sweet knew that he was on to something—but how much? After a discovery well comes in, more wells are drilled to determine the boundaries of the field. Called step-outs, they are usually only several hundred yards from the discovery well. The first step-out at Prudhoe, Sag River State No. 1, was *seven miles* away. It was begun while Prudhoe Bay was still drilling. The rig BP had used punching dry holes all over the map was stacked, gathering snow, at Pingo Beach. Arco, again in partnership with Humble, had it trucked down the frozen Colville, out onto the sea ice, and eastward to Prudhoe Bay. In preparation for it, a platform big enough to accommodate rig and bunkhouses was piled up out of gravel from the Sagavanirktok riverbed, and an all-weather road built from the discovery well. For the first time on the Slope, drilling went on all summer. Sag River, too, hit oil, and from the same strata.

From the tests of these two wells, the internationally respected consulting firm of DeGolyer and MacNaughton estimated the Prudhoe Bay structure to hold from five to ten billion barrels, making it the largest known field in North America, and one of the largest in the world.

In early July Geoff Larminie and four other BP officials decided to make their move. Thanks to the increased production in the Cook Inlet area and the decreased activity on the North Slope, a full inventory of supplies was available in the Anchorage area. In five days, working largely by gentlemen's agreements, Geoff secured a rig, all supplies, and tugs and barges to transport them up the west coast of Alaska to Point Barrow, then north along the coast to Prudhoe. It was one of the great gambles of the industry. The barges were at sea, racing against the ice floes that could at any time block the route, before the actual contracts had been signed. They made it. By September 1, 4000 tons of supplies were sitting on the coast, waiting for the ground to freeze. BP's well, Put River No. 1, three miles south of the first Prudhoe well, hit oil in the same formations as Arco's wells. The great Alaska oil rush was on.

Chapter III

Dillard SPRIGGS, with hair just a bit long, clothes just a bit ranchy, and an easy, earthy manner of speech, would be a perfect Texas oil man if only he weren't an economist, oenophile, and premier Wall Street petroleum analyst. In mid-morning, June 25, 1968, a clerk brought him an item right off the Dow Jones news wire.

No computer could have reacted more swiftly. Spriggs had already programmed the details of Arco's Prudhoe Bay State No. 1, plus the news of the spudding in of Sag River State. Now the confirmation well had hit—*on a seven-mile step-out.* Dillard's hand grabbed his phone like tongs latching onto a string of drill pipe.

His first call was to the manager of a mutual fund, who didn't ask questions but put in an immediate purchase order. Through a coincidence so unlikely that the Securities Exchange Commission later felt called upon to verify it, a block of 25,000 shares of AFI was placed on sale at almost the same moment; Dillard's client got it all, at 125. In the meantime Dillard was making more calls, and writing out a wire that contained the sentence, "We continue to recommend new purchases in Atlantic Richfield stock." The next day the Exchange had to stop trading in the stock; the day after Arco opened up at 142. Dillard's first call made $425,000 in less than 48 hours. In July AFI was up to 195.

"It was the biggest thing that happened here in forty years," Dillard reminisced later, a dreamy look in his eyes. "This was so *damn* big. You know the oil industry's a big mature plodding industry. Oh, there's a lot of romance about Texas millionaires, but basically oil stocks weren't that volatile. This thing touched off the whole Arctic."

And indeed, a quick check of *Forbes* magazine's list of how stocks of the biggest U.S. companies fared from 1964–1969 reveals that only three oil companies were represented among the 130 that doubled in value. Two, Atlantic Richfield and Standard of Ohio—the latter through its relationship with British Petroleum—were directly involved with the North Slope. Even BP, with its enormous number of shares, went from 3½ in 1962 to a high of 24 after Put River hit.

The major oil companies came down with North Slope fever; everybody had to get in the game. Sheer emotion had plenty to do with it; oil-company executives can get carried away just like other human beings. Another reason was based on hard petroleum facts. Oil demand was increasing faster than the supply across the nation, and the gap was projected to become even wider west of the Rockies in the 1970s and 1980s. Alaskan oil would be desperately needed in the West. Further, the nature of the North Slope oil-bearing sands could mean a high profit to the operators on the price of oil at the well-head. Oil pricing is based on many factors, one of which is a deliberate and successful attempt to confuse the hell out of the consumer. In the Prudhoe Bay reservoir, however, the producing strata is so thick that, as Spriggs said, "you just stick a lot of straws down there and slurp it up."

Finally, the unique land situation in Alaska made immediate haste imperative. You and I could have made millions in Alaska oil leases, if only we had known.

PLUS $10 TO GET DRUNK ON

Locke Jacobs is very fond of money. He plays with it. He puts a quarter between his thumb and forefinger and, without using the other hand, walks it over to his little finger and back again.

He tosses three coins into the air and, like a bear scooping salmon out of a stream, catches them separately in quick motions. In his office in Anchorage he has a magnificent polar bear rug, a relief map of Alaska that covers an entire wall, and on his window sill, silhouetted against the Alaska Range, sit oil cores from his wells and chunks of minerals from his holdings. From time to time for no apparent reason he reaches out, picks up his phone, and starts talking into it. He is taking incoming calls, even though no bell has sounded. His secretary gives him a hand signal from the other side of a pane of soundproof glass. "I don't like bells," he explained.

When Locke was nine years old he was working 12 hours a day in his father's filling station in Oregon. On the side he collected pine cones, pieces of pumice stone, and chipmunks to sell to tourists. "Any thing the forest couldn't use, I could," he said. He read all Jack London's books and talked so much about Alaska in school that the faculty chipped in and bought him luggage for the trip. Surely no other college dropout can make that statement. He arrived broke, having lost his money in a poker game en route. In order to see his new home, he got a job as a section hand on the Alaska Railroad. One summer he traveled the Yukon as a steward on board the sternwheeler *Nenana*. The captain was a geologist and Locke badgered him into conducting tutoring sessions as the boat sloshed up and down the river. Convinced that there was oil south of Anchorage on the Kenai Peninsula, he got a job clerking in a surplus store and furthered his education by studying a book on how to file leases on Federal land. He applied for a lease and, six months later, he was notified that his application was rejected because somebody else had already filed on the tract.

This annoyed Locke, but there was no one to take it out on. The Government land office had no interest in oil and gas leases, only in 160-acre homesteads. He stepped into the vacuum. From eight in the morning until he went to work at four, he sat in the land office copying down all the records concerning oil and gas lands. In order to expedite the job he was doing for someone else on his own time, he invested in an early model German duplicating machine. He spent so much time trying to talk his fellow employees at the surplus store into speculating in oil leases with him that the owner gave him $1000 to leave his sales force alone. Jacobs invested it in more oil leases. A group of local businessmen who took their coffee break together and called themselves the Spit and Argue Club heard about his activities. "What do you know about oil?" one of them asked him. "Nothing, but nobody else does either," Locke said. The group rounded up $65,000 for him to play with.

At that time, in the 1950s, a lease cost 25 cents an acre for three years, plus $10 filing fee. Locke and his backers accumulated a sizable amount of acreage, but it did them little good as no company wanted to drill on it. Locke went down to the States and marched into the offices of some 50 companies trying to stir up interest in Alaska, but got nowhere. The one company he missed was Richfield, but Richfield found him. Rollin Eckis, tired of waiting for the North Slope of Alaska to open up, started looking around in the south. His people filed leases in what looked like a likely spot, and then found that Jacobs and his backers had gotten there first. Richfield found him easy to deal with; it was to his advantage for a major company to get in the action.

Locke produced his own hand-drawn maps and told the Richfield people to take their pick and pay him what they thought the land was worth. "Why haggle over a moose pasture?" They offered him three dollars an acre, plus an override, as a percentage of production is called in the oil business, and he took it. Three dollars for a 25-cent investment isn't all that bad. Locke owned some of the leases himself; on the others he acted as broker, at 20 percent commission.

Richfield brought in the Swanson River field in 1957. Now everybody wanted to lease all the land in the Cook Inlet area. Hordes of speculators and oil company representatives descended on the land office. The office ran out of forms and ordered the entire stock from the warehouse. When they didn't arrive, Jacobs went out in search of the messenger and found him with a flat tire. He courteously volunteered to deliver the forms himself, and did so, but not to the land office. He borrowed a friend's office, brought in a group of secretaries, and that night filled out the forms for a quarter of a million acres of land. He hired more girls and the next night turned out leases for a million acres. The land office demanded that he return their forms and he said that was just exactly what he was doing, all filled out. He netted $100,000 in three weeks.

The wells hit, the oil began to flow, and the royalties came in. Locke extended his operations to the western states of the Lower 48. With his own STOL airplane and helicopters he began exploring for minerals. He became involved in all sorts of financial activity throughout Alaska. When I talked with him he was getting a group together to start a bank. In the meantime he had decided to pick up some of the social graces, such as learning how to dance. He married the dancing teacher and retired her.

Independent lease brokers like Locke and company landmen, as oil company representatives who deal with land are called, have only secondary interest in geology and exploration. Their business is wheeling and dealing with landowners and with each other. In most areas of the United States, the companies deal with the individual owners of the land, paying whatever is necessary per acre for the lease, plus a negotiated override on gas and oil, if any is found.

In Alaska, where only a tiny percentage of the land is individually owned, the companies make their deals either directly with the Federal or state government, or with the individuals who got there first. But complicated as these deals may be, what with combinations of payment for the lease in cash or stock, plus varying percentages of production, the real bargaining comes when the companies deal with each other. On the North Slope, for example, so many companies have joined in different combinations on different tracts that I often wonder why they don't just throw it all together and start all over again. The main idea is to alleviate or spread out the cost of both land acquisition and drilling. Richfield, for example, had to run to Standard of California for money to acquire the Swanson River acreage, to Humble for North Slope acreage.

Then come the drilling deals. One type is known as a farm-out. A typical farm-out results when one company has acreage but is either in no hurry or has no funds to drill while another company has the money and wants a piece of the acreage, or has adjacent acreage but not enough to warrant the expenditure of an exploratory well.

A company may contribute to the cost of drilling in return for information on the strata encountered. In a dry hole contribution the company guarantees to pay the operator a share of the cost if the well is dry but nothing if it hits. In a bottom-hole contribution the company pays a stipulated price whether the well is productive or not but first both sides must decide how deep the well will be. The agreed-upon bottom of the hole might be expressed in feet or in rock formation.

In Alaska, prior to statehood, just about all of that immense land mass belonged to the Federal Government. The few people who did want any part of it found the archaic homesteading laws made land acquisition difficult. What privately owned land existed in the territory was mostly located around the towns. This rarely included Indian villages, for an even tinier percentage of land was owned by the people who got there first, the natives.

Whether he was Indian, Eskimo, or Aleut, the original Alaskan never showed much interest in acquiring property. With all that water to fish in and land to hunt on, why bother to stake it out? There are few Indian reservations in Alaska. The people just lived where they wanted to live and, unless that happened to be on a salmon stream or a gold mine, even the avaricious white man let them stay.

When, therefore, following the Swanson River strike, the Federal Government opened up northern Alaska to oil exploration, the land was all owned by the Federal Government. Leases were granted on a noncompetitive basis; that is, would-be lessors did not bid against each other. Rather, simultaneous filings, known throughout Alaska as simos, were held. The tracts were usually composed of four sections of a square mile each, a total of 2560 acres. The rental started at 25 cents an acre for three years, but this was later increased to 50 cents an acre for one year, or a total of $1280 per tract, plus $10 for filing fee, plus, as one Alaskan put it, $10 to get drunk on if you get it. Although there were a few restrictions, such as a maximum number of acres any one individual or company could lease, or the number of tracts he could file on, the tracts were open to any American company or citizen over 21 years old, or group of either, who could afford $1290. All the filings on each tract were placed in a bingo-type contraption, shaken up, and someone pulled out the winner.

Now the obvious question comes up: With millions of acres, many of them unexplored, to file on, how do you know which one you want? In the first simo, held in 1958 in the Lacey Street Theatre in Fairbanks, British Petroleum—which had thoughtfully registered as an American corporation—was just about the only company that had any idea of what it wanted. As far as individuals were concerned, Locke Jacobs was interested, but he was more closely linked with the southern part of the state. That left Cliff Burglin, then 30 years old and running a small stationery store in Fairbanks.

Cliff had picked up a smattering of geology from his stepfather, William T. Foran, the geologist sans peer. He had been fooling around with leases for a few years but he was still learning. "What I had was access to my stepfather's reports and old records," Burglin told me. "I'll put it very simply. If I had had a brain in my head I could have retired a millionaire a dozen years ago."

When the first simo was announced, Cliff broached the subject of filing to friends and business associates in Fairbanks, and eight of them responded to the gambling urge. Cliff filed on some 50 tracts and won a fair share of them. Four were in the Gubik area, which Foran had discovered and named. This was the same area BP was interested in, and Cliff and his associates sat back and waited. The leases were good for three years; at the end of that period they'd have to get up more scratch. Cliff wrote BP letters over a period of two years but received only polite rejection slips. In the third year of the lease, BP made a token offer that Cliff refused. Another four or five months went by, and the BP landman, John Zehnder, dropped by to up the offer to $10,000 for each tract plus a one percent override. Zehnder, an Australian, and Cliff got along well; Australians and Alaskans usually do. Zehnder was honest beyond call of duty; he told Cliff that BP was interested in one tract more than the other three. Cliff agreed to the deal on three, but not on the fourth. Zehnder called BP's Anchorage office which called the Calgary office which called the London office, and back came an offer of $12,500 plus a five percent override. The override figure was unusually good; on the Slope at that time, owing to the expense of exploration, a two percent override was considered maximum.

"We're happy with the override," Burglin said, "but we'd like double the money."

"I'll see what I can do," Zehnder said, and again made the three-hop call to London for directions. He returned with an offer of $22,500. This time he told Cliff, honest Australian to honest Alaskan, "I'd advise you to take it."

Cliff said, "It's a deal."

For a total expenditure of $2560 plus $40 filing fee, therefore (this was in the 25-cents-an-acre period), Cliff and his group received $52,500, plus an override of one percent on three tracts, five percent on the fourth. In addition to his own part ownership, Cliff himself received 20 percent brokerage commission. BP drilled Gubik Unit No. 1 in conjunction with Colorado Oil and Gas and Sinclair and hit gas but not oil. The difficulty of getting the gas to market precluded further development but someday this field will surely pay off.

By the time of the second Federal lease sale in 1964, it would be safe to say that no man in Alaska knew more about oil and gas leases than Cliff Burglin. He had developed friendships with scores of people possessing geological expertise. On occasion he would pay a practicing geologist a consultant fee, but mostly his information came informally from friends and acquaintances. "I was born and raised here," Cliff explained. "And if you have friends, well, they help you."

I asked him if he had personally reconnoitered the area. He laughed. "You could prowl around on the North Slope for thirty years and not know any more than you did when you started," he said.

In addition to having friends, Burglin had a reputation for absolute integrity. Cliff does not come on strong, and in his usual sport shirt he could easily be taken for a minor employee instead of a multimillionaire doing business with the major oil companies of the world. One of his problems as a lease broker is his attempt to be completely fair to all his clients. In the 1964 simo some 600 tracts were put up for filing. Cliff studied them and picked out 120 that he considered to be the best. Now the question was, which of his friends and clients, not to mention Cliff Burglin himself, would be put on what tract?

If he developed some formula for spreading it out equitably I couldn't get it out of him. "I deal with a lot of people," he said, "and I have to be fair. Fairbanks is a small town and everybody knows everybody else and talks to everybody else, and if you think that Cliff is taking care of himself and his friends, then you're going to go looking for another broker. So I try— well, I'm very careful."

Some of his clients could afford to put up the money for an entire tract, others he assigned to a half-ownership with someone else, sometimes himself. As any individual is limited in the number of tracts he can file on, he frequently made the selections, did the paperwork, and made the assignments with no official mention of himself, and consequently no guarantee that he would receive any compensation for it. All he had was the faith that the people who won the leases would come to him voluntarily after the drawing to ask him to serve as their broker for the customary 20 percent. On this basis he was entrusted with more than a million dollars, most of it from people with average incomes, to file on the leases he selected.

Many of the major corporations and thousands of oil-lease speculators all over the United States participated in the 1964 simo. On the basis that the more chances you buy the better your odds, Cliff himself put in over 900 applications on behalf of his clients. The cost of each lease was now $1280 plus $10 filing fee. He got 60. This was during the period when there was little activity on the North Slope, and the oil companies did not offer him fantastic amounts for them. However, of the 60 leases, he sold 40 for an average of about $5000, which tripled his clients' money immediately and left them with an override to dream on. The owners of the 20 leases that were not sold let them go by not keeping up with the 50 cents per acre rent. I know some of these people. They have an easily identifiable characteristic: black and blue spots from kicking themselves.

One of Cliff's best customers was Richfield, which staged a remarkably aggressive campaign. It was headed by Armand C. Spielman, the most popular landman in Alaska. Since his high school days in St. Louis, Spielman had dreamed of coming to Alaska. He had started with Richfield as a title examiner and through the years had picked up the basic elements of what a good landman must know—engineering, geology, geophysical techniques, property description, settlement of claims, accounting, recording procedures. He arrived in Alaska in 1960 and immediately found himself at home. A hard bargainer but a sincere and dedicated man, by the second Federal simo he had an inside track with Alaskans.

For the 1964 drawing he set up headquarters in a motel room in Fairbanks with leased lines to Anchorage and thence to the home office in Los Angeles. He used voice scramblers so that his messages could not be intercepted. Richfield chartered airplanes at the major oil centers—Denver, Dallas, Salt Lake City, San Francisco—with land personnel standing by. If you lived in the Dallas area, say, and had taken a wild chance filing on Federal land in Alaska, word that you had won a lease in the lottery would be delivered to you personally by a Richfield representative, who would then offer you an immediate profit of about five to one plus override. Richfield picked up a lot of acreage that way.

"We were the aggressive company," Spielman explained. "That's what we had to sell, and we sold it. Other companies might offer more money, but we got to you first, and we impressed you with our honest determination to explore the Slope. We had good solid geological information and we were determined to drill. That was the clincher. It meant that your override had immediate potential. It wasn't just a quick profit, but the possibility of a continuing percentage if and when we hit oil. We weren't just going to let that land sit there, we were going to drill."

Richfield, a pygmy among oil companies, built up a large acreage on the Slope.

Between the two Federal simos, Alaska had won its long battle for statehood. Some of the tactics used in the battle were typical of the frontier spirit of the people of the territory. Even when it seemed most unlikely that statehood would go through, a group of Alaska leaders held a convention to write a modern, progressive constitution for a state that might never be. It elected a congressional delegation. Ernest Gruening, former journalist, statesman, and territorial governor, was one Senator. Two well-known Alaska leaders, William A. Egan and Ralph J. Rivers, were Senator and Representative, respectively.

The proponents of statehood had to overcome many obstacles, including opposition by some Alaskans, before joining the union with Hawaii as the 49th and 50th states.

The phase of the campaign with which I'm most familiar, and which has been overlooked in the textbooks, was headed by Ed Merdes, first territorial president of the Junior Chamber of Commerce, newly organized in Alaska.

Ed had been a poor boy in a grubby industrial town in Pennsylvania. "We had rats in our living room," he said. "They came right up through the floor." But he could play football and went through Cornell on an athletic scholarship, then with help from his working wife, Norma, on through law school. On graduation he was offered a clerkship in Utica, where there were 65 other lawyers. He wrote a Cornellian in Alaska to ask if there were an opportunity there. Back came a letter from territorial judge George W. Folta, which read in its entirety:

"If you are sufficiently interested in becoming my law clerk at $6200 a year, please take the next plane to Alaska."

Ed became Judge Folta's law clerk and eventually organized his own law firm in Fairbanks. In 1966 he was president of Junior Chamber International and in that capacity, which carries with it the full VIP treatment, he visited 60 countries in 1966.

"But no matter where I was, and no matter how warm the welcome or the climate, I was always glad to get back to Alaska," he said. Ed and I have known each other for years, and he poured out his love for the Great Land. "Do you know what living in a cold country does? It brings out the best in people. When we see a car stopped we stop, too, to see if we can help. We're less selfish, we're more open, we're all together, we're interested in one another. Listen, we've got something here called ice fog. We'll go for days with the temperature at fifty, sixty, sixty-five below, with ice hanging in the air so thick that you can't see across the street. Going to work, getting the kids to school is a day's work in itself. There's only an hour or so of daylight and all we can do is huddle inside and try to keep warm. Then suddenly the cold snap will break, and the thermometer will go up to ten below, and the air will clear, and friends and neighbors all up and down the block will go outside in our shirtsleeves and talk and laugh together like it was a holiday. Oh, those are wonderful days. Then summer comes, with its twenty-three and a half hours of sunshine, and the flowers, and our own vegetables, and water skiing on the lake and playing baseball at midnight. Oh, this is wonderful, wonderful country, America at its finest and truest. God, how I love it."

That kind of enthusiasm, coupled with the romance of Alaska, had appealed to the U.S. Jaycees, and they made Alaskan statehood a national super-project. Energetic young men from every state, in contact with Alaska Jaycees by ham radio, whipped up pressure on their own Congressional delegations. Some state delegations were opposed to the admittance of Alaska and Hawaii, but others didn't care much one way or the other. These were the poor devils on whom the Jaycees let loose the bombardment, and when the smoke had cleared away they found they'd voted yes.

One suggested qualification to statehood that was narrowly overcome, incidentally, was the division of the state, with the northern section remaining a territory. If that had gone through, the North Slope would not be a part of Alaska today.

The Alaska Statehood Act of 1958 gave the new state the right to select about 104 million of Alaska's 365 million acres—owned almost entirely by the Federal Government—to have for its very own. Apart from the heavily forested lands of the southeast, much of the state acreage consists of barren mountains, muskeg, and tundra. It's difficult to choose when you don't have much to choose from, and even by the beginning of the 1970s only a fourth of the total amount had been selected. Of these 26 million acres, some two million lie along the Arctic coast between the Colville and the Canning rivers, which also form the rough boundaries of the Naval Petroleum Reserve on the west and the Arctic Wildlife Range on the east.

It's interesting to note that this strip, though selected by Alaska when geological attention was directed to the central and southern portions of the Slope, covers only the northern portion. The significance of this, if any, has been almost completely overlooked because of a more controversial aspect, the historical background of which lies in the period following the purchase of Alaska when Congress, apparently not knowing what to do with Seward's Folly, did nothing. During that time there just wasn't any law at all up there. Finally Congress supplanted the absence of law with a ridiculous law, the Organic Act of 1884. The code of the state of Oregon, for example, with its complex provisions pertaining to the functions of counties and towns in Oregon, was applied to the district of Alaska, which had no counties and towns, and no way to create them. With no controls whatever, valuable living resources such as the sea otter and the salmon were almost exterminated. But the Act did recognize the native people of Alaska and provided that they "shall not be disturbed in the possession of any lands actually in their use or occupation or now claimed by them."

When, 80 years later, the State of Alaska, under the provision of another Federal act, grabbed two million acres of the North Slope, it did so on the basis that the land was neither used nor occupied by aborigines. As far as actual occupation went, the claim was probably correct. Though native villages had once been scattered along the Arctic coast, their inhabitants had moved into gas-heated Barrow to work for the white man on Pet 4. The only other coastal village was Kaktovik on Barter Island, well east of the chosen area. In strict compliance with the law, the state published a notice in *Jessen's Weekly*, a small Fairbanks paper since defunct, notifying any claimant of the land involved to file an objection. Considering the number of Eskimos living 400 miles to the north of the offices of this great publication who saw the notice and could comprehend its legal jargon, it's not surprising that no one came forward to claim ownership.

The question of prior claimants was thus doubly taken care of. The Act of 1884, however, refers specifically to use as well as ownership. Instead of sitting in their igloos reading *Jessen's Weekly* by the light of a seal-oil lamp, Eskimos had been wandering over this frozen land for millennia in search of the caribou. The state appropriation of these not-so-happy hunting grounds was going to have repercussions later, even to the point of uniting the Eskimo, Aleut, and Indian against state, nation, and white man, but at the time no protests were forthcoming.

The state sold leases to tracts totaling some 900,000 acres of this land in 1964, 1965, and 1967. Proceeds of the sales brought $12 million into the state treasury—more money than the Federal Government had paid for the entire territory and but a tiny fraction of what the oil underneath the surface is worth. But who knew that before Prudhoe? Many tracts placed on the block in those sales couldn't attract the minimum bid of $1 an acre.

Unlike the Federal bingo system, the state put the leases up for competitive bidding. The land itself was not sold, only the oil and gas rights. Rental was set at $1 per acre per year on a 10-year lease—$25,600—but the real money was in what the state called the bonus. If you wanted to take a crack at what lay beneath the surface of four square miles of tundra, you would decide how much money you were willing to pay to get the lease, have a certified check made out for 20 percent of the amount, and enclose it in a sealed envelope. If your bid was high, you got the lease, whereupon you'd pay the remaining 80 percent of the bonus bid and a year's rent. The state reserved the right to reject the bid if it didn't think it high enough. What you got really amounted to an oil-hunting license. In addition to the initial cost, any oil produced, prior to an increase enacted by the 1970 legislature, was subject to 12½ percent royalty due the state, plus a tax of four percent.

Only four companies bid on the area covered by the two discovery wells, Prudhoe Bay and Sag River. Atlantic was low bidder with $6, then came Mobil Oil and Phillips Petroleum and BP with $12 and $47 respectively. Richfield, with financial help from Humble, won the prize with $93. (In the Atlantic Richfield merger the low bidder absorbed the high.) BP was high bidder on tracts immediately to the south and to the northeast.

One of Cliff Burglin's friends in Fairbanks is a pharmacist named Tom Miklautsch. The first time we met, Tom and I quickly discovered we have something in common: the crazy, mixed-up U.S. Army of World War II. I, a journalist in civilian life, made the Normandy invasion with, of all things, a medical depot company, doling out pharmaceuticals. Tom, a quiet pharmacist in tortoise-shell glasses, wound up in the MPs with an equally harrowing assignment, MP duty in San Francisco on VJ night.

One day, Tom told me, Cliff called him to say that a state lease sale of 40 tracts on the North Slope was coming up and he ought to get in on it. Tom was hesitant. He was still paying rent on tracts nobody wanted to buy. But Cliff was persuasive—he had learned that only four companies were going to bid—and Tom went to the bank and borrowed $50,000. Other friends of Cliff's also got in on the deal, but without much alacrity; action was slow on the North Slope at that time. Cliff bid the minimum of a dollar an acre—$2560 plus filing fee—for each of the 40 tracts. He got just two, the two he had put Tom Miklautsch on. He wouldn't have gotten them if you and I had gotten together and put up one cent more per acre.

Ownership on both was split 80 percent Miklautsch, 20 percent Burglin. In June, 1968, Miklautsch and Burglin found themselves sitting on the hottest piece of property on the North Slope. They were ten miles due north of Arco's original well, Prudhoe Bay State No. 1. Land men for every major oil company made their way to Tom Miklautsch's drugstore and to Cliff Burglin's cluttered office. Cliff couldn't study his maps; Tom couldn't count his pills. One man was particularly persistent, and they kept passing him back and forth. He was Robert E. Swesnik of General American. They threatened to take him out to the airport and put him on a plane three different times. The first time he had offered a quarter of a million dollars, the second time a half-million, and the third time one million.

"It got to the point," Cliff said, "where Tom would call me and say I had to see him, that he was busy, and I'd say okay, I'd see him this morning but that Tom would have to see him that afternoon because I was busy, too. Bob Swesnik and I are good friends and I wasn't trying to give him the runaround, but I just didn't think we'd ever get together. Incidentally, let me tell you a little bit about Tom. If Tom were a greedy man, or if I were for that matter, we couldn't have made this deal. We'd have accepted the first offer. Tom is honest and fair and courageous."

"Wait a minute," I said, "I don't dig you. It seems to me that the word greedy means holding out for the most you can get."

"Yeah," Cliff said, "but what I mean is, it takes courage for a man who doesn't have a lot of money, and has never had a lot of money, to turn down that kind of offer. But we had made up our minds what we thought it was worth, and Tom stuck to it."

Eventually General American came through with two million dollars, but that was only part of the deal. Burglin and Miklautsch have a most unusual override. Usually the override, whether it is one percent or five, starts paying off only after all the drilling expenses have been accounted for. Cliff and Tom have a 25 percent override, and it is net, off the top. They not only have their two million, but they get 25 percent of every drop of oil that comes out of their holdings, from the first barrel to the last.

There's a sequel to this story. General American has since sold the two leases to Humble for $4.7 million, plus, hold your breath, *another* 25 percent override. With all this, Cliff and Tom haven't changed a bit. When I last talked to Tom he was involved in a real estate venture that involved glassing in a couple of blocks in Fairbanks and using excess steam from the power company to keep the temperature at 60 degrees even when it's 60 below outside. He's interested in it not only from the profit angle, but because he wants to develop the downtown area of Fairbanks, which sure needs it. He is still the general manager of the Fairbanks Goldpanners, one of the nation's top semi-pro teams (Tom Seaver of the Mets started out there). This doesn't leave a great deal of time to continue pushing pills, but he still checks in his drugstore every Saturday. "Some of my old customers want me to fill their prescriptions personally," he said, almost apologetically, "so I work Saturdays to take care of them."

THE RUSH TO THE SLOPE

Tom Miklautsch, Ed Merdes, a couple of other fellows and I were having dinner together one night—Tom picked up the check—when Ed began needling Tom about a trip they had made to the North Slope in August, 1969. Atlantic Richfield had asked Tom, Ed, and Mayor Red Boucher of Fairbanks to take a look at what the company was doing at the Prudhoe Bay base camp —Arco is justifiably proud of its housekeeping there—and had furnished a helicopter for the trip. After leaving Prudhoe Ed suggested that they go take a look at Tom's property. Tom was hesitant, but finally agreed. The helicopter pilot was even more hesitant, but after radioing ahead and receiving permission to land he went ahead.

"We set down on the landing pad," Ed said, laughing, "and I opened up the door and got out. Red was right behind me, but Tom wouldn't leave the copter. 'Come on,' Red and I said, but Tom wouldn't budge. He kept saying he'd be trespassing. Here's a guy with two million bucks and a twenty-five percent override and he's trespassing!"

Tom just grinned, and Ed kept sticking the needle in. "The guards came up and there were Red and I on the ground and Tom, the only one of us who really had any right to be there, still sitting in that chopper and refusing to get out. Can you beat that? Those guys had guns, too. Were you scared they'd shoot you for putting your foot on your own property, Tom?"

Tom had obviously had a few shots of the Merdes needle before, and had taken it like a man. But suddenly he leaned toward me intensely. "You were in the Army, too," he said, and I knew he was going to tell the real story. "Well, I was in one of the best MP detachments in the Army, and I got so I could sense things. When those guards first started toward us with their guns I could *smell* danger. When they got close enough I could see they had their fingers on the trigger, and their safeties were off. I wasn't scared exactly, but I sure didn't want to get those guys excited. I can tell you from experience, you just never know what a guy with a gun and the authority to use it is going to do."

State Senator Merdes and Mayor Boucher were able to identify themselves and their reluctant friend and they were eventually permitted to take a look at the well. All they saw was a Christmas tree, which is oilfield terminology for something that looks like a fire hydrant with extra nozzles on it sticking out of the ground. But that was all they needed to know. You don't put Christmas trees on dusters; General American had hit something there. They looked at it, then went back to the helicopter and headed for home.

This was the type of security practiced on the North Slope during that period. The place was lousy with oil spies—pardon, *scouts.* Helicopters were constantly buzzing around the top of rigs, with observers peering out through binoculars to see what was going on. They came so close that the men on the night shift couldn't sleep. Every rig on the Slope had a security guard; one was patrolled by guard dogs. A female dog went into heat. Her condition aroused the interest of the local canine population, and as she made her rounds she was followed by a pack of panting, passionate wolves.

Oil scouts can learn a great deal about what's beneath the surface just by observing the activities on the rig. When a well makes a trip, the 90-foot lengths of pipe are stacked vertically in the racks on the rig floor. Count the lengths of pipe and you know how deep the well is. If you can get a look at the bit through binoculars you've got a good idea what type of rock it's drilling in. These activities are all considered fair in the oil game. Stealing drilling records is a different matter; two men who attempted to sell information to another company were caught, turned over to the F.B.I., and charged with grand larceny.

Even under normal conditions, oil companies like to keep

their operations to themselves. Most exploration wells are known as tight holes: no information is supposed to leak out. But no wells in the history of drilling were ever tighter than those on the North Slope following the Prudhoe Bay discovery; the president of one company drilling a multimillion-dollar well couldn't get past the guard house at the airstrip. The reason for the super security was the lease sale scheduled for September 11, 1969, at which the state of Alaska would sell 179 tracts totaling 450,858 acres to the highest bidders. In what came close to mass hysteria in the oil industry, just about every company of any size at all was itching to get in on the action on the Slope.

The determination of which barren chunk of land to bid on, and how much, is one of the most complex activities of the oil industry. The pioneers on the Slope, chiefly BP and Arco, had been studying it for 11 years. The newcomers had only months in which to acquire sufficient information. Geophysical crews poured into the area. Companies that already had holdings rushed in drilling rigs, not only in hopes of hitting oil, but to study the stratigraphy of the basin. Not even in the height of the Gold Rush was there such activity in Alaska as in 1968 and 1969. It seemed to me that the State of Alaska, or at least the most populous part of it, the Anchorage-Fairbanks corridor, was going nuts.

If I could sum up the whole activity in one set of statistics, this would be it: In May of 1968, Fairbanks International Airport recorded 591 revenue landings and handled 1236 tons of cargo. In May of 1969 there were 2921 landings and 17,448 tons.

Aviation couldn't handle the load. Arco, BP, and other companies joined together in a barge shipment of 65,000 tons of oilfield equipment from Seattle to Prudhoe Bay. It has been called "one of the most daring and almost incredible feats in maritime history." A fleet of 24 tugs and 36 barges was assembled for the voyage to the Slope. The flotilla, largest ever to penetrate Arctic waters, proceeded up the Pacific coast, across the Gulf of Alaska, through the Aleutians, along the western coast of

Alaska to Barrow and then to Prudhoe Bay. The barges carried mammoth trucks, timber, rigs, food, prefabricated buildings, and fuel oil. It takes oil to get oil. Four barges were especially made to be sunk at the end of the gravel causeway at Prudhoe.

Going around Prudhoe the flotilla ran into ten-foot blue ice; the Coast Guard icebreaker *Storis* suffered gaping holes in two places in its successful attempt to free a tug and barge. But the biggest risk was along the northern coast. Strong winds held the ice floes offshore, but the skippers had to maneuver delicately to keep from grounding; the barges drew up to 18 feet of water and there are places eight miles off the coast where the depth is only five feet.

The first string of barges arrived safely. The four designed for that purpose were filled with sea water and sunk. Giant cranes started unloading cargo as curious seagulls circled about. The whitecaps of the gray-green Beaufort Sea slapped up against the sea's first dock.

Then the oil barges came in. Pillow tanks, which can be rolled up like huge sleeping bags, were unloaded and stretched out on the gravel-insulated tundra. Fuel oil was pumped into them until they resembled bed pillows for giants. Half of the barges were heading home unloaded and the other half were coming in, when, about the first of August, a sudden cold snap froze the Beaufort Sea solid. The homeward bound flotilla couldn't get out; the Prudhoe-bound shipment couldn't get in. It could have been a long winter, but the ice broke up in September and some 200 longshoremen worked around the clock to get the barges unloaded and back out to sea again. Having slept in the comfortable bunkhouses they brought in, warmed by the heat from the fuel oil, I'm thankful that the deliverers got home safe.

Thousands more tons of cargo came down the Mackenzie, in barges built at Hay River and Port Smith. More cargo came in overland, by Cat train from Fairbanks. Once on the Slope, the trains were kept busy moving rigs around, for the big companies were now punching holes in the ground as fast as they could get rigs to the sites. Bennie Loudermilk supervised one move in which the rig was transported, standing up, 36 miles over the tundra. The 152-foot rig, weighing 400,000 pounds not including its crust of ice, was mounted on tracked flatbed trucks called Athey wagons, and pulled by five Cats around the pingoes, over the grassy hummocks, and across frozen lakes with the ice cracking like rifle shots.

"I'd never have bet a nickel it would get there," Bennie said. "I followed it in a pickup truck and we broke every shock absorber. Nothing like that had ever been done before, but hell, we were desperate. When we got to the drill site there was nothing there but a mat on a piling, but we set up the rig and were drilling in six days. It cost twelve thousand dollars but it paid for itself several times over. We must have made a half-dozen moves like that in the winter of 1969–1970."

For the long hauls the Cat trains were inefficient. Frontier Rock and Sand Company, which ran the first Cat train to the Slope, had also pioneered in building roads out of that plentiful Alaskan substance, snow. Two Cats, scraping snow from the sides into the middle, could build 6 to 12 miles of road a day.

To bridge the Yukon, they used the river itself. First they put down a layer of brush on the ice, then augered holes, put down hoses, and pumped water from beneath the ice to on top of it. After several repetitions, they had a reinforced ice bridge capable of holding the heaviest truck. Trucking companies proposed to Governor Walter Hickel that the State Department of Highways take over the route for a winter road to the Slope, over the Yukon and through Anaktuvuk Pass. Hickel authorized the department to go ahead, and it built the now famous winter haul road or Hickel Highway. Like Theseus in the Labyrinth, an airplane laid out the route by dropping a trail of twine.

Though the concept of a winter road was not new—gold miners had used similar trails decades before—the construction of such a road on so large a scale was certainly another first. The road began at Livengood, 80 miles north of Fairbanks on a year-round gravel highway. The first leg was to the Yukon, 60 miles north. There, in December and January, a brutal cold wave struck the construction men. One night the temperature fell to 75 below. In such cold hydraulic hoses burst, dozer blades snap. This was one of the times in the great oil rush when even the white man had sense enough to quit.

This is an area of forest patches and muskeg swamps that turn to soup in summer. The southern foothills of the Brooks Range begin at Bettles, 130 miles north of the Yukon and across the Arctic Circle. Winds gusting to 80 miles an hour attacked the men as they climbed to Anaktuvuk, 110 miles farther on, then down the other side and out on the slope to the Sagwon strip, final destination 550 miles north of Fairbanks.

Unfortunately, in its haste to get the winter road in while it was still winter, the highway department apparently did not consult the experts, Frontier Rock and Sand. The Frontier men looked on with shocked amazement as the road builders from southern Alaska scraped up chunks of dirt and vegetation and packed them on the road. The dark splotches absorbed the heat, melted the snow, and more dirt and vegetation had to be packed on. When summer came the exposed permafrost on either side of the road melted so that the road looked like a causeway winding through a narrow lake.

One summer day I was flying up to Barrow with a group of legislators and state officials from the Anchorage area who had never seen the winter road. The pilot announced that it was beneath us, to the right, and everyone on the left side of the plane jumped up and moved across the aisle to look down on it. The sudden shift of weight rocked the plane like a boat in a cross wave, but in the shock of seeing the blight on the landscape beneath, no one even noticed. No one but me, that is. I prefer to fly horizontally, and I'd already seen the road.

It was in such terrible shape that it cost $1.5 million to reopen it for the winter of 1969–1970. Nevertheless, thousands of tons of cargo, and the heavy trucks and equipment needed on the Slope, traveled the Hickel Highway that first winter. One convoy of 36 trucks loaded with cargo made the trip all the way from Odessa, Texas, up the Alaska Highway and the winter road to the final destination on the Slope.

Few companies scouring the Slope had sufficient time to bring their equipment in by barge or truck. Within less than a year after it had taken a meeting of two chief executive officers to get a Hercules airplane in Alaska, at least nine were flying from Fairbanks to gravel strips, snow strips, and frozen lakes on the North Slope. They rattled the windows of Fairbanks day and night. Each plane could make three, sometimes four, round trips a day, and carry up to 25 tons.

"It's a money machine," a Herc maintenance man for Interior Airways said. "Three hours and ten minutes round trip, four to five thousand bucks a crack, two and a half million per plane—hell, we can pay for it in six months and then it's all gravy."

But he left out a significant factor. As the number of aircraft in the Arctic skies increased, so did the number on the ground —permanently. The cost of insurance rose to $400,000 on a Herc, and it was available only from Lloyd's of London. Tonnage delivered to the North Slope rivaled that delivered in the Berlin Airlift, but in comparison to that minutely planned military execution, the North Slope operation was a disheveled mess. In August, 1969, the Federal Aviation Administration estimated that some 200 aircraft, from Hercs to helicopters and light twin-engine planes, were flying more than 1100 operations a day to and on the Slope. Small planes were also flitting around.

"It gets to be terrifying sometimes," a Hercules pilot said. "Conditions here are archaic. There's nothing like this in the United States any more. It's basic instrument flying in high performance aircraft."

Flying up to the Slope with Jerry Newman of Aviation Contractors in a Piper Navajo one day, we noticed the tail of an airplane sticking out of a lake beneath us. "Is anybody lost?" I asked.

"There's always somebody lost," Jerry said. He put the plane into a steep bank and we went down and circled the lake repeatedly, looking for some signs of life. We couldn't land as the plane was not equipped with floats.

After making sure that there was no downed pilot on the lakeshore, we resumed course. "A pilot I know was flying a float plane," Jerry said, as we waited to get within talking range of a DEW Line station, "and lost his engine and tried to make the nearest lake. He hit the trees going in and knocked the float up on top of the cabin. He broke both legs and most of his ribs in the crash. The float was sticking out of the water. Somehow he managed to get out of the cabin with his bedroll, tied it to the float and got in it. He hung there for four days. He could scoop up lake water with his hands to drink. He caught lake shrimp and ate them alive. He was in such pain that on the third day he decided to cut himself loose, drown, and get it over with. He gave himself one more day, and that's the day they found him."

By that time we could get the station on the radio. Jerry gave the operator the approximate location of the downed plane. The operator checked his records and said the plane was accounted for; it was a World War II bomber. Russian ferry pilots, picking up planes in Fairbanks for Lend Lease delivery during the war, had, in their unfamiliarity with American instrumentation, splattered the things all over Alaska. Jerry and I both knew the plane we had seen was no bomber, and said so. The operator checked again, and said it must be a Stinson, but that didn't meet the right description either. The operator then described a couple more.

"For Christ's sake," Jerry said, "how many have you got down there?" Finally the operator promised to make a full report on it, and we proceeded on to the Slope. There was nothing more we could do.

Helicopters are almost helpless in bad weather on the Slope. One pilot, trying to land in an ice fog, couldn't see the ground and came down tail first. The rotor hit the frozen ground, deflected, and sliced the pilot's head off; his co-pilot and passenger didn't get a scratch. Two huge Sikorsky Sky Cranes were brought in to airlift a drilling rig for Rowan Drilling Company. They moved an entire rig and a 52-man camp, bunkhouses and all, from one location to another in summer, over the impossible tundra. On one lift a glass of water inadvertently left on a kitchen table was delivered without spilling a drop. But on a later trip a cable dangling from one of them hit a small bluff, bounced up into the rotor and severed the blade. Three men killed and a two-million-dollar craft demolished. In spite of these perilous conditions, some 75 helicopters were active on the Slope.

Even the old flying adage that a good landing is one you can walk away from doesn't hold true in this demanding wilderness. On Christmas Eve, 1968, a Hercules, flown by a pilot fresh out of Miami, was coming in for a landing at the BP field at Prudhoe. It was a clear night, and he could see the lights below. But a gale was blowing in from the Arctic, sweeping snow along with it. The pilot came down out of a clear sky into an opaque 20-foot layer of blowing snow. The plane broke up as though it exploded, strewing metal over the area and killing the co-pilot and engineer.

The pilot and loadmaster survived and could have walked away—but in which direction? They waited for someone to come rescue them. But though the bunkhouses were less than 200 yards away, in the roar of the wind not one of the 50 men inside heard the sound of 100 tons of loaded Herc hitting the frozen ground. By the time the two men were discovered they were close to death from exposure.

Many a pilot in the Lower 48 has crashed, recovered from his injuries, and flown again. But any injury severe enough to keep a pilot from crawling in his sleeping bag can mean death in the Arctic. Bob Fawcett of Interior Airways once spotted a plane reported lost sitting apparently undamaged on a frozen lake. He landed and found the pilot in his seat. He had been knocked unconscious, and then had frozen stiff. When Bob delivered the body back to Fairbanks several hours later it was still frozen solid in a sitting position.

You get so you know the pilots, how long they've been in

Alaska, how many crashes they have survived, the jobs they've been called on to do. Bennie Loudermilk was telling me one time that he used to ride C-46s to Susie the way the average guy takes a bus to work. In Alaska apprehension of flying develops calluses, but I saw the muscles on his face tighten up at the memory. I asked him if he had flown with Bob Fawcett, and the relaxation of his facial muscles was instantaneous. "Bob's the best!" he said. I agree. To me happiness is trudging out to a small plane, trying to look casual in spite of the knot in your stomach, and finding Bob Fawcett in the driver's seat.

What I liked about Bob was that, after 20 years of flying missions impossible, the flights he took me on were routine. Bob had flown in the miserable fog of the Aleutians, following the coastline in a 100-foot ceiling guided only by the thin dark line on the beaches where the tide washes away the snow. He delivered 100,000 pounds of dynamite, 4000 pounds at a time in a DC-3, in subzero temperatures. When dynamite freezes the nitroglycerine separates, and Bob let that DC-3 down awful easy. That's the way I like to land, like frozen dynamite.

Bob used to be called upon to fly into an Air Force detachment at the foot of the 1000-foot bluff at Cape Lisburne. It was normally serviced by the Air Force, but regulations restricted pilots from landing there when the cross winds were blowing at more than ten knots. As such winds persist for months at a time and the detachment had to have food and mail, the Air Force had to find a civilian to make the run. Bob flew it in a C-46, which has big wheels suitable for rough runways, but a big tail surface sticking up in the cross wind. He'd have the plane loaded heavy in the tail and come in practically sideways, one engine idling and the other revved up all the way.

The sudden demand for pilots brought in many men with thousands of hours, but not enough of those hours flown in such extreme conditions and with so little traffic control. It was a bad year for flying. Of the 13 Hercs brought in, for example, one was totaled and two were severely damaged. In the winter of 1970 six near-collisions involving Hercs alone were reported.

In addition to the Slope traffic, of course, there was the usual busy flow of regular air travel including the big jets high over-head on the polar routes.

These, too, have an impact. I was in a small plane coming into Anchorage one time when it ran into a brick wall. Everything in the plane, including me, went forward. Debris came flying from the rear of the cabin all the way up to the cockpit, where I was in the co-pilot's seat.

"What the hell was *that*?" I asked the pilot when I got my breath back.

"A wind spiral from a big jet, I guess," he said. We both looked up, down and around, but didn't see another plane in the sky. "Don't quote me," he said, "because they're supposed to dissipate, but that isn't the first time I've hit one out in the middle of nowhere with no plane in sight. It's like a horizontal twister. We banged into the edge of one. If we'd hit the other edge it would have thrown the plane forward. In the middle we'd have bounced up and down."

Flying in Alaska can still be a delight. Glowing in the red sunset of an early winter afternoon, Mt. McKinley and its rivers of ice—the Indians called it Denali, the High One—is glorious. Even on the North Slope, with herds of gray caribou and stately moose grazing over the soft heather and the pale sun, setting over Siberia and illuminating the thousands of lakes, all mys-teriously pointing to the northwest, the scene beneath has its own beauty, soft and strange.

ALASKAN CRESCENDO

I bumped into Ralph Cox at the Atlantic Richfield base camp at Prudhoe Bay one afternoon. From the eager look in the eyes of Texas that were upon me I'd have thought he was on the way to the Cotton Bowl with two 50-yard-line tickets. "I'm go-ing out to look at the grass," he said. "Want to come?"

"Sure," I said. I didn't know whether the grass was for mow-ing or smoking, but with all that enthusiasm, count me in.

Geologist Marvin Mangus prepares to break camp during oil explorations in 1947.   *Mangus*

Bush pilot Sig Wien flew in many of the early geological parties.
Photo by Marvin Mangus, courtesy Wien Consolidated Airlines

Rollin Eckis, then chief geologist for Richfield, visited the North Slope in 1949. The visit was to pay off nearly twenty years later. *Eckis*

Dry Navy well at Oumalik. Note vehicle tracks and polygonal cracks, a natural phenomenon.

Alaska Travel Division

Barrow, America's northernmost town, sits on a natural gas field. The gas pipe runs along the top of the oil cans in the center of the picture.

Alaska Travel Division

The Weasel was used to get around during the summer thaw. Marks from these and other tracked vehicles are still visible on the tundra. *Eckis*

British Petroleum got into the act in the early sixties, using helicopters.

F. G. Larminie, right, led the BP party.   *BP*

Larminie, right, assesses the day's work with members of the party.   *BP*

With the development of the Hercules, heavy equipment could be flown in to the Slope. *Lockheed-Georgia Co.*

Arco's well at Prudhoe Bay.   *Arco*

By the mid-sixties techniques had been developed for operations on perma-frost. Wooden pilings are set in holes and water poured in around them, re-sulting in a wood-in-ice foundation that will last practically forever.   *Arco*

BP gets back into action.   *BP*

Drillers at work.   *Grossman-Granger Productions Ltd.*

BP's Christmas tree at Put River. *BP*

The infamous winter road, rushed through to the Slope, is a disastrous mud
river in the summer. Modern technology bypasses the problem with the
giant Sikorsky Sky Crane.   *Sikorsky Aircraft*

This is the way it is.   *Arco*

Alaskan Jules Wright, part Athapascan, stands on the ice bridge built over the Yukon River by the company he owns. The rush to the Slope has meant profits for many besides lease-holders.

Tundra Contractors

Base camp at Prudhoe Bay. Airstrip is in left center and two rigs show in
the background. *Grossman-Granger Productions Ltd.*

Cliff Burglin and Tom Miklautsch, on the left, just back to Fairbanks from
a happy inspection of North Slope property. In their party are the top
executives of General American Oil, which paid them a fortune for their
Slope lease. *Cliff Burglin*

Cranes unload cargo at Prudhoe under the northern lights.

Grossman-Granger Productions Ltd.

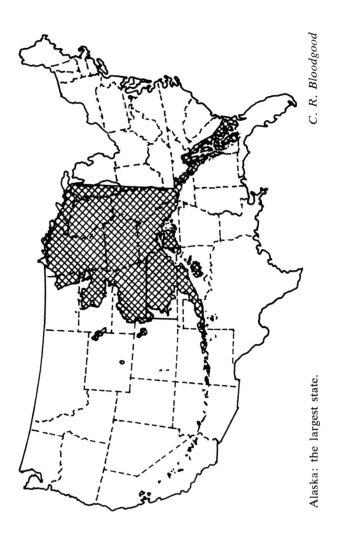

Alaska: the largest state.

C. R. Bloodgood

BELOW: Shaded area at top of map shows location of tracts sold in the billion-dollar lease sale. To get the oil to market, the route shown was proposed for the TransAtlantic Pipe System.   *C. R. Bloodgood*

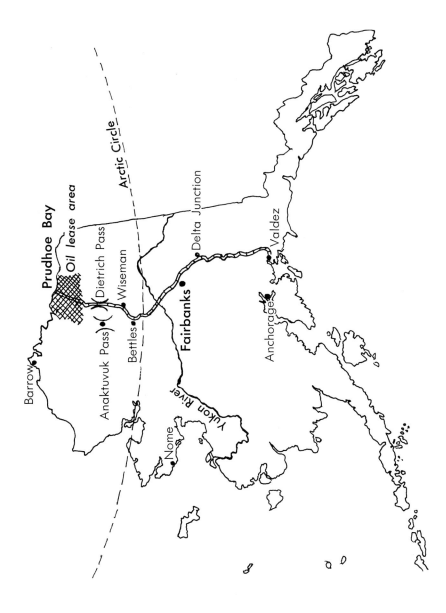

Work began immediately on access roads to the route of the pipeline.
Alyeska Pipeline Service Co.

The world's largest order of pipe arrives from Japan and is unloaded in Alaska. *Alyeska Pipeline Service Co.*

The forbidding and barren Brooks Range. This is the area through which the pipeline will pass on the north side of the range.

The *Manhattan*, the world's largest tanker, crunching through the ice.

The victorious *Manhattan*.

The south side of the Brooks Range, where the pipeline will emerge, has stands of small evergreens.

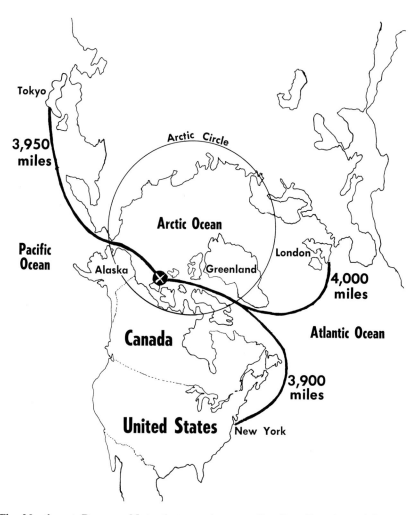

The Northwest Passage. Note that a point near Prudhoe Bay is equidistant from three major cities of the world.   *C. R. Bloodgood*

When the pipeline project was halted in 1970, Republican Governor Keith H. Miller, center, led a bipartisan delegation to Washington to fight for its continuance. Left, Democratic State Senator Ed Merdes; right, the author.

The bipartisan fight for the pipeline brought together in Washington Republican Senator Ted Stevens, front left, who organized the trip, and, right, Democratic gubernatorial candidate Bill Egan. Stevens was reelected in 1970, and Egan defeated incumbent Miller.

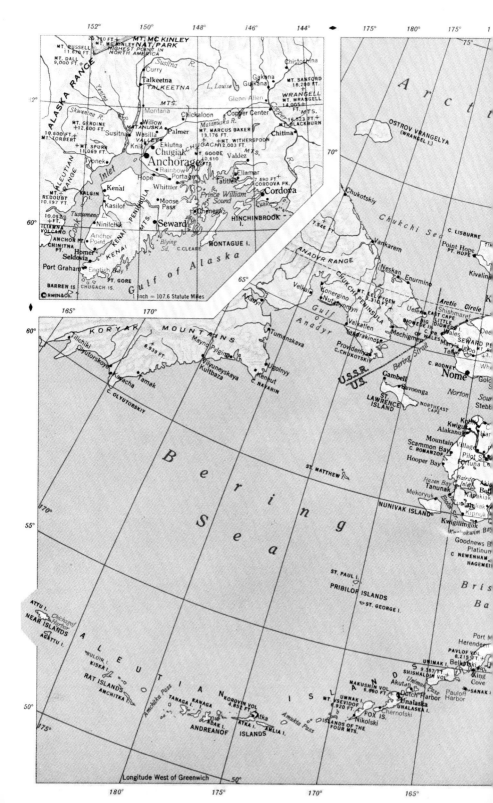

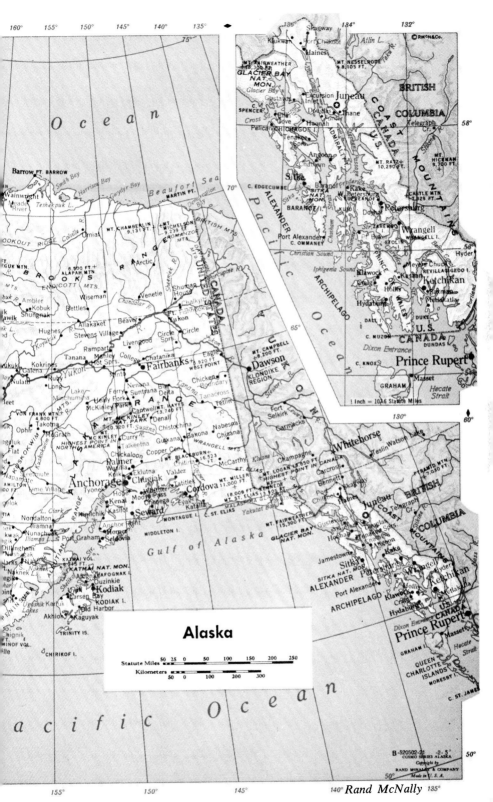

Alaska

Statute Miles 50 25 0   50   100   150   200   250
Kilometers   50 0   100   200   300

Walter Hickel, while Secretary of the Interior, inspects Alaskan fire fighters.

Engineers experimented with many ways to pipe oil to an icebreaker-tanker at Prudhoe, including these two ice islands. The project didn't work.

Humble Oil

Senator Mike Gravel took his 1970 campaign to the natives.

"Red" Boucher, former mayor of Fairbanks, with his Finnish wife Heida and their son. Boucher, elected Secretary of State (lieutenant governor) in 1970, has long been a leader in Alaska's number one sport, baseball.

Three important Alaskans: left, Mrs. Ted Stevens; center, Brideen Milner, who sold her bank to the man who beat her in a game of gin rummy; right, Mrs. Wally Hickel.   *Ward W. Wells*

Dog sleds today are used mostly for tourists, and the big races.
Alaska Airlines, by Bob and Ira Spring

Traditional Alaska: Eskimos put out to sea in their umiaks, walrus-hide boats.
Alaska Airlines, by Bob and Ira Spring

This is Alaska—a moose and the ubiquitous camper coexist tranquilly within sight of Mount McKinley.
Alaska Travel Division

Alaska Travel Division

Some native fishermen.

"You've seen the tracks churned up in the tundra," Ralph said as we walked to the helicopter. "Plant life grows so slowly up here that under normal conditions it would take years to eradicate the marks. Well, we're experimenting with different kinds of vegetation and fertilizer to see if we can't speed things up and get this land back the way it was."

We got in the helicopter and took off. Over a section of tundra that looked just like any other he told the pilot to put down. "We've got company," the pilot said, and pointed. A big grizzly was looking up at us. We circled around him, and he loped away.

"Gee, I'm glad he left of his own accord," Ralph said. "We could chase him off easy enough, but there's a regulation against buzzing wildlife. And I want to see how this grass is doing."

We landed and Ralph stepped out and started across the tundra, picking out hummocks to step on like rocks in a trout stream. After a few yards he stopped and pointed down to a few straggly blades of grass. "This crop didn't do too good," he said. "But over here we've got some broad-leafed stuff that's doing a lot better."

We zigzagged on farther, hummock to hummock. Suddenly he stopped, squatted, and peered at a little green nubbin. "I'll be damned," he said. "Something's been eating it."

Sure enough, the Arco re-tundration project looked like a lettuce patch after a rabbit raid. "Damn ducks," he said. But what was left did look healthy. Ralph straightened up and looked around at the plot of nibbled plants the way a rancher surveys a lush river bottom. Then he caught himself and grinned. "Isn't this a hell of a thing to be proud of?" he asked.

But he was still proud. Ralph, from Dallas, had visited the East Texas oil fields with a friend when he was in high school, and from then on his life was oil. A petroleum engineer from Texas A&M, before coming to Alaska he had been coordinator for the North Slope in Arco's Dallas office. "Someday," he had told his wife, Barbara, "we'll be going up there to live." Now he was here, the company's top man in its most exciting dis-

trict. He stopped and looked around at the bleak tundra stretching endlessly in every direction. "I'd rather be here than anywhere else in the whole world," he said.

After dinner that night I looked in the little room in the bunkhouse that serves as parlor, bedroom, and office for Landon B.
Kelly, in charge of activities on the Slope itself. Landon is tech-
nically on duty 24 hours a day, seven days at a stretch. I knew
he'd had a long rough day and I just wanted to say good night.
Next thing I knew he was dragging me out to his four-door pickup. The tired look in his eyes had disappeared; there's nothing
like a captive audience to turn a man on. "You've got to see our
topping plant!" he explained.

In the next hour I learned more about topping plants than I
really cared to know. A topping plant is a small refinery. Its
sophisticated equipment had been installed in a neat metal building supported by wooden pilings with the bark still on. The
company was using 20,000 barrels of oil a day in its North
Slope operations, at a dollar a gallon, while sitting on one of
the world's great reservoirs. ("The turning point of this field
will be when they ship out as much as they've brought in," an
oil man had told me.) The topping plant would draw crude
from the Sag River confirmation well, distill it, and withdraw
the fuel oil from the seventh level of the condensation tower.
That would furnish all the oil needed on the Slope. The remainder would be pumped back down into the ground until
there was a use for it.

Landon, a drawling mountain man from Montana, told me
that he really didn't know much about oil refining and then explained every piece of equipment in the plant in detail. He
couldn't have been prouder of it if he'd had invented the whole
thing.

On the way back he pointed out a stretch of built-up gravel
road. "That one-mile section cost $200,000," he said. "It's
sprayed with polyurethane at different levels, and there are
thermocouples buried in it all along. We want to test the in-

sulating quality of polyurethane to see if we can use less gravel in roads and airstrips." He laughed. "All that to save dirt."

The day before, at the drill site of Nora Federal No. 1, 60 miles up the Sagavanirktok, I'd been talking with Bruce Johnson, the mud engineer on the well. Johnson had had his own company in New Mexico, but had taken the job with International Minerals and Chemicals in order to work on the Slope. "This field is the United States's hole card," he said. "We've been using up our oil, now we've got a new supply. I wanted to get in on this deal. I don't know if you've noticed it, but this operation is kind of like the beachhead. The combat troops made the landing, and now the old pros are coming in to run it. They're hauling in things like they're going out of style. You see something new every day. Hercs, Sky Cranes, Hovercraft . . . I wouldn't be surprised to look up and see a space craft or a big balloon hanging up there."

Thirty-four men made up the Nora community, living in a comfortable bunkhouse of modular construction. Each cell, 9½ by 39 feet, had been especially fabricated to fit inside a Herc, then flown in and joined to the others. The two-man sleeping quarters, with built-in bunks and bureaus, were neat and attractive in pastel colors, as were the recreation room and mess hall. The well was a joint venture of Arco and Home Oil Company of Canada. Arco was the operator, but each company had a drilling engineer and a geologist on the job. The drilling company had a crew of 18 men under a tool pusher. There were five cooks and helpers, one mud engineer, and two mud loggers, a radio operator, truck driver, and forklift operator. Seven companies were represented on that one site, each with its own pay scale and working schedules. Jerry Schmidt and Bill Congdon, Arco's engineers in charge of both camp and operations, relieved each other every seven days. The drill crew worked 20 days on, 10 off. The cooks were apparently there for the duration.

All the cooks on the Slope seem to have the same compulsion;

they have to stuff people. They remind me of Alsatian women feeding geese. Two service companies, Universal and Boatel, supply all the rigs on the Slope and the employees of each say that the other is no damn good. The head cook at Nora was John T. Hanson, half-Norwegian, half-Swedish, and a former head chef on the Swedish American Lines now whipping up enchiladas in Alaska for Universal. He averaged about $30,000 a year, which, he said, was a lot more than the owner of a successful restaurant can make, and without the headaches. He demanded, and got, everything he ordered from the main supply depot, including mignonette pepper and whole sweet basil— "ground basil is bitter." The tables in the mess hall were so loaded with ketchup, steak sauces, pickles, jams, and jellies and condiments of all kinds that there wasn't much room for the plates.

Hanson just likes to see people eat. On the morning I was leaving he insisted on fixing my breakfast himself. I'd been up most of the night rapping with the roughnecks, eating my fourth meal of the day at midnight and sampling the pastry tray from then on, but I told him bravely that I would enjoy an omelette *aux fines herbes*, and he made an excellent one.

The Red Baron (Andris Vagners, born in Riga) was supposed to bring the Otter in around 9 o'clock, but he was fogged in at Prudhoe and I was still at Nora at 10:30, eating fresh doughnuts. Hanson became panicky over the possibility that I might get into the base camp too late for lunch, so he opened up the mess hall an hour early and heaped my plate with a smorgasbord built around stuffed cabbage and enchiladas. I was eating a dessert of fresh baked apple pie with ice cream on the side when the Red Baron came in. As Hanson was watching I had to choke down the pie before waddling out to the plane.

We were at the base camp in half an hour, and there the cook, learning that I had been starving to death in the wilderness, insisted on piling up my plate again. Later that afternoon I visited another rig. Boatel had the concession there and Murray Marshall, the chief cook, learning that I had just come from a

Universal rig, began shoving samples of pies, cakes, puddings, and ice cream at me.

For dinner that night he was serving five entrées—barbecued spare ribs, meat loaf, liver and onions, Hungarian goulash, and brisket of beef. Vegetables consisted of spuds cooked in two different ways, two frozen vegetables, two canned vegetables, three salads, three kinds of pie, two kinds of cake, and an assortment of cookies. Regrettably I could not stay, but I was back at the base camp in time for the main meal of the day. Later that night I couldn't sleep for some reason, and got up and strolled into the recreation room. There again was a table laden with pastries, plus coffee, tea, cocoa, milk, and soft drinks. On another table were boxes of fresh fruit—apples, pears, oranges, bananas, grapes. I had a little snack to settle my stomach and went back to bed; breakfast would not be far off.

Nobody's young any more up here, Bruce Johnson had said, and they've all got stories to tell. He was right on the stories, and in the long hours between shifts I heard plenty, mostly with women involved. But two of the men were still young. The radio operator was Dick Collins, 22. He'd been shot down twice in Vietnam, caught up in the riots at Watts and the march on Washington.

"No matter how long I live," he said, "I don't ever want to be in the position of looking back on my life and knowing I blew it. I still don't know what I want to do, but at least I'm finding out what I don't want to do. Sometimes the thermometer hits bottom at minus seventy, but I don't care. Here there is peace and tranquility and the opportunity to be alone with myself and figure out who the hell I am."

The Arco geologist was Murk Dirk Otto Lels, 30, born in Bandung, educated at Utrecht, and a former geologist with a British company. To get to the Slope he had written a dozen companies and picked the best. "This company is committed to exploration," he said. "A geologist can experience both exploration and the development of a whole new field. It's so fantastically exciting. Look at all the money being spent here—we're in the limelight."

It was a peculiar kind of limelight. Murk's operations seemed to me to rival the CIA's in secrecy. Though he told me what a geologist does on a well, he sure didn't tell me what he was doing at Nora. He wouldn't even tell his counterpart for Home, Ken Parsons. Periodically he locked himself in the isolated little laboratory with the cuttings sifted from the mud, ground them up in a Waring blender, and examined them minutely in several tests utilizing different techniques. When he had a core brought up so he could test it, the entire drilling crew was banished from the floor of the rig. It takes two men to remove the core, but only the drilling engineer could assist him. If the drilling engineer didn't happen to be available, he would call on the tool pusher, but in that case a canvas screen would be hung between the pusher and the precious cylinder of rock. The pusher would stick his hands under the cloth and perform his duties strictly by feel.

Though the rig had radio communications with the outside world, Murk sent in his daily reports in a far more elaborate manner. Each morning, as soon as the fog cleared, the company's chartered Otter, piloted by the Red Baron, would fly up from the base camp at Prudhoe. Murk and the Arco drilling engineer would board it, as would Ken Parsons with the Home engineer. They would all fly together, cordially but noncommittally, to the base camp at Prudhoe. There Murk would go to the company telephone and talk via scrambler with the Anchorage office. The engineer would make his report, also by scrambler, and then they'd return to the well.

Riding in with the solemn mission one day, I asked Ken Parsons if he also reported in by scrambler. He carefully unbuttoned the flap on his shirt pocket, took out a small circular code card, flashed it for a split second, grinned mysteriously, replaced it in his pocket, and carefully rebuttoned the flap. He would make his report to the home office in Calgary, talking in code to the chief geologist who would be using a similar card with the same prearranged combination for that day.

Just a daily routine mission, but it was on just such a mission, going to Prudhoe to make his report, that Parsons was killed. His epitaph in my mind is the amused little grin and the furtive flash of the code card, for that was the last time I saw him alive.

Before I went up to the Slope I thought of the activity there strictly in terms of those drilling for oil. People talked about the enormous sums paid to drilling crews—$4.60 an hour for a roughneck, for example, with time and a half for 44 of the 84 hours he puts in a week. Working schedules vary from rig to rig, but for a man working 28 days on, 14 off, that can mean almost $2000 for a working month, and an average of $1500 a month for a man who can endorse his paycheck with an X.

But there are many other types of workers on the Slope. I was walking in from a plane one day when the fellow I was with pointed to a dinky little scraper smoothing out the strip. "See that guy?" he asked. "He's making $1500 a month doing that."

A few days later, flying back to Fairbanks on Fat Albert, I got into a conversation with the fellow sitting next to me, and it turned out that he was that fellow on the scraper. Carried away by envy, I suppose, I asked him if it were true he made $1500 a month smoothing out gravel. Instead of punching me in the nose, he pulled out a couple of paychecks. He was not making $1500 a month, but $1300 every two weeks—*after taxes*.

But that was only part of the story. His name was Tommy Sentell, he was from Little Rock, Arkansas, and he'd been running heavy equipment since grade school. He'd driven to Fairbanks in a new Chevrolet pickup, selling it there for a net profit of $500 after the expenses of the trip, and applied for work at Frontier Rock and Sand Company. They tested him out on a front-end loader.

Nine out of ten applicants jump up on the machine, start

it up, and start moving sand around. Sentell first checked the oil and water, then started the engine, built up the hydraulic pressure, checked the gauges, raised and lowered the loader a couple of times to get the oil circulating, *then* started operating. The foreman yanked him down off the loader and put him on a bulldozer. He went through the same meticulous detail.

"Can you cut blue tops?" the foreman asked, and Sentell, knowing he was referring to the blue tops on grading stakes, allowed as how he could. After that virtuoso performance, the foreman accepted Sentell's word that he could also run a dragline, shovel, crane, scraper, end dump, forklift, D7 and D8 Cats, backhoe, and any truck made, including the huge western Peterbilts and Canadian-French Kenworths so popular on the Slope.

"You can tell where a man's from by the way he works heavy equipment," Sentell said. "City fellows like to showboat. New Yorkers just fuck around. But you can always tell a Southern boy off a farm. He can't afford a mechanic every time anything goes wrong, so he learns how to service his own equipment and take care of it so it won't need servicing. That's where my money comes from; I save the company money by making the best use of their equipment. I was running that scraper because there wasn't anything else at the time. I usually make a hell of a lot more than that. I'm going home now and just lie around for a while with my wife; she runs a beauty shop. Then I'll buy a Buick Riviera, drive it up here, sell it in five minutes at a profit, and work on Cat trains this winter at $2300 a week before taxes. I'm investing in oil stocks and in another year I'll have enough to put both my daughters through college."

I even ran across a boy from my hometown in Alaska. He's a college student named Matt Murray, and although he didn't have Sentell's ability, or his paychecks, he had luck and earned $1500 during summer vacation. Driving 10 to 12 hours a day, he made the trip from Charlottesville to Fairbanks on a motorcycle in nine days. "I'll never do it again," he said with authority. The Alaska Highway in summer is a column of dust. Road scrapers are constantly at work smoothing out the gravel surface, and it's easy to run right up on top of one in the dust-out.

Matt's plan was to get a job as a firefighter at $48 a day, but he arrived at a good time for Alaska but a bad time for him: no forest fires. He went to the office of a geophysical company in a trailer near the airport. A man took his name but said there wasn't much chance of a job; there were 20 names ahead of his on the list. Just then a call came in from the Slope. One of the helpers was quitting. Matt was on the Slope the next day.

In contrast to the big money paid to men on the drill sites, helpers on geophysical crews get a big fat $2.10 an hour. In the summer they work out of helicopters, drilling holes in the tundra and packing in explosives. In the winter, when travel across the tundra is possible in the tracked vehicles manufactured by Nodwell of Canada, the explosives are detonated and the results recorded. But seismic crews have been known to jump the gun in the fall before the tundra is frozen solid, and continue on too long in the spring.

Much of the reaction against the oil industry in general on the Slope has been brought about by the grubby practices of some of the geophysical companies. They usually operate on a low-bid basis, pinch pennies and louse up the countryside. Most of the 55-gallon oil drums, so ubiquitous as to be called the Alaska State Flower, have been scattered about by the geophysical companies.

"When they'd refuel the helicopter," Matt said, "there'd always be a few gallons left over in each drum and they'd just kick over the barrel and let it spill out on the tundra. The drums were brought in in clusters of eight, bright blue Gulf barrels, and we'd just go off and leave them lying there."

Matt's crew loved to shake up the helicopter pilots. They'd plant a charge in a lake and detonate it when the chopper was directly above. I don't imagine the wildlife liked it any better than the pilot. This kind of thing is prohibited by the Alaska Fish and Game Commission; but with fewer wardens in Alaska than in the state of Rhode Island, it's a little difficult to enforce it.

I never saw a gun on any drill site on the Slope. A couple of
Texans told me they had brought in six-shooters as a matter of
course and kept them stashed away but hadn't used them. One
drilling company went to the extreme of searching the luggage
of incoming crews for guns. These stringent regulations, en-
forced by the companies themselves, have largely been brought
on by the needless slaughter, or, more likely, crippling, of wildlife by the roughnecks with nothing else to do. But though
the big operators and drilling companies make an effort to heed
the restrictions, the geophysical companies apparently don't.
Matt said that at least ten members of his 40-man crew had
guns. "They were always popping away at birds, but they rarely
hit any," he said.

When the annual summer curse of forest fires began, Matt
left the seismic crew. He started firefighting at $48 a day and got
a $5 raise. He brought home about $700 of the $1500 he made.
He also brought home the conviction that the land is being
ruined. He saw the marks being made.

Only a handful of the men working on the Slope come from
the Slope. Although Alaskan natives have the lowest per capita
income of any segment of our population, and would consider
even a geophysical company's paycheck a fortune, few were
hired. I don't think the reason was discrimination. Oil in Alaska
is comparatively recent and neither natives nor non-natives have
absorbed the romance of the oil field as have the Texans and
Oklahomans who grew up with it. In the hectic days prior to
the lease sale, drilling companies wanted experienced men, and
they came from Outside.

A tool pusher who had employed Eskimos said they developed into excellent hands and, of course, could take the weather.
"But they always want to take off and go after a walrus or something," he said.

BP, which has learned to work with native populations over
most of the world, has had the most success with Eskimo workers. "First of all," Geoff Larminie explained, "All you have to
do is look at their way of life to realize that they have excellent

hand and eye coordination. You couldn't support yourself in this climate with handmade tools without it. They make excellent oil field workers. But where a Bedouin, say, who leads a lonely desert life, would welcome the opportunity to earn money on an isolated rig for a long period of time, an Eskimo would go completely out of his mind. They're friendly and gregarious, and they have to take time off for whale hunts, walrus hunts, fishing, dances, get-togethers celebrating any and every occasion. The idea that an Eskimo can live away from his family for a long period of time is preposterous. Instead of insisting that they adjust to our life in the field, we adjust to theirs. We ask only that they put in a good day's work, which they do, and that they give us some advance notice before they take off on a caribou hunt so that we can replace them with other Eskimos who have just returned from one. It works out well, and it will work out better as we go along."

BIG DEALS

During the Gold Rush the sourdough who scrabbled and mucked like a slave for gold was usually the first man to lose it. It was the traders, the cardsharps, the madams, the shipping companies, and the suppliers who wound up with money in the bank—and don't overlook the bankers. It's the same thing all over again, and to a greater degree in the oil rush. Although the big oil companies provided the impetus and the money for exploration on the Slope—with an indirect assist from the taxpayer, for they enjoy generous deductions—most of the actual work has been done by other companies: drilling companies, transportation companies, geophysical companies, service companies. Though the oil companies have been exclusively footing the bill for operations on the Slope since 1958, they cannot expect a nickel's return on the hundreds of millions of dollars invested until the mid-1970s, the earliest date they can get their oil to market.

But plenty of financial world-shaking action was going on

back in the home offices. The Atlantic Richfield merger had proved so successful that Arco's chairman, Robert Anderson, engineered another one. Arco took over Sinclair Oil Corporation, a major company of approximately its own size, to become the seventh largest oil company in the country with assets of some $3.7 billion. Alaskan oil was a major factor in the deal, as Sinclair was long on stations but short in crude; Arco thus got a substantial outlet for its new reserves.

And so, with incidental assistance from the Federal Anti-Trust division, did BP. It was able to purchase from Arco, for $400 million, Sinclair assets including two refineries and some 10,000 retail outlets in the eastern states and Texas. By 1970 the green and yellow BP shield marked handsome new stations, and TV commercials called attention to "the new boy on the block."

This was just a warm-up exercise for the enterprising English, however, for next came the announcement that BP was merging with Standard Oil of Ohio. It was such a stunning surprise that the stock exchange couldn't handle the demand the day after the announcement. Sohio just didn't open the first Tuesday in June, 1969. Then it zoomed up 30 points in a week.

The merger was based completely on North Slope oil. Sohio had excellent outlets throughout the Midwest; BP had the oil. As production from Prudhoe Bay increased, so would BP's equity in Sohio, to a maximum of 54 percent. It took Dudley Knott, vice president of BP North America, Ltd., and a master of clarification, about ten minutes to explain it to me, but you might be interested in a simplified description of the way it works. The British Petroleum Company Ltd., BP London, or The Group, as headquarters of the international giant is known, owns Sohio. Sohio, with headquarters in Cleveland, owns the North Slope properties. BP Alaska, Inc., owned by BP London and based in New York, operates the North Slope under contract to Sohio. BP Oil Corporation runs the BP stations you see in the eastern states; it is a subsidiary of Sohio. You see?

If Dudley is any criterion, and he says he is, the British love working in America. ("What he loves is American martinis," said his secretary, who calls him by his first name.) They like the friendliness in America and match it with natural warmth. They are fascinated by the way Americans get people to repeat their names ("In England we never know whom we're talking to") and they first-name you on first meeting.

Meanwhile, back in Alaska, in those halcyon years following the strike at Prudhoe, everybody was raking in the oil companies' money. Special companies, or divisions thereof, were set up to fulfill the new Alaskan demands.

Take suitable clothing, for instance. When I first went to Alaska I had no idea of what a man would wear on the Slope, and the more people I asked, the more confused I got. The one point on which everybody did agree is that Eskimo mukluks are the best Arctic footgear known to man. But as mukluks are made of sealskin softened in urine, crimped by biting, then hand sewn by sinew to caribou leggings, it hardly seemed likely that local shoe stores would keep a sufficient inventory.

It occurred to me that somebody should make a comprehensive study of Arctic wearing apparel, determine exactly what was needed by whom, and then make the whole outfit available at a price. The next thing I knew I was in touch with a young man named Patrick F. Charles of Olympic Products in Seattle which had done just that. If Pat's luck and timing holds up he's going to make a mint. Just as Alaska oil exploration was getting hot, Pat and a group of other young people went into the fine old mail order house of Eddie Bauer. I've known of Eddie Bauer sleeping bags since I went on my first Boy Scout overnight trip.

"We already had a reputation," Pat said. "For example, Mr. Bauer long ago learned that only the inner down from Northern geese provided the insulation he demanded. Don't take this personally, Boo, but Southern geese aren't good enough for us.

With this kind of detail you can be comfortable in one of our North Slope parkas at one hundred ten below zero, including chill factor."

Pat has put together various packages for companies operating on the Slope. For drilling crews, who today work in enclosed rigs, the package includes goose down underwear with insulated canvas coveralls. The best boot is the Canadian-made Sorel felt-lined boot with neoprene sole—it doesn't slip on oil—and safety toe. Without spares, the complete outfit comes to about $200 per man.

For the poor bastard who really gets out into the cold, like the member of a geophysical crew, the package deal on company orders runs to $260. This includes down underwear, down-filled windproof trousers ($39) and parka ($105). The parka hood has three inches of wolf fur, one inch of wolverine. (Contrary to sourdough opinion, wolverine fur is not frost free, but because of its natural oils the frost can be easily brushed from it.) The package also includes five pairs of thermal socks and nylon inner socks. The Sorel boots come with extra felt liners. Also included are mitts with palms of goatskin, which remains supple in subzero weather, and backs of mouton fur, which enables you to wipe your face without having the gloves stick to it. There's a wool face protector, too. Men have been caught out overnight in this gear without great discomfort. If you really want to play it safe you can spring for a $150 Mt. Everest parka that has a comfort range down to minus 85 degrees plus chill factor.

For aircraft pilots Pat has a rescue kit including sleeping bags, emergency rations, small heating unit, strobe light, and radio homing beacon.

By 1970, Olympic Products was doing so well that it organized a separate North Slope division, with 85 percent of its business serving the oil industry.

Another unique demand on the North Slope is for a vehicle capable of transporting heavy equipment over the tundra, winter or summer, without roads or airstrips. Cities Service Company and its seismic contractor, Olympic Geophysical, aware of the environmental problems, tried out two Hovercrafts. Next to oil itself, I don't think anything caused as much conversation on the Slope in the summer of 1969 as these odd-looking land-going airplanes. Whenever we flew over one of these things, scuttling across the tundra like a low-flying space ship, we'd all crane our necks to look at it; the pilots would make scathing remarks.

When the Olympic-Hovercraft charter came to an end, Ralph Cox, Arco's top man in Alaska, chartered them for an emergency operation. I went on one of the trips, to get some drill pipe, and I'll be talking about it the rest of my life.

The Hovercraft, or ACV, air-cushioned vehicle, was about 50 feet long and about half again as wide. ACVs squat down on rubber skirts like an old peasant woman picking sugar beets when at rest, but when the huge fans powered by gas turbine engines start blowing down on the ground, the craft slowly rises up on the four-foot rubber skirts and hovers there. A propeller mounted toward the rear of the vehicle pushes it along at speeds up to 65 miles an hour.

The one I was on was surely the world's most beatup ACV. Designed to carry a total of 38 passengers on scenic tours along the Thames, the British-built craft had been brought up the Mackenzie from Yellowknife and over the ice pack to Prudhoe, had served the seismic crews for months, and was now hauling 25 tons of drill pipe at a crack over the tundra. Its skirt was torn in several places, part of the rudder was missing, and most of the instrumentation was busted. The door would fly open if I didn't hold it tight with a rope. I sat on the left side, of course; it had right-hand drive.

The pilot, Jimmie Sober, former Navy flier of both fixed-wing aircraft and helicopters, was the Number 3 Hovercraft pilot in the world in seniority. By now he had been away from his wife for several months and he was sick of blasting the battered thing over the tundra.

"Don't get me wrong," he said, "I love the concept. I'm just goddamned tired of doing it."

He started up the engines, and the craft rose slowly like a ballerina in a full skirt coming up from a grand plié. It started forward, and headed for the six-foot drop off the built-up airstrip. Sober was pushing rudders with both feet, jiggling controls with both hands, bitching to me over the roar of the engines and fans, and picking up speed all the time. When we came to the bank I thought we'd shoot straight out and then splatter all over the tundra, but the craft went down it as smoothly as a rubber raft on a small wave. We roared on across the tundra with Sober, having forgotten his homesickness, selling me on Hovercraft at the top of his voice. Sometimes we yawed to starboard and went sideways for a few hundred yards, sometimes to port.

A road embankment was up ahead, but again he didn't bother to slow down or stop talking. As we hit the bank I held up my hands to cushion the shock, almost dropping the rope that held the door closed, but all I felt was a smooth little roller-coaster effect as we went up the bank, across the road, and down the other side. We crossed streams with ten-foot banks, and a dozen lakes. The Hovercraft didn't care whether it was over water or tundra. A white fox came up out of nowhere and we raced it for a while, then skirted around a few grazing caribou.

"We can outrun 'em," Sober hollered, "but I don't like to get them excited." He also admitted he kept a sharp lookout for nesting fowl and tried to avoid them. Sometimes, he said, when operating on San Francisco Bay, he couldn't help going over a duck or a seagull sitting on the water. They usually pulled themselves together and flew away, but if they appeared damaged he'd pick them up and take them to the S.P.C.A.

At the drill site we stopped and hovered motionless as the other Hovercraft came down the high embankment with drill pipe stacked up on steel racks welded on both sides. "I don't want to get in his way," Jimmy said, "that's a pretty tricky maneuver." It sideslipped down the bank, then on over the tundra. I looked carefully at its wake. I could just barely see the track.

"We've made thirty or forty trips," Jimmie said. "You can hardly tell where we've been. You can run these things over the tundra winter or summer and leave it completely undisturbed."

A half-hour or so later, with a few tons of drill pipe a couple of feet from my left ear, we maneuvered the embankment easily and proceeded on to the delivery point. "This thing will haul heavy cargo a hell of a lot cheaper than a Hercules or a Sky Crane," Jimmie said, "and we don't need landing strips or anything more than a ten-foot ceiling. On this seismic operation we just finished, it would take a helicopter a month to shoot a mile. We could do a mile in two days."

The total distance over the triangular course was about 60 miles; including loading and unloading, it took us only a little more than two hours, and we didn't disturb a square inch of tundra. The next day, on the unfamiliar run up to Nora with another pilot at the controls, the Hovercraft crashed, killing Ken Parsons, who was sitting in the same seat I had had. These things can happen. The North Slope experiment was considered such a success that Bell Aerospace, which has pioneered in ACV's in the United States, began bringing out a larger model with a payload of 25 tons. They can be used over coastal waters, lakes and rivers, ice and snow, tundra, marshland and grassland, and even more difficult terrain. They're also fun to ride.

OPPORTUNITY

With the promise of oil opening up transportation in Alaska, people interested in heavy minerals were taking new hard looks at the Great Land. Iron, copper, mercury, titanium—they are there.

Lives were being changed. Alaskans who had learned the Gold Rush lesson—that there's more money in gold miners than in gold—were applying it. Bonnie ran into a typical example, Ken and Olga Carson. It was Sunday morning, Olga was doing the ironing, and she shooed the kids out of the kitchen while she bubbled over about her new residence on Cloud 9.

Olga was born in Alaska, daughter of a gold miner. "Daddy made a lot of money," she said, "but all he did with it was spend it. Ken and I are going to be a lot smarter with the money we make—and we're making it."

Ken was a special assistant to Governor Hickel when the Prudhoe field came in. "Politics," Olga said, "is working hard for other people. You don't make a dime. Wally influenced us to go into business for ourselves. He said, 'anything you want to do you can do.' "

Ken, who knew the Slope, started Carson-Fairbanks Services, with the high-flown description of Oil Expediters. At first he served as a guide to the Slope. A representative of Ardent Dairies said that he wished they could get some of that Slope business. Oil field workers drink buckets of the stuff and gripe when it's not available. Ken moved in quick, and arranged to make guaranteed milk deliveries. This meant personally scrounging space on planes and rearranging shipments when at the last minute a flight was cancelled.

Geophysical companies learned that he got milk in on schedule and began asking him to provide immediate delivery of drilling bits. Next came a back haul: empty oil drums. As there is always some fuel left flushing around inside a drum, they are in effect 55-gallon Molotov cocktails; Ken had to hire two men to rinse them out. He himself would spend two or three days on the Slope each week while Olga ran the office. But they were in business.

Another example of enterprise and self-confidence is Jules Wright, raised in an Athapascan fishing village. Today Tundra Contractors, Inc., is a highly rated Fairbanks firm, but at one time it consisted of Jules on a rented Caterpillar. He took jobs that nobody else wanted on a pay-on-completion basis. One of these jobs was a particularly difficult dam that kept washing out.

Jules had seen beaver dams all of his life, and he figured that anything a beaver could do he could do better. Instead of using the textbook methods of dam construction, which had failed, he literally worked like a beaver and the dam held. Tundra Contractors became the outfit to call on for tough jobs, and Tundra Contractors was paid commensurately when the job was done.

"I like to tackle jobs everybody thinks are impossible," Jules said, "because then nobody tries to tell me how to do it."

Another impossible job that I saw performed would be appreciated by any newspaperman. One day I dropped in the *News-Miner* office to see Joe LaRocca, one of the best journalists in the country, and found him even quieter than usual. Joe had started out in his hometown of Erie, Pennsylvania, then got a job in which he covered every state but Alaska. The omission bothered him so he went there, and he couldn't have picked a better time. He fell in love with the Great Land and became so interested in the oil boom that he talked his publisher, C. W. Snedden, into putting out a weekly four-page tabloid section on oil and resources development with Joe as editor. It was so successful that Snedden decided to increase it to 32 pages—two days before deadline. Joe turned out copy for 28 more pages in 48 hours, and still remained cordial to dropin visitors.

"I still love it," he said. He later found a home in radio and T.V. with the statewide Alaska Broadcasting System.

As we traveled around Alaska I usually talked to the men and Bonnie talked to the women. But I guess I neglected to tell her that the chairman of the board of the Alaska State Bank was a lady, a good-looking, redheaded lady named Brideen. Her first husband, Ben Crawford, was about as Alaskan as you can get. His parents were married in the Gold Rush village of Hope, and promptly after the ceremony took off on a 70-mile, two-day trip on snowshoes to spend their honeymoon in Seward. Crawford started the Alaska State Bank with a total of $25,000. Brideen was a director. When Crawford died in 1961, Brideen was 39. The suggestion was made to her that she sell the stock Crawford left her and get out. She said that if her husband hadn't thought she could run the bank he wouldn't have left her that stock.

"Besides, I thought it might be fun to be the youngest lady chairman of a bank. I'd been handling the public relations and I wasn't overly fat. Maybe I could open some new doors."

When the J. C. Penney Company opened up new stores in Alaska, Brideen went down to Chicago to see Mr. Penney himself. He was 90, "a dear old soul, and bright as a bird." After Brideen turned her blue eyes and hearty laugh on him, the dear old soul turned to his treasurer and said, "I hope we bank with her." They did.

As the oil activity heated up in Alaska, Brideen, having heard the Gold Rush tales from a third-generation sourdough, figured that history would repeat itself. "I wanted some of that oil money in my bank," she told me. "But oil men are funny people, they talk their own language. Instead of trying to make bankers into oil men, I thought I'd get an oil man and make a banker out of him. So I hired Bill Bishop—you know, the man with the golden shoes."

This was the kind of banking that caused Wall Street's Louis Starr to call the Alaska State Bank the most aggressive in the state. With the oil discovery on the Slope and the big lease sale coming up, financiers all through the Lower 48 began looking for a foothold in Alaska. Around this time Brideen and Andy Milner got married. Andy was a man with plans of his own; he set up North Slope Sales and Services, one of whose projects was buying the bunkhouses at the Sagwon airstrip and making a hotel out of them. "We've got the only hotel in the world with wall to wall carpeting and outdoor toilets," he said proudly. Andy does things in a big way. When he quit smoking he wanted it to be a historic event, and it was. At 5:56, Anchorage time, July 20, 1969, he snuffed out his last cigarette. (Astronaut Neil Armstrong happened to set foot on the moon at the same time.)

"Andy didn't want to be married to a chairman-of-the-board type lady and I figured that the time was right to sell," Brideen told me.

Syndicates were formed from Wall Street west to buy out her
interest. She was alternately hounded and wooed. Brideen was
negotiating with one group when Ralph F. Whitmore, Jr., a
New York financier, approached her. She liked him and his
progressive banking ideas, brought him home, served him tacos,
and played gin rummy with him. But because of the current
negotiations with the other group she wouldn't sell him the bank.

The impasse was solved in traditional Alaskan fashion: The
stakes of the gin rummy game became the purchase of the bank.
Whitmore won, but Brideen got what she wanted and held back
a nice little chunk of stock for a souvenir.

Big ideas, big deals, and big money were being dreamed up,
hatched, and changing hands in both Anchorage and Fairbanks.
Ed Merdes lobbied the Arco lobbyists into promising an oil refinery for Fairbanks. "If you want the good will of the people
of this community," he said, "the way to get it is to sell us fuel
oil at a reasonable price." Red Boucher, knowing that the housing shortage was going to get shorter, entertained representatives
of companies with revolutionary housing ideas. His counterpart
in Anchorage, George Sullivan, was working for unification
with the borough. "They say our propulation is only fifty thousand but we've got thirty thousand kids in public school," he
said. "They must be coming from somewhere."

Tandy Industries of Tulsa, Oklahoma, announced plans for a
whole new city to be connected with Anchorage by tramway.
It would have moving sidewalks, climate control, cost $500 mil-
lion, and be the world's first twenty-first century city. It would
be called Seward's Success.

In this frenetic atmosphere anything could happen. One
Alaskan plopped down in the dentist's chair and said, "Drill
anywhere, Doc, I feel lucky today." An Outsider came into
town with plans for a $20 million building. He was readily ac-
cepted and lived high on the hog for days, leaving just before
his checks bounced.

The restaurants and night spots of both Anchorage and Fairbanks could surely have absorbed a few bad checks. In what was

recommended as the best restaurant in Fairbanks I had some pink papier-mâché coated with cod liver oil that was called salmon on the menu, accompanied by a nice warm rosé. The bill for three without cocktails was $45. As per Alaskan custom, the waitress presented toothpicks with the bill. In Anchorage reservations had to be made days in advance not just for the hotel restaurants and the Mexican restaurants—where there's oil there's chicken mole—but for the in place as well, a quonset hut called The Garden of Eatin'.

The modern equivalents of the Malemute Saloon were going strong in both Fairbanks and Anchorage. Several Anchorage nightclubs feature the something-for-everybody combination of topless waitresses with female impersonator MCs. Oilfield workers, lousy with dough, blew it in the bars. In one of the most elaborate ways of frittering away money yet invented, they'd spend 15 minutes making a ring with a little rosette on it out of a $20 or $50 bill, then slip it on a B-girl's finger.

As for the whores, it was rare indeed when a girl had to make a complete tour of the block around 4th and C. They have a unique method of solicitation in Anchorage. Late one misty night I was walking home along the vapor-lit street—you can walk around by yourself at night in Anchorage—when a car pulled up beside me. "Wanna ride, honey?" said a soft sweet voice. Behind the wheel of a brand-new Thunderbird sat a comely smiling miss, white teeth and black skin luminescent in the greenish street lights. I'll always wonder whether she had a place to take me to or whether the shiny T-bird had optional equipment for her profession.

She cruised off into the fog. That night was September 9, 1969. Tomorrow would come the orgiastic ceremony, the billion-dollar lease sale.

$ $ $ $ $ $ $

Pandemonium to a classicist may be a conglomerate of shrieking devils; to a sports nut it's what happens in the stands when

the quarterback connects with the bomb. I saw it in a conglomerate of middle-aged men one afternoon in an auditorium in
Anchorage. A state official droned out the figure $72,277,133
and the place went wild. Men representing multimillion-dollar
companies jumped up and down and screamed like kids at a
rock festival. It was the largest amount of money ever bid for
one lease. It amounted to $28,253 per acre for nothing but what
might lie beneath the ground. Many millions were yet to be bid,
but that was the climax. It had been building up for months.

At 7 o'clock that morning when the doors of The Sidney
Laurence auditorium—named after an Alaskan artist—were
opened, the line of people waiting to get in stretched halfway
around the block. But these were only the onlookers, the applicants for the 200 general admission seats. Representatives of the
oil companies, their bankers, the Wall Streeters, the politicians,
the brokers, all had made their reservations, in effect, months
before. There wasn't a vacant hotel room in Anchorage—or even
in Alyeska, the ski resort 27 miles away down Turnagain Arm.
People were sleeping in their private jets.

It's a rare game when, at the opening whistle, nobody knows
for sure the names of the teams or players, but is primarily interested in the total score. It was the *Wall Street Journal* that
first speculated that this third state lease sale on the North Slope
would bring in one billion dollars. From then on there were
betting pools all over Alaska on what the bids would total.
Leases on 179 tracts totaling 450,858 acres would be let out for
bid. The date of the sale was originally set for September 11, a
Thursday, but then somebody realized that the cashiers' checks
accompanying the bids might not be cashed in the one banking
day remaining that week. For three days the money wouldn't be
working!

The date was moved up a day and the Bank of America, appointed to handle the money, chartered a DC-8 for $23,000
to fly the checks Outside so they could be cashed. The plane
would take off immediately following the sale with the booty,
and fly direct to New York. This was not because of the number

of checks that would be written on New York banks, but because the sun rises in the east. From New York, as the sun proceeded westward, prolonging the day, bank officials would follow it, cashing checks at other financial institutions en route.

The question of who would put up the money provided the best guessing game in Alaska. In coffee shops in the morning, in bars and restaurants at night, that's all you heard. Rumors, rumors, rumors. One of the best, passed around early in the week, concerned a group of oil company executives supposed to be coming across Canada in a sealed train. The next version I heard was that the train had mysteriously broken down. Then came the report the train, still with its petroleum passengers on board, was simply roaring back and forth between Edmonton and Calgary.

Would you believe that this last was true? It was. Ten companies had chartered a train for $10,000 a day. Sixty executives boarded it on Friday, September 5, and rode back and forth between the two cities preparing their bids undisturbed and in complete security. Only two of the 60, by prior arrangement, were allowed to leave the train at all. When newspapermen heard something was going on and showed up at the station on one of the turnarounds, the guards shone bright lights at the cameramen to foil their attempts, and nobody answered any questions. Before dawn September 10, the group snuck off and boarded a plane for Anchorage and the sale.

Bids could be turned in to the State Department of Natural Resources, which conducted the sale, up until 8 A.M. the day of the sale. All the big operators waited until the last minute. Each bidder brought along a representative of his company's bank, usually a vice president, authorized to sign a cashier's check. Certified checks were acceptable, but they had to be prepared in advance, and somebody might talk. Close-mouthed as a bank vice president might be, nobody wanted to tell him the figures to write on the checks—one check for each tract bid on; some bidders went for all 179—until Wednesday morning. The banker-boys in their pin-striped suits gave an outward appearance of great cool, but one later admitted that he had taken his slim-line attaché case containing his checks to bed with him.

At 8 A.M. sharp the Commissioner of Natural Resources, Thomas E. Kelly, a tall and handsome young Texan who had come to Alaska originally as a landman, closed the bidding and introduced Governor Keith Miller. The Governor uttered the truism of the century: "After today, Alaska will never again be the same."

Kelly had a couple of hours to fill while the clerks were sorting the bids into the appropriate tracts, and he had arranged a little program that, he announced earlier, would be "something with a little class." He showed us a film. A man with a beard and a yellow parky read an interminable ballad into the microphone. Then we all stood and sang the Alaska Flag Song. I was sitting in the press section and directly in front of me was Philip Jacobson of the London *Times*, with ringlets around his face, and Richard Kilian, of the London *Express*, with a long bob in back. Neither of them was singing the Alaska Flag Song. I chided them.

"I'm sorry, old chap," Jacobson explained, "but the words escape me."

Locke Jacobs was sitting on my left; he apparently thought we in the press had the best seats. He had come early and secured his seat by placing on it a piece of paper on which was written, *The News*. I told him *The News* was a fine paper, and he thanked me. He was constantly jumping up, looking around, peering this way and that, jamming me with his elbow, and pointing out the celebrities, the oil company representatives.

On the stage of the auditorium stood a huge map of the North Slope, divided into square-shaped tracts. Those to be sold were scattered all across it, running in numerical order generally from left to right. As the Prudhoe Bay area is about the center, and in this area would come the highest bidding, most of us sat back to relax during the warm-ups.

Tract No. 1 sat way up on the Colville delta, almost 100 miles northwest of the Sag River well. It was one of a block of six in

that area. F. J. Keenan, director of the Division of Lands, began reading the bids, droning out the list of companies that
had combined on each bid, the price per acre, the total price.
He came to the bid made by British Petroleum in combination
with Gulf Oil Company and read $15,528,960. The two Brit-
ishers in front of me looked at each other incredulously, saw that
each had heard what the other had heard, and began writing
notes. On my left Locke Jacobs bounced as though he was on a
pogo stick. "Holy mackerel!" he said. BP-Gulf took the tract.

Then came Tract No. 2. This time the BP bid was $20,705,-
280. The *Times* and *Express* in front of me were now ready for
anything, but I thought Locke was going to have a heart attack.
People were shouting all over the auditorium but I heard him
distinctly. "Oh, this is gonna be a big sale," he hollered. "They
came to buy." He put the heel of one hand under his chin,
grabbed the back of his head with the other, and twisted. His
neck popped like a cap pistol.

Then came Tract No. 3. BP-Gulf, $31,000,000. Moans and
groans, cheers and hollers. Now Locke was indignant. "They're
gonna take it all," he cried. "They're not gonna let anybody take
anything. They're gonna wipe the whole block!"

Locke was incoherent. The *Times* and *Express* were scribbling
away. I looked around for somebody who could tell me something about what was going on, and saw George Sullivan, the
mayor of Anchorage. "What an indication!" he said. Everybody
was talking in exclamation points. "What does it mean? It means
that the companies not already active on the North Slope are
coming in. Gulf is using BP's information, and BP is using
Gulf's money. That's what it means."

The combination took the solid block of the first six tracts.
It was about 10:45 A.M.—8:45 P.M. in London. Jacobson was
just going to make his deadline. He looked around in desperation, saw the easiest way out was up and over, and leaped, nearly
kicking me in the face. He made the aisle and ran toward the
press phones. Having been exposed to the British reserve during

bombing raids on London, I was curious how he would report such an event. The words that he screamed into the phone actually appeared next day in the *Times*. "Staggeringly high bids from British Petroleum and a major new combination with U.S. giant Gulf Oil has swept the board in the early results of lease sales here," his lead began with quiet understatement. ". . . People in the crowded auditorium gasped and then cheered wildly . . . oil experts here are utterly astounded at the prices the group has been paying, but all agree they can only be based on totally encouraging exploration work."

Of the total of more than $92 million paid for the six tracts BP put up just $3 million. It received an interest of ten percent in five tracts and 25 percent in the sixth. It was pretty obvious both that BP had discovered something in the Colville River area, and that Gulf wanted to be on the Slope mighty bad.

After the BP-Gulf overture, the performance steadied down for several bids. One local outfit bid $1 per tract for each of the 179 tracts, and I got awful sick of hearing it.

The longest name of all, repeated in full over and over, was: Amerada-Hess Corporation, Louisiana Land and Exploration Corporation, Marathon Oil Company, Getty Oil Company, Placid Oil Company, Hunt Industries, Carolyn Hunt Trust, Herbert Hunt Trust, Lamar Hunt Trust and Hunt Estates combine. But when it came to Tract No. 57, it was only Amerada-Hess and Getty, who went 50-50 on the bid of $72,277,133. The next highest bid was $72,113,000. The shouting was so loud that the man who put in the bid didn't know for several seconds whether he had won.

Company officials later revealed that J. Paul Getty, generally considered the richest man in the world, had asked a simple question, "Why aren't we on the North Slope?" and they had done their best to oblige him. Leon Hess, chairman and chief executive officer of Amerada-Hess Corporation, had the same idea. The other groups came in for varying percentages. Hess and Getty agreed on a bid of about $70 million for No. 57, but just before the sale Hess, who likes to get what he wants, strongly suggested $80 million. Getty wouldn't go that high, but he went enough to get ol' 57.

The three big holders of acreage at Prudhoe Bay, Arco, Humble, and BP, didn't bid anywhere near that much on 57. Of the 179 total, Arco picked up 19 tracts, Humble only three. The two owned well over a million acres on the Slope. When you have a whole cow, why pay through the nose to get one filet? Each bid separately in the sale.

After the shouting was over I went downstairs to the lounge for a cup of coffee. A group of men were talking.

"If we'd thought we could have gotten that tract for eighty million," one man said, "we'd have bid it. We thought it would go for ninety, and we didn't want to go that much."

"They won't know for two years whether they've got a nickel's worth of oil," another man said.

"We won't know for two years what this whole sale means. It may have been a complete farce."

A young man broke in. "Look, that seventy-two million tract is a gut cinch," he said.

An older fellow who was listening to the conversation with me winked. "That's youth talkin'," he drawled.

Outside a half a dozen natives were picketing the entrance of the auditorium. They carried hand-lettered signs to the effect that Tom "Oilcan" Kelly was selling their land. Some of the Chamber of Commerce types seemed perturbed over the effect the pickets might have on the prominent visitors from Outside. I thought that in comparison to an everyday college demonstration it was pretty mild, and said so.

Another fellow came up. "Do you know what they want?" he asked and then answered the question himself. "They want the equivalent of ten thousand dollars for every native. Look at that fellow there. The worse thing you could do for that man would be to give him ten thousand dollars. He'd drink himself to death in a year and his dogs would eat him."

By the end of the day a total of 1087 bids had been put in. All the pioneer companies improved their position to some degree; a score or more majors came in for the first time. One combine, Mobil Oil, Phillips Petroleum, and Standard of California, all of which already had acreage on the Slope, wanted one tract so much that they bid $41.2 million for it; the next highest bid was $1.6 million. That's known as leaving money on the table.

The total amount bid, including the losers, came to more than $1.4 billion. It *was* a billion-dollar sale, but the final total of accepted bids was only $900,220,590. Bids were later rejected on 15 tracts and the total dropped to $900,040,000. It was still the biggest lease sale in history.

The entire territory of Alaska had been sold for two cents an acre; on this day, one tiny portion had brought $2180 an acre for the oil and gas rights alone. And the state still had more than 800,000 acres on the Slope left to sell.

The gambling fever spread to stock exchanges and investors around the world. I know of three telephone lines held open between Anchorage and brokerage houses in New York for a period of ten hours and up, and there must have been more. In Tulsa, a radio station distributed free maps of the North Slope, showing blocks to be leased, and a friend of mine borrowed his teen-age daughter's transistor radio to take to work with him so he wouldn't miss one word of the action. Three separate stockbrokers in Charlottesville, my hometown, called me late at night, their time, to find out what was going on. At about 15 bucks per call all I could give them was the truth: I hadn't the faintest idea what was going on and nobody else did, either.

During the afternoon I began wondering how a big-time oil analyst operated. I knew that Dillard Sprigg's assistant, Phil Dodge, was at the auditorium, while Dillard himself was back in the hotel with a direct line to his New York office. I called him and asked him if I could come over and see what he was doing.

"You'll see a guy looking at a television set," Dillard said, "but sure, come on."

In his hotel room Dillard was lounging on the sofa watching

the lease sale proceedings. He had pulled a chair in front of the TV set and put a telephone, off the hook, on it. He waved at a used-up yellow pad, with figures scribbled on every page. "I thought my damned arm was going to fall off," he said. "Now I've got somebody in the New York office taking all this down. But it's tough when they break in with commercials."

"Have you figured out what's going on?" I asked.

"Well, it's pretty plain that some people think the structure extends to the east, and others think it extends to the south," he said. "Other than that, no, I haven't figured it out, and I better get started doing it. I've got to get a wire out tonight."

When the sale was over he and Phil Dodge wrote out a wire for Baker Weeks to send its clients. It was about 6 P.M. Anchorage time, 11 P.M. New York time, and they composed the report in a hurry so that the people in New York could go home. Its tone was fairly optimistic. When they'd finished and called it in, both dead tired, they sat and pondered the sale. From the bidding it looked to both of them as though the original estimate of five to ten billion barrels was low, and that the big companies probably figured there were 15 to 20 billion barrels there. But this had already been speculated on, and the market had already taken it into account.

"We've all been sort of wondering in the backs of our minds whether there might not be thirty or forty billion barrels up here," Dillard said. "But if there isn't, well, the market has already taken this into account. Maybe there ain't no more good news to come. No more big romance."

He and Dodge went out to dinner with an investor and independent oil operator. The more they talked, the more they convinced themselves that, in terms of the market, the North Slope was big, but not much bigger than it had been before.

By this time it was after 11 P.M. "Let's grab a couple of hours sleep," Dillard said, "and get up early in the morning and redo this thing."

They left a call for 3 A.M.—they were in adjoining rooms— and sat down immediately to work out what they wanted to say.

They wrote it out in long hand, carefully, to make sure there could be no misunderstanding. When they were satisfied, they called the New York office and dictated the statement over the phone. It turned out to be a page and a half, single spaced. Four words leap from the middle of the penultimate paragraph. They are: "We would cease buying . . ."

In an official wire of this kind, the phrase "cease buying" is a euphemism. To the salesmen in the institutional service department "cease buying" means SELL. They immediately started calling their clients, advising all aggressive funds to sell.

Trading in oils was heavy September 11. Most of the people at the sale the day before had envisioned a great spurt. Some had made purchases on the West Coast exchanges, others were seriously considering staying up to catch the London market when it opened. The big bids and the $900 million total fed their enthusiasm. I know several people who placed orders with their brokers before they staggered off to bed that night, but I won't name them.

Because they were wrong, and Spriggs and Dodge were right. Arco was off 5⅞. Sohio, with which BP had announced plans to merge, was down 6½. Gulf was down 4, BP 1⅜, and Home dropped 8⅛.

This was months before the general decline of the market; in spite of these losses, oils held up well even after the decline began. The drop in oil stocks following the lease sale was no reflection on the companies involved; it was simply proof that emotion plays a major role in investments.

Alaskans, however, were jubilant. The lease sale had not brought in the magic figure of one billion dollars, but it had come close. Immediately following the sale, the chartered DC-8 took off for New York and arrived well before the banks opened the next morning. From there representatives of the Bank of America hurried westward. With cashiers' checks the transfer of funds is a simple procedure. Take them to the Federal Reserve Banks and the money is transferred from the account of the issuing bank to the payee bank in a jiffy.

The Bank of America had been quietly purchasing securities for almost a month. As the money was deposited to its account in Reserve banks across the country, these securities were transferred to the State of Alaska's account. A total of $180,000,000 was deposited on Thursday, and the securities purchased earned interest of $41,000 for the State of Alaska that day. By the tenth day, when the remainder of the 80 percent was due, the state was receiving $185,666 a day in interest.

Many of the sale's participants and concerned onlookers arrived days early and stayed days late, and, all on the expense account, they were big spenders. The state also picked up a large amount of that intangible commodity known as goodwill. All the people I talked with were pleased with Alaska and Alaskans, and many said they were going to bring their wives back for a vacation visit. The sale itself had gone off smoothly. Though not yet 12 years old, on that day the new state came of age.

Postscript: MARSHALL'S FOLLY

In all the exciting conversations before, during, and after the lease sale, and all the millions of words written about it in newspapers and magazines, I knew that something was missing, but I guess I was just too close to put my finger on it. When I did get the hint it was not from an Alaskan, or any representative of an American oil company, but from Geoff Larminie, the BP Irishman with the French name.

Late one night after the sale, and also after a little Scotch, he was dishing out encomiums to my country. He talked of the foresight of Seward, who almost singlehandedly arranged the purchase of Alaska, and, even earlier, of Thomas Jefferson, who engineered, over great opposition, the Louisiana Purchase. Then he came back up through time to the lease sales on the North Slope, and how there had been so little interest at first. "It was only a bloody good lemming pasture." But the state officials had persevered.

And then it hit me, what had been missing from the columns

of type and the hours of conversation on the lease sale. Out of 365 million acres of Alaska, who was it who had selected those two million on the North Slope?

"Why, Tom Marshall, of course," Geoff said. "Oh, he's a good hand. We used to call that area Marshall's Folly."

I had never heard of Thomas R. Marshall before. When I called him and asked for an appointment he seemed a little surprised but said to come on out, he was there. I gave the cab driver Marshall's address, and we started out bravely, but within a half an hour we were hopelessly lost. Finally, on a dirt road tucked behind a construction yard, we came across a small, government-looking building. And there, in what was obviously a geologist's office—full of maps, rocks, and other assorted junk—I found Tom Marshall.

He had come to Alaska from Wyoming when the territory first became a state. He was interested in the challenge of the transition—"that's why I am here." He found that there was no geological expertise in the state, that someone with some knowledge in that area was desperately needed. "That's what kept me here."

At one time he was petroleum geologist, petroleum engineer, and petroleum consultant for the Department of Natural Resources. His main efforts were directed to arranging his budget so that he could get somebody to help him. Today there are plenty of professional geologists around. "I'm not so lonely any more."

The influence of the Gold Rush had lingered on; the Commissioner of Natural Resources in the early Sixties was Phil R. Holsworth, whose background was in mining. Still, Holsworth had the vision to see a petroleum potential in Alaska. He gave Marshall a free hand in selecting lands under which there might be oil-bearing sands.

The magnitude of the job almost floored Marshall. On the one hand, the total acreage of Alaska and the 103 million acres the state was entitled to select under the Statehood Act comprised tremendous areas. On the other hand, so much of the state was eliminated—Pet 4, national forests, wildlife ranges, national parks, and, from a practical standpoint, unlikely areas such as the Alaska Range. So difficult was the choice that after 12 years of statehood, Alaska still had 83 million acres left to choose.

Marshall asked the few individuals exploring for petroleum in Alaska for their advice in selecting acreage, and all recommended the area around the upper Colville, in the southern part of the North Slope east and south of Umiat.

"It's a beautiful structure there," Marshall said wistfully. However, all indications were that the oil-bearing sands in the Umiat-Colville geosyncline were of the Cretaceous period. Back home in Wyoming, Marshall had had an unfortunate experience with Cretaceous sands. The oil was there all right, but so was a swelling clay that clogged the pores of the rock. Two important words in petroleum geology are porosity and permeability. No matter how many billions of barrels of oil may be in a formation, they are valueless if they can not permeate through a porous formation into the well.

Marshall turned down that beautiful structure of Cretaceous time and looked instead to the north, where the formations were of an earlier period. He selected a strip of 30 miles along the coast. Holsworth approved the selection on trust, and Marshall posted the announcement in the public room of the Division of Lands. Somebody wrote across it in red ink, Marshall's Folly.

"It was not funny to me," Marshall said. "I was out on a limb. This was a matter of public funds. It was a tremendous responsibility. I tried to laugh about it, too, but I didn't feel like it."

What *is* funny, Marshall candidly admits, is that since he has left Wyoming the Bell Creek field has been brought in there—from a Cretaceous formation. "If they'd brought in Bell Creek before I made the selection," he said, "I'd have probably gone along with Colville and I'd have shrunk a little smaller with every one of those dry holes BP and Sinclair drilled there."

The first lease sale on the acreage Marshall selected brought in $5 million. That's not much compared to $900 million, but it paid for the cost of selecting the entire area, and Marshall felt vindicated. The second sale, in 1965, brought in $6 million, and included the guts of the Prudhoe Bay anticline. That sale, incidentally, included the tract for which, four years later, Amerada-Hess and Getty Oil paid $72 million. Not one bid was made on it the first time it was opened. Other tracts which had been passed over in the two earlier sales were also included in the $900 million sale. It consisted mainly of odds and ends that nobody wanted before.

I had one more question. Regulations require all geological data to be turned over to the state within 30 days. All records must be kept confidential for two years, unless the company itself chooses to reveal them. And so the question: Where did Marshall keep the records—in a bank vault?

"Oh, no," he said, and nodded toward a green filing cabinet in the corner. "Right in there. We locked it up at night."

When I had come in Marshall's office he wasn't there; somebody had gone out to look for him. The cabinet was wide open. The office was on the ground floor; you could almost step over the window sill. A Junior G-man could have picked the lock with a hairpin. I thought of all the money spent trying to find out what was in those records, of helicopters circling rigs, of scouts counting stacks of drill pipe.

Marshall grinned. "Well," he said, "about a month before the sale I began thinking what you're thinking and I started taking them down to a bank vault at night."

"How?" I asked.

"Oh," he said, "I drove them down myself in my car. No problem."

Chapter IV

EVEN if all the people involved in putting up $1.4 billion in the lease sale had blown their minds and their stockholders' dollars—if not one of the 179 tracts ever produced one drop of oil—there's still plenty of oil already located on the North Slope of Alaska. After the sale, companies began announcing the results of wells already drilled. Five of Mobil's wells were productive, three drilled with Phillips, two with Socal. Arco announced five new ones, four with Humble, one with BP. And BP, pardon, Sohio, boasted the enormous flow rate of 21,500 barrels per day from one of its new wells.

Before the sale Arco had begun sticking its straws down into the ice-cream soda. I knew, because I had helped deliver drill pipe to it—well, at least I held the door shut on the Hovercraft. In one stretch of a few hundred yards, a brand new turbine-powered rig punched six holes in the ground, bending them out underground in every direction so that from one small strip they could slurp up the goo from the entire tract.

For well over a year, experts in oil transportation had been working, efficiently and expensively, on ways to get that oil from its cozy resting place north of the Arctic Circle into your gas tank. They were talking in terms of producing two million barrels a day by 1980. That's enough to take care of all the needs of the entire Northeast, or of all the states west of the Rockies.

But how would they get that oil out of Alaska? Even the

mighty Hercules could carry only a drop of that bucket; they might as well use dogsleds.

The standard methods of transporting crude petroleum are by pipeline over land, tanker over water. The three big pioneers on the Slope, BP, Arco, and Humble, went in together to study the pipeline route. Humble took it largely on itself to investigate the possibility of water transportation. Humble's Marine Division has America's largest domestic fleet—23 tankers flying the U.S. flag. Its parent company, Standard of New Jersey, operates well over 100 ships over the world.

Stanley B. Haas, a big, affable Missourian, headed the special project. Haas fell into a dream that has intrigued the romanticists of the sea for 500 years. Northwest Passage! What history, adventure, hardship, suffering, tragedy, that phrase evokes. All across the island expanse of northern Canada are scattered the names of the men who sought the Northwest Passage from Europe to the Orient. Beginning with Giovanni Caboto, or John Cabot, who reached Newfoundland in 1497 and thought he'd found Asia—the King of England gave him ten pounds—scores of mariners have picked away at the Passage from both sides. Their names are on the map. Frobisher Bay, Davis Strait. Hudson Bay, where Henry Hudson and his young son were cast adrift by his mutinous crew, and were never heard of again. Baffin Island, Baffin Bay; William Baffin, one of the mutineers, navigated the ship to the actual entrance of the Northwest Passage but he never knew it. He named the strait after one of the financial backers, Lancaster. Franklin Inlet, Lake Franklin, M'Clure Strait. Sir John Franklin gave himself, his two ships, and 129 officers and men three years to make it through the Passage. When he didn't get back within that time Lady Franklin encouraged a search for him. She spent her fortune in keeping the search alive and over the next 12 years some 40 expeditions went out looking for her husband. They never found him, his ships, or his men, but one of them did find the Northwest Passage. He was Commander Robert M'Clure, who led the search from the west.

M'Clure's ship was stuck in the ice in the strait that bears his name for two years and finally he gave up and started walking. He and his men hiked 200 miles across the floes to connect with another rescue expedition. His is the name that has gone down in history as the first man to make the Northwest Passage. Others eventually traversed it, leaving their names—Amundsen Gulf for one—but they didn't carry any more goods from Europe to China than did M'Clure.

By August of 1968, when Stan Haas got involved, the field was still wide open, although he was concerned only with the difficult part of the route, U.S.A. to U.S.A., New York to Prudhoe Bay.

The motivation of Humble and Standard of New Jersey was not just to make history; economics had something to do with it. It was estimated that transporting oil by tanker from Alaska to the East Coast would cost 60 cents a barrel less than by pipeline. At, say, 50 million barrels a day, that's worth looking into.

The cost of the venture was estimated at $40 million. For what was readily acknowledged to be an out-and-out gamble, Arco and BP put up $2 million each, and Humble the rest. Humble chartered the biggest and most powerful ship ever made in America, the tanker *Manhattan*. Three football fields long and 115,000 tons dead weight (Cabot's ship was 100 tons), it was powered by engines capable of grinding out 43,-000 horsepower forward, 14,000 astern.

But the *Manhattan* was no icebreaker, and to make it into one in one shipyard would take years. Haas had only months. To get the work done in a hurry he had the huge ship chopped up into four chunks. They were towed to shipyards from Maine to Mobile for the necessary modifications. The pieces looked awful funny being pushed around in the open sea by tugs. When the ship was reassembled—at one time 10,000 men were working on it—it had a revolutionary new icebreaking prow sticking out in front. There wasn't anything new or subtle about the principle; the prow would ride up on top of the ice and smash it through sheer weight and force. But the angle of the 70-foot prow was 18 degrees instead of the customary 30. The new bow was eight feet wider than the rest of the ship. Tankers are squat-looking vessels anyway; looking at this one head on from the water line, or ice line, I thought it resembled a hammerhead shark.

To transport oil through the ice pack a tanker should have sides of thicker, stronger steel. But there was no time for that; besides, all the ship was going to carry on the trial voyage was sea water for ballast. The compromise was to reinforce the sides at the waterline with a band of steel.

The path to Prudhoe lay right over the magnetic pole, which made any compass useless for hundreds of miles on either side. Sophisticated navigational equipment to work with Navy satellites was installed. To measure the pressures of the ice, electronic gauges were placed along the ship's sides. Two helicopters, operating from special pads installed aft, would buzz around ahead of the ship scouting out a path through the ice. Radar, laser beams, and infra-red photography would also be used to measure the thickness of the ice ahead. The ultimate in ice-measuring devices would also be used: cold humans twisting hand-powered augurs.

As word of the impending attempt to smash through the Northwest Passage got around in marine circles, applications from men—and one woman—eager to participate began pouring in from all over the world. Enough members of the Humble fleet volunteered to make up the 54-man crew. Captain Roger A. Steward, a bristle-mustached veteran of 30 years with Humble, was picked as master, with two staff captains to assist him. All three, with Haas, prepped for the trip on American and Canadian icebreakers and flew over the route from Greenland to Alaska.

Two icebreakers, one Canadian, one American, would accompany the ship. A group of some 75 specialists and scientists went along. Captain Thomas C. Pullen, a veteran of the Royal Canadian Navy's Arctic Patrol, accepted the invitation, although he termed the trip "an exercise in self-destruction." Another Arctic veteran was Martti Saarikangas, Finnish designer of most of the icebreakers in use over the world, including the huge Russian vessels. Saarikangas demonstrated how far ahead of the American novices he was by ignoring the great forward horsepower of the *Manhattan* and inquiring how much power it could muster astern. Told the ship could muster only a third of its total horsepower in reverse, but that the ship intended to go forward, not backwards, he let out a Finnish horselaugh. And it turned out he knew what he was laughing about.

Just as it takes a while for an ice cube to freeze, so it does for the Arctic seas; they build up their greatest expanse and thickness of ice by late spring and early summer. In the open western Arctic north of Alaska the ice may remain in massive floes the year round, but in the protected waters in the east by August and September there are great areas of open water. The *Manhattan* had to steam northward in August for nine days until in Baffin Bay, between Baffin Island and Greenland, 1000 miles north of Hudson Bay, Haas found a floating ice pack to play with.

A low white wall rose from the blue sea. Its height was deceptive; ice rides low in the water. It had to be 15 feet thick. This was a $40 million moment of truth, and the first ice Captain Steward had ever laid a ship on. He approached it warily. As Haas later said, they didn't know whether the ship made contact with the ice or it made contact with the ship. Under the onslaught of that tremendous weight and force, the ice pack cracked. A chunk the size of a city block broke off. Steward called for more speed. The ice grew thicker, but the ship didn't hesitate. The bow bore down on the ice, cracked it, and threw boulder-sized chunks to each side as though they were mere slush.

The ship broke through into open water, but ahead lay another floe, this one thicker and a mile across. Everyone braced for the shock. The prow hit. A geyser of spray shot into the air. The entire ice floe split with the sound of a thunderclap. Chunks of ice the size of boulders scraped the reinforced sides with shrieks and groans. Yet so big was the ship, so heavy with dead weight and ballast, that it only trembled slightly. The men on watch, working below deck about the ship, heard only faint sounds if any. No ship in history had ever broken through ice of such thickness, yet only those who actually witnessed the show would have known it.

I had always thought that an icebreaker, even as gargantuan a one as the *Manhattan*, butted into the ice, came to a shuddering stop, then backed up and butted again. I guess I had the impression that it was something like a tank battering into the brick walls of a fortress, and that everybody and everything in it would be tied down. When I first boarded the *Manhattan* and went up to the bridge, I passed by the quarters of one of the staff captains. The door was open, and I looked in. Something was wrong. It took me a second to realize what it was. The bunk was built into the forward wall, and it was made up head forward. I have put in many a mile in sleeping cars, where you always sleep feet first, in case the train comes to a sudden stop. But on this ship, designed to smash into ice ridges, the captain slept head first.

I learned that even when the ship was deliberately propelled into more ice than it could smash, its weight and velocity were so great that it came to a slow stop, not an abrupt one. Sea ice, at least to an icebreaker, is not as hard as I had assumed from my contact with it on frozen fresh-water ponds.

Sea ice is of infinite variety; an Arctic climatologist says the Eskimo language has more than 70 words meaning ice. One of the important discoveries made by the scientists on the *Manhattan* was just how little they knew about ice. Stan Haas's greatest surprise on the voyage came when he first encountered ice more than a year old. His previous training experience had been with so-called rotten ice, fresh frozen that winter.

The *Manhattan* encountered first-year ice, second-year ice, and multi-year or polar ice. The first, new ice, contains salt and is milky white, spongy, and easily broken. Second-year ice, usually aquamarine in color, has suffered some summer melting, in which the salt has leached down, leaving pure water on top to freeze harder. In polar ice this process has happened over and over, and the leaching of the salt and the compacting of the lower strata result in great hardness. It also results in a beautiful blue color, like the sky.

As the *Manhattan* proceeded westward it began encountering pack ice, piled up into thick jagged ridges by the wind pouring down across 2000 miles of Arctic Ocean; the wind drives the ice into the straits and sounds between the northern Canadian islands through which the Northwest Passage runs. Here was where the *Manhattan* first ran into major resistance, but still it kept going, chomping its way through the floes, threading between ice ridges 30 and 40 feet thick. In Viscount Melville Strait the ship deliberately, for this entire voyage was an experiment, bit off more than it could chew and came slowly to a full stop. To test the ice ahead the ice parties, who came to be called the chipmunk brigade, made the first fully comprehensive scientific studies of ice.

Frequently the ship would stop at night, for even the light of the aurora borealis, intensely brilliant in the peak year of the 11-year sun-spot cycle, was not enough to keep the *Manhattan* from slamming into building-sized ridges. Every morning, during a special testing period, the chipmunk brigade would go out on the ice and go to work. Using hand-powered augers (engine-driven equipment would create friction capable of changing the character of the ice), the icetronauts, including University of Alaska students, would collect cores of ice to be tested in laboratories on board. They worked at times in subzero temperatures made even colder by the strong winds. Once their search for knowledge came to an abrupt halt when a couple of curious polar bears ambled up. The parties carried heavy rifles for self-protection, but, thanks to swiftness of foot, never had to use them.

One striking property of icebergs, which could put the sparkling water manufacturers out of business, was discovered when the ship deliberately banked off an iceberg. Fragments fell on the deck. When placed in a drink, they fizzed.

The advance eyes of the *Manhattan* reported that strong westerly winds had piled up great pressure ridges in M'Clure Strait, the western exit of the Northwest Passage opening up into the Arctic Ocean. It would be a feather in Captain Steward's tamoshanter and Stan Haas's orange fur-flapped cap if the *Manhattan* could break its way through that famous strait. Another route, the protected Prince of Wales Strait that runs southward into the eastward extension of the Beaufort Sea, was less hazardous, but Haas wanted to take a crack at the stretch that had bottled up M'Clure for two years.

Knowing what they were letting themselves in for, Haas and Steward headed into the strait. To compound the difficulty, one escort, the American icebreaker *Northwind*, underpowered and 25 years old, damaged two of its six engines and had to go home. That left only the Canadian *John A. MacDonald*, vastly superior to the *Northwind* but still possessing only a fraction of the power and weight of the *Manhattan*.

Battering her way into M'Clure Strait, the *Manhattan* was stopped six times by the massive pressure ridges. Five times she was able to back up, build up speed, and bull her way through. But on the sixth time—the third that day—still only at the halfway mark, the *Manhattan* was stopped dead. Ice floes, driven by a 20-knot gale, piled up against the ship's sides. The channel behind was freezing over, and it was filled with massive chunks of polar ice broken loose by previous efforts. The 14,000 horsepower the *Manhattan* turned up astern wasn't enough. Further, there was always danger that the big blocks of ice would damage the 22-foot propeller blades. Captain Pullen, serving as liaison with the *Johnny Mac*, as the tough little Canadian icebreaker was called by the Americans, sent a message to her captain: "Would you mind nibbling at our quarters?"

Bucking and smashing, coming up to within 100 feet of the *Manhattan*'s great bulk, the *Johnny Mac* cleared out the way astern and enabled her to get a running start. Darrah Moore, an Esso International representative, suggested shutting off all power and heat on everything not absolutely essential to moving the ship. Lights were extinguished, hot water heaters cut off, and even radio communications shut down. Another few thousand horses were added.

The extra power was just enough. The *Manhattan* slammed into the ridge, split it, and kept going. Moving steadily now, even building up speed through the pack, the *Manhattan* turned in a two-mile circle, breaking ice as she went. After M'Clure Strait, nothing could stop her. The *Manhattan* broke through the Prince of Wales Strait in less than a day and came out into the open sea.

The first commercial ship had completed the Northwest Passage. When a helicopter dropped me on board the *Manhattan* at Point Barrow, westernmost part of the passage, I had a tickling feeling in the soles of my feet; the deck I was standing on was part of history.

Offshore at Prudhoe Bay one gilded barrel, filled with oil from Sag River No. 1, was put on board by helicopter. T. J. Fuson, head of Humble Marine Division, commented that at $40 million it was the world's most expensive barrel of oil. Somebody suggested that he go back and get another; then each would cost only $20 million. T. J. smiled politely.

Returning to New York, the ship grazed an ice floe and tore a hole in its side large enough to drive a truck through. The rent occurred in an area that had been strengthened and proved only what everybody already knew: commercial tankers playing the Northwest Passage must be designed and built for that purpose. Stan Haas said repeatedly that the voyage of the *Manhattan* proved that it could be done. The only question remaining was: Could it be done economically?

T. J. Fuson candidly enumerated some other problems. "We know we can build tankers to ply between the East Coast of the United States and the north coast," T. J. told me over dinner one night. "That's what this trip set out to prove. As a matter of fact, the necessary shipbuilding program would be an enormous boost to the national economy. But another thing we have to think about is how we're going to get that oil on board. As you know, we couldn't get the *Manhattan* within thirty miles of Prudhoe Bay. We couldn't *see* Prudhoe Bay. The water's just too shallow there. We've thought of running a pipeline out to an offshore landing platform but the problem would be withstanding the terrific pressure of the ice pack when it comes in. It would cost $500 million! Dredging a harbor at Prudhoe Bay would be a fantastic engineering project, and fantastically expensive."

I had talked with a University of Alaska scientist who had spent some time on an ice island off the coast. These are fascinating things; the most famous one, Fletcher's ice island or No. T-3, has been floating around the pole for God knows how long. Two ice islands had floated south to ground near Prudhoe Bay the year before. To hold one there a team of scientists and assistants had set up quarters on the island and pumped millions of gallons of sea water on top of it. The water froze and added to its weight. Could this provide protection from the pack?

"Aw, that was only a wild idea," T. J. said. "The thing split. It would be a lot more practical to use real islands for protection. The biggest one is Hershel Island. It's about 300 miles east, off the Canadian coast in Mackenzie Bay. There's oil there, too. But that involves running a pipeline along the coast and I don't want to spoil my dinner thinking about *that*. Yeah, the *Manhattan* made history, all right, and we all know that bigger and better ships designed for that sole purpose can make the trip, week in, week out, all year round. But when you add up the cost of the ships and the cost of loading them, you're talking about a billion dollars and more. Is it worth it? That's what we've got to figure out."

T. J. pooh-poohed the ecological dangers of tankers running through the Northwest Passage. "We're not going to pour money into a fleet of icebreaking tankers just to dump oil in the Arctic," he said. "We can't sell it to polar bears. Any ship we send up there to get oil will be designed and built to withstand any possible catastrophe."

That spring Stan Haas took the *Manhattan* back to the Arctic for further testing. The trip, with BP and Arco again picking up a token part of the bill, ran the total expenditure up to some $50 million. This time, without fanfare, the big ship proved it could run for hours through first-year ice. Haas repeated his conviction that oil can be delivered by tanker through the Northwest Passage, but the stupendous cost of building both a fleet of icebreakers and loading facilities remained the prime consideration.

During the two voyages cost estimates had risen. Ships of 200,000 tons dead weight, capable of carrying one and a half million barrels of oil, powered by engines ranging up to 200,-000 horsepower and built of special steel, would cost from $60 million to $100 million each in domestic shipyards. (The Jones Act prohibits use of foreign-built vessels between American ports.) Figuring on the basis of a round trip of 30 days, to deliver a million barrels a day would require 20 ships. Add to that the cost of building a loading facility on the north coast.

And to the economic pressure add that of groups concerned with environment and ecology. Conservationists question whether anyone can give an absolute guarantee on so vital a project. On its return trip from Prudhoe Bay the *Manhattan* passed over an uncharted undersea pinnacle that reached up to within 20 feet of its bottom. Even with steel of the thickness and strength American plants can manufacture, can civilization be certain that no rupture could ever possibly occur?

Both the State of Alaska and the Department of the Interior were perturbed by oil slicks on the southern coast and in Cook Inlet in 1970. They resulted from the discharge of sea-water ballast from tankers coming in to load up. This ballast contains what is known as clingage, the film of oil adhering to the sides from the previous load. Though only a comparatively small amount of oil compared to that from a wrecked or damaged vessel, it was still enough to take a heavy toll in aquatic wildlife.

A major oil spill in the Arctic would be horrendous—and not just to the local population of seals and polar bears. Foreign substances break down slowly in the cold regions of the world; the dark blot could lie there for centuries, absorbing the solar energy that now bounces back from water and ice. A change in temperature of only a few degrees over such an expanse would upset the balance of wind, sea, water, and climate in the polar regions—about which we know so little. We do know that if the polar ice cap melted, the water released would raise the level of the oceans and flood tidelands and coastal cities.

However alarming, this potential is still speculative. Another pot of trouble brewed up during the *Manhattan*'s junket is a reality.

Although little has been printed of it in the United States many Canadians and a large segment of the Canadian press have expressed bitter opposition to the idea of foreign ships traversing their archipelagic waterway. Many of the Canadian newspaper accounts I've read of the voyage were bitterly hostile; the reporters seemed to go out of their way to find fault with the exploit and to poke fun at the ignorant, clumsy, and over-cautious Americans involved in it.

The Canadian Government had cooperated closely and cordially with the leaders of the project; the presence of Captain Pullen on the *Manhattan*, and the *John A. MacDonald* nibbling at its quarters, had been easily arranged. Economically, Canada has everything to gain from the opening of the Northwest Passage. The Canadian North Slope has oil, too, and the Arctic islands are a mineral bonanza. Baffin Island iron is so pure it can be fed directly into the blast furnace—but there aren't any blast furnaces on Baffin Island.

In spite of the camaraderie with which the project began, reporters covering the trip had the crew of the Canadian icebreaker chortling with glee when the *Manhattan* called on it for help. When one of the *Manhattan*'s helicopters broke through the ice and had to be rescued by the *John A. MacDonald*—no one was hurt—the incident was reported with great relish.

Captain Pullen joined the *Manhattan*'s crew in referring to the *John A. MacDonald* with typical American familiarity as the *Johnny Mac*. Some reporters, however, felt that this belittled the Canadian hero for whom it was named. "How would the Americans like it if we talked about Georgie Wash?"

Humble ships, like most others, fly the flag of the host country when in a foreign port but not in coastal waters. The fact that the Canadian flag was not flown by the *Manhattan* when underway became a cause célèbre in some circles. The very question as to what constituted Canadian waters became an intense political issue. A Canadian official declared that the Government should station a destroyer at either end of the waterway.

The question of jurisdiction over the Northwest Passage is indeed intriguing. The three-mile territorial limit is generally recognized by most nations; by close navigation a ship could conceivably manage to stay three miles from land all the way through, using M'Clure Strait. In the Prince of Wales Strait, however, at a point where it is 10.8 miles wide, stands Princess Royal Island, 5.5 miles from one shore, 4.8 from the other. Aha!

Another intriguing debate involved the two schools known as ice-is-water and ice-is-ice. When you can walk from one Canadian island to another, regardless of how far apart they are and whether you are a polar bear, does this not make what you walk on Canadian? Under pressure Prime Minister Pierre Trudeau issued a proclamation extending the three-mile limit to 12, with pollution control to 100 miles and the further stipulation that this would continue to be in effect whether the World Court liked it or not. If other nations got into this act, international shipping interests would have a fit. The Philippines, Indonesia, and Malaysia would become a land mass.

As in most international controversies, the U.S.-Canadian problems contain both a lack of communications and a surfeit of chauvinism. It just happens there is in the U.S. Senate a man thoroughly conversant with and concerned about Arctic ecology, and who can talk about it in Canadian French with Prime Minister Trudeau. He is Mike Gravel of Alaska, young and forward-looking, whose parents were Quebeçois.

Mike, né Maurice, was born in Massachusetts and as a boy determined to be a U.S. Senator. He put himself through Columbia University driving a hack, then headed for Alaska. He was speaker of the Alaska House of Delegates at 35, and a Senator at 38.

While angry diplomatic notes were being passed between Washington and Ottawa, Mike talked with Trudeau quietly, and publicly endorsed the 100-mile pollution control feature of the Canadian declaration.

"I for one admire the decisiveness of Pierre Elliott Trudeau's position," he told a Conference on Canadian Affairs. "If it takes a unilateral political act such as the Canadian declaration to focus our attention on the issues, then that act is well worth the ruckus . . . I find it hard to fault the Prime Minister's argument that this is an area in which the law has not yet caught up with technology. Until it does, concentration on legalisms will not save our wildlife from an oily death nor clean up our beaches."

Canadians have pointed out that if the United States considers the Northwest Passage a waterway open to the ships of the world, we could hardly complain if ships of the Soviet Union or Red China use it, too. Japan has expressed great interest in the Northwest Passage: it would lop 3300 miles off the distance between Tokyo and New York and save the Panama Canal toll to boot. The combined savings from importing coal from the East Coast and exporting manufactured goods right back again would pull the rug out from under European competition. Japan could compete in automobiles, say, right on the home grounds of European manufacturers.

Regardless of who owns the route, who would maintain it? Without the *John A. MacDonald* the *Manhattan* would have been in trouble. But icebreakers are expensive to build and maintain. The United States has none capable of the job. Canadians laughed at the poor old *Northwind*. The *Staten Island*, which substituted for it when the *Northwind*'s engines conked out, was not much better. Its crew members pointed out to me Russian stencils on a bulkhead; it had been built for lend-lease in World War II. It was no strain for the Russians to give it back; they've got lots better ones.

Alaska's Congressman Howard Pollock, a Navy veteran, complained loud and long over the condition of American icebreakers following their performance during the *Manhattan*'s voyage. He demanded an immediate buildup of the American icebreaker fleet in both quality and quantity.

Senator Mike Gravel found some sugar for the bitter pill. After conferring with the Coast Guard, he pointed out that America had had no great need for icebreakers before the Northwest Passage. Now we can start from scratch with more efficient, nuclear-powered modern vessels.

General Dynamics Corporation has proposed a fleet of nuclear-powered submarine tankers to move Alaskan oil under the ice. Each could carry 1.2 million barrels and make the round trip between Greenland and Prudhoe Bay in two weeks, including loading time. Even loading could be underwater—or under ice. As oil is lighter than water and would exert outward pressure on the hull to balance pressure at normal depths, some unique construction methods could be utilized. And the skippers would not care what the Arctic weather was like on top.

The Northwest Passage can become a world waterway if anyone wants to spend the money. Based on Humble's figures, it can result in a gross saving of $900 million a trip. But, as we have seen, the voyage of the *Manhattan* did more than make feasible the delivery of Alaskan oil to eastern ports. It lopped off thousands of miles between the industrial centers of Europe and Asia. It gave a practical lesson in global geography: that a hitherto inaccessible point in the Canadian Arctic just north of Alaska is equidistant from Tokyo, London, and New York, which makes Tokyo the same distance from both, and by the shortest possible route.

Economics and oil aside, the *Manhattan*'s realization of a 500-year-old dream will always remain a tribute to the perseverance of man.

WINTER OF DISCONTENT

Drifting from group to group in the big, high-ceilinged hearing room in the new Senate office building in Washington, now crowded with Alaskans, I had the feeling that I was in with a bunch of cornered wolverines. The hearing was over and two bars and an hors d'oeuvres table had been set up. Two days before Governor Keith Miller had brought in a group of a hundred Alaskan leaders in hopes of finding a way out of the snarl preventing the Great Land from getting her oil to market. They had been preached to in hearings, briefings, and special appointments with Senators and Representatives. They'd gotten nowhere, and though they were now drinking, nibbling, and talking, their anger and frustration were just barely under control. An inocuous remark, a mild question, and off they'd go.

I sidled up to Stanton H. Patty, who covers Alaska for the Seattle *Times*, in hopes of a brief respite from these explosive emotions; journalists usually look on such gatherings with a kind of cynical objectivity. "Do you sense a little antagonism around here?" I said.

For objectivity, I'd come to the wrong man.

"You're damn right I sense it," he said. His face got red and I thought the muscles in his neck would pop his bolo tie. "What's more, I condone it. We opened up this country, we fought for it, and now we deserve the fruits of our labor. These hypocritical critics make me and all Alaskans sick to our stomachs." He glared at me. "It's Alaska against the nation and it's not the first time, either."

Stan Patty was born in Alaska. His father, Dr. Ernest Patty, had become president of the University of Alaska when it was a rundown little technical institute and built it into a handsome and highly regarded center of learning.

Stan expressed the fury that had been building up all winter in practically all the Alaskans I know. It was popping out in ugly ways. Not for a generation had there been overt enmity between natives and white man. But that winter, incidents began to occur. A man and his wife were eating dinner in an Anchorage hotel when a native couple sat at the table next to them. They angrily pushed back the table, got up, and left.

Later, in the spring, when the vanguard of college students began arriving in naive hopes of landing the lush summer jobs they'd read about, there was open talk in Anchorage and Fairbanks of forming vigilante groups and rapping them on their long-haired heads. The Anchorage City Council passed an ordinance giving police extra powers to deal with the newcomers, who had no idea of the real situation there. Because times were tough. The Fairbanks jail had triple its normal number of boarders, a sure sign of unemployment. The unemployment rate was 13 percent, triple that of the rest of the nation, even before the arrival of the summer crowd.

Heavy equipment worth up to $50 million was sitting idle in stands from the Gulf of Alaska to the Beaufort Sea. Its owners were paying out high interest. Housekeeping costs were $100,-000 a day. The men who were counting on running it had to take any job they could get, if they could get it.

One Christmas when I was a child I was counting on getting my first bicycle, a real two-wheeler. It took me all Christmas Day to realize fully that I wasn't getting that bicycle; the enormity of the loss was too much to comprehend. It was a much longer Christmas for the Alaskans and the gung-ho oil people; they couldn't believe it either. Anyone could see the big new office buildings going up in Anchorage, the activity in Fairbanks. The world was hungry for oil, Alaska had it, and some of the world's great corporations had bought their share of it—$900 million in one day. What could possibly go wrong?

What went wrong, simply put, was the sudden discovery in the Lower 48 of the word ecology. The great Alaska oil rush was only one of the many victims, innocent and guilty, of the exploding concern with the environment in which we live.

The immediate target in Alaska was TAPS—the Trans-Alaska Pipeline System. It came to a halt slowly, still struggling uncomprehendingly, like a gut-shot moose.

The man I worked with most closely on the pipeline was a likable Louisiana Cajun named A. F. "Buddy" Morel. He was so full of pipeline that he didn't even miss Mardi Gras. As far back as 1964, Buddy remembers, there had been some discussion of a pipeline across Alaska. It would hardly be wise to continue exploration on the North Slope if it were not possible to get that oil to market. When the Prudhoe Bay field was discovered, plans for the pipeline began immediately.

The *Manhattan* cut no ice in TAPS headquarters in Dallas, Texas, in the spring of 1968. Oil men tend naturally to think first and foremost of a pipeline as a means to transport crude. Even had the icebreaking tankers been a proved success they would have persevered with the pipeline, for the immediate market of North Slope oil was the West Coast. The most practical way to get it there would be by pipeline to an ice-free port, by tanker to Pacific ports. The three major operators on the Slope at that time, Arco, BP, and Humble, each already operating great complexes of pipelines, formed the pipeline consortium and assigned their best men to it.

But as it turned out, getting North Slope oil to market caused as many international reverberations as the oil itself. To lay pipe, four feet in diameter, more than 700 miles across the mysterious tundra and its underlying permafrost, four mountain ranges and the Yukon River, is not only the world's largest private construction project (the original estimate of $1 billion increased by the hundreds of millions as time went on), but one of the most challenging and controversial.

Flying its route, especially through the confused wind patterns of its narrow, twisting, glacier-hung passes, and studying the

ιs its contractors would face, I thought the Trans-Alaska
e mighty exciting.

major construction job is exciting. There's always a new
challenge coming up, and the engineers with their slip sticks,
the supervisors and operators out on the job, respond to it with
the aggressive and predatory instinct of an Eskimo on a hunt.
Though a comparatively recent breed, pipeliners have a romance of their own. I know men in their 50s who remember
when they bent pipe in the field by heating it in bonfires made of
fence posts. They also remember skedaddling down mountainsides in the southern Appalachians with rifle bullets nipping at
their heels; they may not have been revenooers, but the moon-
shiners up in the hills weren't taking any chances.

Pipelines require geologists and surveyors to lay out the route,
landmen and lawyers to obtain the right of way over it. The pipe
is usually laid in a ditch, welded together, and neatly covered
over. As it goes around obstacles and over hills and mountains
it must be bent. Try to bend a curtain rod without putting a
crimp in it and you'll understand why this requires special expertise. Pipelines cross rivers by bridge or on the bottom; that's
two separate areas of engineering right there. The Arctic adds
mystery, for little pipelining has been done in those regions.
The Russians have laid huge pipelines in Siberia, but few American engineers have been able to study them.

To get started, TAPS lined up several consultants, from the
international firm of Pipeline Technologists to individuals like
Dr. Harold Peyton, the Alaska geologist.

They knew where the oil was; they had to determine where it
would wind up, and work back from there. The decision nar-
rowed down to the town of Valdez, 120 miles east of Anchorage.
Ice never gets to Valdez. It is 12 miles up a natural deep-water
fjord from the protected waters of Prince William Sound.
Though Valdez dates back to the Gold Rush days, it is para-
doxically a brand-new little town. The original Valdez was partly
destroyed by a series of great waves in the earthquake of 1964.
The people abandoned their soggy homes and buildings and

moved to a new location on more stable ground about four miles away. From the air the neat little town looks like a lot of little loops, and indeed it is. Every street is a cul de sac; children don't have to cross the street to get to school.

For years the cheechakos landing at Valdez crossed the Chugach Mountains on the glacier north of the city on their way to the Yukon. Then Thompson Pass was discovered. It was a steep hike, but better than a glacier. Today the highway north to Fairbanks runs through Thompson Pass. Some years 100 inches of snow fall in the pass, and some days the wind blows at 100 miles an hour. Crossing it is like taking a ferry. You wait for the snow plow and follow it over. In the summer the beautiful scenery and the lush foliage make up for the winter hardships. Southern Alaska is the land of berries and you can stop and stuff yourself. The TAPS people took a series of survival courses in which they learned how to determine what's edible.

"I pick every berry I see and squeeze it to test it," Buddy said. "If it's okay I eat it. I don't know what I'm eating but they sure are good."

To determine the route from Valdez north, several survey parties, working with helicopters, went out into the berry fields. In the Lower 48, pipeliners must secure permission from property owners along the route, skirting such man-made obstacles as towns, factories, and houses. In Alaska most of the route was over Federal land, with no sign of habitation for miles. The bears showed a strange form of inhospitality. Helicopter pilots began having trouble returning to sites already marked with cloth panels. Bits and pieces of markers indicated the markers had been destroyed. One day a helicopter arrived to find a bear busily tearing up the piece of cloth. The helicopter came in anyway, and the bear departed, leaving unexplained the reason for this ursine vandalism.

The Yukon, half a mile wide, presented some unusual problems. Bush pilots frequently follow the river in bad weather, flying at tree-top level under the clouds. It would be most discomfiting to see an elevated pipeline suddenly loom up ahead;

the decision was made to cross the river on the bottom. However, at spring break-up, ice floes frequently pile up in the big river, creating a partial dam. With the channel restricted, the surge of water flows under the ice dam, flushing 50 or more feet of silt and gravel away and scouring the bottom down to bedrock. The pipe would therefore have to be laid in a trench blasted out of the bedrock.

Through the Chugach and Alaska ranges the route would follow the highway. Through the Brooks Range the original intention was to use Anaktuvuk Pass, following the route of the caribou, the Eskimos, the Cat trains, and the winter road. With an elevation of only 2100 feet, it is the lowest pass in the range. North of the Brooks Range, where there is an almost solid expanse of permafrost to Prudhoe Bay, the planners originally decided to lay the pipe above ground. This is more expensive but there was good reason for it. Prudhoe oil comes out of the ground at a temperature of more than 160 degrees. Offhand, it would seem that it would cool down quickly in a steel pipe at 60 below zero, but it doesn't work that way. Pumping stations along the route would move the oil through the 48-inch pipe at a speed of 300,000 barrels a day to begin with—eventually two million barrels a day. Pressure and friction would maintain the high temperature all the way to Valdez.

Placing a container of hot oil in permafrost would cause thawing. The hot pipe would wind up in the middle of a huge puddle. If weighted it might keep on sinking; if not, it might be heaved up to the surface. There was no choice but to elevate it. The alternatives were whether to set it on pilings or to lay it on gravel piled up high enough, say four feet, to provide sufficient insulation.

It was at this point that the conservationists got into the act. I was playing tennis one day, far, far from Alaska, with a friend named John M. Rhea, when, between sets, I mentioned that I was going up to Alaska to take a look at the pipeline. His face turned red and I thought he was going to have a heart attack. It turned out that, as president of the Boone and Crockett

Club, an office once held by Theodore Roosevelt, John and his fellow big game hunters were taking off after the pipeline as though it were a trophy grizzly. One of their objections was that the elevated line, four feet of pipe on four feet of gravel, would constitute a man-made barrier to the normal migration of wild-life, particularly caribou, on the North Slope. The half-million or so caribou—nobody knows exactly how many there are—are divided generally into two herds. One migrates southward in the fall through the Anaktuvuk Pass. The other sifts through un-named passes in the mountains to the east. Sealing off either herd or portions of both with an eight-foot blockade would cre-ate nobody knew just how much havoc in the entire chain of wildlife in Alaska.

The pressure brought to bear by conservation groups on this one issue caused the route planners to take another good look at both the North Slope and the Brooks Range. Tracing the Sagavanirktok River and one of its tributaries, the Atigun, south-ward into the Brooks Range, they found another pass. On the other side of the divide is the source of the Dietrich River, one of the tributaries of the Yukon. The pass had no name. It had no need of one. Its elevation is 4100 feet and there's a steep as-cent at the top; neither man nor caribou could cross it. I saw some Dall sheep jumping around the rocks but they don't count; Dall sheep can go anywhere. But so can a pipeline. The problem is not in pumping oil up the steepest grade, but in braking it, with chokes in the pipe, coming down on the other side.

A rough measurement of the entire line from Prudhoe Bay to Valdez through the Anaktuvuk Pass came to 789 miles; over the Dietrich Pass, as it has come to be known, the total route was 22 miles shorter. (The current management, reorganized as the Alyeska Pipeline Service Company, refers to the length as "almost 800 miles.") By laying the pipe in the Sagavanirktok River's gravel bed, which is not permafrost, the caribou could roam at will and TAPS would save money. In this one instance, at least, conservationist pressure and TAPS response opened up the possibility of a superior and cheaper route.

As routes were proposed, crews went out in the field to examine the ground more closely. Surely no other pipeline project ever involved such a wide variety of terrain. It would cross mountains, permafrost, and a major earthquake zone. There also proved to be wide variations within the separate categories. I had thought that permafrost is permafrost is permafrost. It turns out, however, that the characteristics vary greatly from the North Slope to the central part of Alaska.

You get so you can make an educated guess as to what lies beneath the surface of the ground from what grows on top of it. When you look down from a plane and see birch trees, brilliant green in the summer, pale gold in the fall, it's a pretty good indication that there is no permafrost beneath. But the dark year-round blue-green of spruce is no help, for this hardy conifer can thrive on a thin layer of soil over permanently frozen ground.

Flying over the proposed route, Buddy Morel pointed out to me a two-way feature of the line. When fully completed with vegetation planted ("I'd sure love to have the tomato-growing concession on it," Buddy said) it would be an obvious pathway from Valdez to Prudhoe. To the Alaskan bush pilots, whose many flights are nearly always by visual flight rules, it would provide a handy landmark. On the other hand, the pilots would provide a free surveillance service. In the Lower 48, pipeline companies usually check the routes regularly by air, looking for any discoloration that would indicate a break or seepage.

"Up here," Buddy said, "with half the pilots in Alaska getting their bearings by it, this line will be overflown hundreds of times a week."

From Valdez through the Alaska Range, the route would cross an active earthquake zone. Seismologists studied the fault lines and laid out the route so it would cross these lines on bedrock. Though a 48-inch pipe looks pretty rigid, pipeline engineers say that on the grand scale of an earth-shaking disturbance the pipe is actually flexible and elastic.

While groups of technologists were studying the terrain and

possible routes, another group was determining the specifications of the pipe itself. Any pipeline should be tough; a pipe laid across Alaska has to be tough in Arctic temperatures. Yet it also must have properties that make it possible to weld the lengths together in those same temperatures. This metallurgical contradiction kept slide rules and laboratories busy. When the specifications were announced, it turned out that no steel mill in the United States could begin immediately to turn out such huge pipe in the enormous quantity required. Normally, steel industry representatives said, a big pipe job is preceded by discussions over a period of several years.

One American company proposed fabricating the pipe in Alaska. Business interests in the state were delighted at the prospect, but TAPS said it could not wait the 18 months required to build the plant and start production. The oil was there, the market was there, and the route was being laid out. Construction would begin in the spring of 1970 and oil would be flowing south in 1972.

A group of three Japanese steel companies with the capability of producing 48-inch pipe almost immediately came in with a bid estimated to be from $50 to $75 a ton less than American estimates, and promised 120,000 tons in 1969, another 300,-000 tons in 1970, and 80,000 in 1971. They got the contract.

In September, 1969, eight months after the first specifications were announced, the first shipment of pipe arrived in Valdez on board a Japanese freighter. An official delegation flew to Valdez to welcome it to Alaska. I had to take its unique metallurgical composition on faith, as steel looks like steel to me, but I do know that I could walk through the pipe, stooped over. TAPS sent lengths of the pipe, each 40 feet long and weighing five tons, to Anchorage and Fairbanks for exhibit. Adults ogled it; schoolteachers took their classes to see it. Meanwhile, in Japan, shipyards built special barges to transport pipe to the northern terminus on the Arctic Coast, the longest barge trip in maritime history.

To build the world's most difficult pipeline, you don't start out at one end and keep welding one length to the other until you finish. That way would take years. Rather, you break it up into spreads, thirteen in the case of TAPS, and work on each. Nor can these be done simultaneously. "Man, we'd tie up every piece of heavy construction equipment in the world that way," Buddy Morel said.

Setting up headquarters and stockpiling areas for these spreads was in itself a major construction project. In Alaska, remember, you don't just dispatch pipe and equipment to where it's needed by normal means of transportation; normal means of transportation to most of the site locations would be by bush plane on floats or skis. First, therefore, haul roads would have to be routed, and contracts let to build them.

Contractors and subcontractors, big and little, from the Lower 48 and from Alaska, purchased and transported massive and expensive pieces of equipment to Alaska in order to build the haul road. One major stretch, from Livengood to the Yukon, was underway during the summer of 1969, pushing out from great natural sources of gravel. Other contractors had to wait until the winter, when they could run their equipment in across country over the frozen ground.

By the winter of 1969 TAPS had put up $200 million of BP, Arco, and Humble's money, but although it had pulled up a chair, it had not been officially invited to get in the game. For during the period that TAPS was exploring the route, letting the contracts and buying the pipe for a pipeline across Alaska, it had no permit to build a pipeline across Alaska. It was hardly a matter of concern, of course. Where would the permit come from? From the Department of the Interior. And who was the Secretary of the Interior? Wally Hickel, former governor of Alaska. And whom did the oil interests have in their hip pocket? Again, none other than good old Wally. Wally would issue that permit.

But Wally didn't.

As I observed to him one time after he had surprised a lot of people with strong and positive actions on behalf of the American environment, "when you take a rough, tough son of a bitch and put him in a job like yours, you shouldn't be surprised if he keeps right on being a rough, tough son of a bitch." The secretary's press aide, sitting in on the interview, turned a few shades paler at the language, but Hickel, who has been called worse, didn't disagree.

CRUSADE OF THE SEVENTIES

I doubt if any of my history professors would okay my qualifications to chart the paths of nations, but it seems to me that a country can be very much like an individual. And many an individual has waked up one morning to think, My God, what has happened to me. I'm overweight. I've got to do something about my hair. I'm spending more than I'm making. I'm behind in my work. I haven't done my math assignment. The kids are getting sassy; I don't spend enough time with them. The crabgrass is taking over. I haven't dusted the shelves over the sink in *weeks*. After the realization that time is running out, after the guilt and remorse, comes the sudden explosive determination to tighten things up around here.

A few dedicated people had been carrying on a lonely fight to save America from herself for years, but all of a sudden, all over the country, men, women, and children from all walks of life became concerned. Whether it was caused by the beer cans on a country road, the litter in the streets, smarting eyes from the smog, the wildlife that will be no more, or the conditioned response to TV programs and magazine articles on the subject, ecology became the word of the decade. Given this situation, it's awful easy to get mad at the internal combustion engine-oil complex, particularly when you're stuck in a traffic jam, burning premium gas in a car you still owe money on.

Like the automobile industry, the oil industry is particularly vulnerable. Everybody knows that oil people are unlettered and reactionary millionaires, mostly from Texas, who get away with murder on their income tax. Oil companies buy legislators the you and I tip the newspaper boy, and play footsie with dictators of foreign countries. They make us pay more for gas by restricting oil imports. They gunk up beaches and kill birds.

In the ecological crusades, the oil companies are the infidels. And Alaska, whether it likes it or not, is Jerusalem.

Led by such eminently respectable groups as the Wilderness Society and the Sierra Club, the conservationists struck at the most vital organ, the pipeline. First came the Seventy-nine Questions dealing with such major issues as laying pipe in permafrost, and details such as sanitation facilities and use of DDT.

These questions, and subsequent studies, called the attention of people in the United States and Canada, and in the United Kingdom and Europe as well, to the possible dangers of the pipeline. I've already discussed these in terms of the North Slope's easily scarred tundra and easily melted permafrost. Crossing hills and mountains in the central and southern parts of the state, the heat from the pipe could melt the frozen topsoil and cause it to lose its grip on the bedrock; great landslides could occur. The pipe could settle suddenly to bedrock on the hills and be buried under tons of mud in the valleys. Should a break in the line occur, and indeed during 1968 there were nearly 500 leaks involving 50 barrels or more in pipelines in the United States, the quantity of hot oil pouring out over the wild and fragile area of nesting birds and innocent animals could cause irreparable damage. The amount of oil that could be released has been estimated at 51,000 gallons a minute.

And what about the haul roads, and the camps necessary to house thousands of men? Conservationists who have seen the ravages of man in the Lower 48, as well as in parts of Alaska, could envision the ruination of America's last great wilderness. Men like Sigurd Olsen, president of the Wilderness Society who has hiked, canoed, and flown over much of Alaska, pleaded, with a note of desperation and sadness, for the preservation of the Great Land as it had always been. Men like John Rhea of the Boone and Crockett Club are dedicated to the preservation for their sons and grandsons of the very species they themselves selectively kill. And though the average guy trapped in a world of asphalt, concrete, and steel may spend his vacations with his wife in an air-conditioned hotel and get no closer to nature than the golf course, he can still dream of fishing in wild waters, camping under the North Star far from the world of the but- toned-down shirt. He'll probably never do it, but it's nice to know that it's there waiting for him anyway.

The first victim of the conservation crusade was almost Wally Hickel. National Republican Committeeman from Alaska, he was appointed Secretary of the Interior by President Richard M. Nixon following the 1968 elections. The Interior Depart- ment issues pipeline permits. Although he made some of his millions from piping natural gas from the fields south of Anchor- age into the city, ex-railroader Hickel's dream was of transport- ing North Slope oil over an extension of the Alaska Railroad from Fairbanks to the Arctic Coast, rather than via pipeline; still he came to be associated in the public mind as a captive of the oil interests and a diehard pipeliner.

In an unfortunate press conference after the appointment was announced, he said, "I think we have had a policy of con- servation for conservation's sake." In the next sentence he ex- plained that what he opposed was locking up a large area. Rather, it should be used to benefit the American people both in recreation and development of natural resources. But "con- servation for conservation's sake" came back to haunt him. The Senate's approval of his appointment was held up while he was grilled for three days by the Committee on Interior and Insular Affairs. He was the only member of the new cabinet who didn't make the Inauguration ceremony.

I asked him later how he felt about the hearings.

He said that they weren't really hearings, they were an inter- rogation. "I made up my mind first that I wasn't going to get excited. Secondly, I was going to win, and thirdly, when the hearings were over, they would look worse than I did. I think all three things happened."

Hickel acquitted himself well under difficult conditions; the popular Democratic chairman of the committee, Henry M. Jackson of Washington, said later that the charges against him simply blew up. But there's another story that his approval was the result of a deal in which Russell E. Train, a highly regarded conservationist, was appointed undersecretary.

When public pressure against the Trans-Alaska Pipeline built up to the point that President Nixon appointed a task force to look into it, Train was named to head it. Composed of representatives of many Federal and state agencies, the task force worked out a set of stipulations for the pipeline. In presenting the stipulations in the fall of 1969, Train pointed out that no private construction project had ever been asked to accept such strong constraints or such direct control by the Federal Government, and that TAPS had agreed to those conditions. The stipulations created the position of Authorized Officer with the broad power to close down the operations if he didn't like what was going on, and TAPS agreed to foot the bill for inspections.

The stipulations, which make up a small book, deal with all aspects of the construction of the line in and out of permafrost. They require protection of the environment and wildlife from moose to mosquitoes, and require a $5 million bond.

Still Hickel held off issuing the permit. The U.S. Geological Survey was not satisfied with the information provided by TAPS as to how it proposed to meet some of the problems. In the meantime, five more oil companies—Mobil, Phillips, Union, Amerada-Hess, and Home—joined in participation in the pipeline.

As the months went on, all the operators on the Slope began to get panicky. Activities were curtailed. Construction on one section of the road was going ahead, and contractors were moving in heavy equipment over the winter road to be in position to get going in summer. But TAPS was beginning to get the message. A friend with one of the oil companies told me in confidence early in the spring that if TAPS didn't get the permit by April 15 they were going to close down the whole damn thing. They didn't, and they did. Two Federal court decisions enjoining Secretary Hickel from permitting either the pipeline or the road made it official. One was brought by three conservationist groups, the other by some of the native villages through or near which the line would pass.

In May, 1970, an official of another company told me that they were seriously considering scrubbing the project completely, canceling all contracts, disbanding TAPS headquarters, and leaving the pipe there to rust. "Then in about five years, when the oil shortage in the United States becomes so critical that even the goddamned conservationists come crawling to us on their hands and knees, maybe we'll be nice and reconsider it."

This was sweet talk compared to what you could hear in any bar in Alaska. The Alaskans were outraged. Putting in the line would mean jobs for at least 3000 people, many of them natives. The haul road paralleling the line would mean year-round land transportation to a whole new area of Alaska—an area larger than California. And finally, of course, on the completion of the line, Alaska would be rich from the royalties and severance taxes on the oil rushing through it. Education, health, transportation, communications, prosperity—utopia!

But it wasn't just the immediate loss of the money, the postponements, or even, if worst came to worst, the cessation of the dream. What made the Alaskans madder than anything else was the hypocrisy of it all, and the general belief that the people in the Lower 48, that cesspool they had run away from, were still treating them like immature children.

For all the swagger of the Alaskan male as he sets out in mukluks and parky to shoot his annual moose, or the quiet strength of the Alaskan woman through the long winter, Alaskans have the thin skin of insecurity when it comes to the Outside. Alaskans import consultants by the planeload ("The farther away you are the more impressed they are and the more they pay you," one consultant told me) and then go ahead and do what they were going to do in the first place. They particularly hate criticism and interference from big cities and the industrial East. An editorial in *The New York Times* recommending that the pipeline be postponed was answered furiously by editorials in the Anchorage and Fairbanks papers, as well as by the Nome *Nugget*, and bitterly discussed throughout the state. A CBS television show that portrayed a simulated break in the as yet unbuilt pipeline set them in a frenzy.

To illustrate how wild and confusing the continuing battle of Alaska vs. the U.S. can be, let me tell you about the Wolf Man. One day in November Governor Keith Miller received a score or more of furious telegrams protesting the vulgar and barbaric slaughter of wolves in Alaska. Then letters began flooding the Juneau post office. Hundreds were obviously written by children as classroom assignments, others by responsible members of conservation societies. These were painful enough, for nobody likes to be thought of as barbaric and vulgar, but other letters hit where it hurt, in the pocketbook. Tourism produces a good-sized segment of Alaskan income, and many letters were from people announcing the cancellation of vacation trips in protest.

The governor was in the position of a man being pummeled in the dark. He knew that a TV program had brought on the attack, but he hadn't seen the show, and wouldn't for weeks. Routine TV shows don't get to Juneau until three weeks after they are shown in the Lower 48. All those Christmas shows in January are sometimes depressing.

It had been a rough year for Keith anyway. Lightning had struck several times. Grandson of Government employees stationed in Alaska for many years, he'd come up himself as an Internal Revenue Service agent, stayed, gone into politics, and run for Secretary of State on the Republican ticket. Thanks to a squabble among the Democrats, the Republicans, headed by Wally Hickel, squeezed in. When Hickel went to Washington, Miller took over as governor in the biggest year in Alaska state history. He kicked off the lease sale, and was charged with the responsibility of providing leadership for the disposition of the money it brought in. He welcomed the *Manhattan* at Prudhoe. He saw pressure develop against the pipeline. He was caught in the middle of the fight over the Atomic Energy Commission's underground test of a nuclear device on Amchitka Island in the earthquake-prone Aleutian chain.

Now here come 5000 letters about Alaskans slaughtering friendly wolves from helicopters and eating them raw.

Finally the film came in and he and other Alaskans got to see the TV show that caused the outburst. Most of it was devoted to heart-warming scenes of wolf families in the wilds, but there were also short bloody episodes showing the slaughter of apparently half-tamed wolves from a helicopter, an airplane hunt, and an Alaskan eating raw wolf meat. The commentary said that wolves were being hunted to extinction, and blamed the $50 bounty paid in Alaska for encouraging the termination of the noble species.

It turned out that much of the objectionable portion of the film was misleading. The wholesale slaughter of the wolf pack from helicopters had occurred in Siberia; the helicopters bore Russian insignias. As for the Alaskan bounty hunter who ate raw wolf meat, he was an Alaskan bush pilot named Howard J. Knutsen who had been hired by a camera crew to put on a wolf hunt. One wolf had been shot, and Knutsen had been asked, as a joke, to raise a bloody knife to his lips. Knutsen said he'd been told that the scene would never be shown. He was so angry that he tried to get a court order prohibiting it. Far from being a bounty hunter, he disapproved of both the bounty on wolves and hunting them from planes.

Governor Miller had to scratch up $800 to reply to his correspondents. He sent out individual letters, mild in tone, assuring people that there were plenty of wolves in Alaska and that they were not being hunted to extinction. But the tumult raged on. State Senator Lowell Thomas, Jr., called for the termination of the bounty and introduced a bill that would prohibit the use of airplanes as what he termed gun platforms. On the other side, a spite bill was introduced raising the bounty on wolves from $50 to $100. And while in Juneau the legislators were debating the bills, and the governor's assistants were licking stamps, the peo-

ple of Alaska, from Ketchikan to Barrow, from Coldfoot to
Eek, ranted about the interference from the Outside with Alaska's private affairs.

The whole episode is so typical of the areas of misunderstanding between the Great Land and the Outside that it de-
serves a little further exploration.

The TV film had some basis in fact. Alaska does pay a $50
bounty on wolves; a wolf skin can bring up to $250 from parka
manufacturers, and hunting wolves from airplanes is permitted
under controlled conditions. It would be hard to hunt them
otherwise; in Alaska there are few highways leading to wolf
dens. But the Alaska professional hunters association, to which
many of the 400 registered guides in the state belong, opposes
what they call "unfair chase," which includes shooting from
planes or using planes to run animals to exhaustion.

The reason for the bounty on wolves is because they kill caribou and moose. The game-management question as to whether
wolves actually improve the herds by culling out the weak and
sick, or whether they slaughter more healthy animals than they
can eat, just for the hell of it, has caused barroom wrangles
throughout the state. The point remains that caribou and moose
are to Alaskans what cattle and sheep are to the farmers and
ranchers of the Lower 48—food on the table. For every bounty
paid on an Alaskan wolf each year, thousands are paid on
coyotes in the Midwest and West.

This is the true area of conflict. It bugs Alaskans to be told
that they shouldn't do what everybody else does. They hate hypocrisy, even when it stems from ignorance, and they are natural
victims of it. It's so easy for someone sitting in front of a TV
set in the Lower 48 to get mad over something 5000 miles away.
Alaskans live close to the land; they know the game laws of
their state. But do you know yours? After hearing my neighbors
in Virginia rave about the slaughter of wolves for bounty in
Alaska, I asked a game warden about the wolf bounty in
Virginia. He said there isn't any, because all the wolves have long
since been exterminated. If a wolf or a coyote did poke his nose

across our sacred borders, he said, all the game wardens in the area would themselves lead a posse of local hunters to hunt him down and kill him. As for bounties in general, in some Virginia counties you can get 15 cents for crows, 50 cents for hawks and owls, $4 for foxes, $5 for wildcats, and $50 for any bear known to have killed a sheep. Alaskans tend to think that before I get excited over a wolf in their state, I show some concern for a fox in mine.

In the late nineteenth century, crews of trains going over the Great Plains used to pass out rifles to the passengers who could stick them out the windows and, as they clattered by in comfort, shoot the grazing buffalo. As a result, the home where the buffalo roam is now pretty limited.

The depletion of wildlife, and the parallel ravaging of the environment in general, Alaskans tell you over and over, is just what they went to Alaska to get away from. In the Lower 48 we reacted too late. The Alaskans believe that they reacted in time. Their game laws are strict, and everybody knows them. They care about their animals, too, in their own way. Ed Merdes's 12-year-old son came back from an overnight duck hunting trip on Chena Slough—less than five miles from the Fairbanks city limits—to report, almost tearfully, that he'd seen a dead moose on the bank. He theorized that it had been shot, had swum the stream, and died, and the hunter had left it there. In the boy's mind it was okay to shoot the moose—it was in season—but not to waste the carcass.

"It's easier to get away with shooting your wife than a female moose," Red Boucher, the mayor of Fairbanks, told me. "Not long ago a state official was fired because he gave the wrong address on his fishing license. I'll tell you the way Alaskans think about these things. I was taking a friend on a fishing trip and the pilot who flew us in said we'd better take guns along to protect ourselves from the bears. We borrowed a couple of guns from the fellow who outfitted us. There were some bears fishing in the stream, but we didn't worry about them because we were armed. They fished and we fished and we all caught some nice ones. Waiting for the plane to come get us we thought we'd shoot the guns, just target practice. They wouldn't go off. The firing pins had been removed. Now wasn't that a nice way of handling the situation? That fellow wanted us to feel safe, but he wanted to make sure the bears were safe, too."

Though the laws are strict and the attitude good, Alaskans do tend to oversimplify them. The handful of protection agents can't possibly cover the state. In 1970 Alaska had 44 agents; so did Maryland. You hear of game shot out of season, and also immediately after being spotted from the air. To animal lovers, even the legal taking of polar bears, which requires two planes, is a cruel and ostentatious display of atavism and money. The much-discussed "harvesting" of musk oxen by so-called sportsmen who'd pay thousands for the privilege of shooting a beast so helpless and appealing is to me but the rationalization of greed and brutality.

Alaskans have not always had respect for the game laws. "When I was a prosecuting attorney for the Federal Government before statehood," Ed Merdes said, "I used to prosecute poachers who were guilty as sin, but the juries would acquit them just the same. Breaking a Federal violation was no crime to the Alaskans, it was something to be proud of."

Clem Tillion, a red-headed, blue-eyed part-Cherokee who went to Alaska after World War II and walked most of the way from Anchorage down the Kenai Peninsula to Halibut Cove where he built his log cabin, used to keep his neighbors in moose meat the year round. Since statehood, however, Clem has never shot game out of season. He would never break an *Alaska* law. Although he is a licensed hunting guide as well as a commercial fisherman, Clem doesn't cater to trophy hunters from the Outside anymore. "I don't approve of people coming up here and shooting our animals just so they can stick their heads up on the walls down in the Lower 48," he said. "I like to take out people with cameras. That way I can sell the same bear over and over."

But the thought of Federal gun control sends Clem right up his log wall. This is a subject Alaskans get paranoic about; it is a land of guns and, in Clem's house at least, *loaded* guns. "If a hawk comes after my chickens, or a bear after my livestock," he said grimly, "you think I'm gonna take time to load?"

All this ties in with the Trans-Alaska Pipeline in a very concrete way. Alaskans, rightly or wrongly, believe that they can take care of their own state without interference from the Federal Government or the Outside conservationists. They aver that they are the very last people to permit its being messed up. They get along well with the oil and pipeline people, many of whom have become Alaskans—Arco's chief explorationist, John Sweet, went Alaskan to the point of getting elected to the House of Delegates. Most of the Alaskans I've talked to believe that the pipeliners know what they're doing. As Buddy Morel, the Alaskan with the Louisiana accent, said, "Why in the world would we put a billion dollars into a pipeline that's gonna bust?"

Most of the Alaskan leaders who have visited drilling sites on the North Slope as well as the producing fields in the Kenai Peninsula are convinced that they can have their oil and their nature, too. In the Kenai moose range, for example, the moose are getting fat in the oil field development. They stroll along the access roads, browsing the brush on either side. On the North Slope, the caribou also stroll the access roads, though for a different reason. Geoff Larminie, a zoologist before he became interested in geology, thinks that on the long still summer days there's more air stirring on the built-up roadbeds, hence fewer mosquitoes. Ducks and geese nest by the side of the road.

As for the wells themselves, the operating companies have worked out a unitization system. This means, in effect, that the companies combine to operate the field efficiently, each taking its proper percentage. The Prudhoe Bay wells are gas-driven. In the underground structure, which is like the cover of a butter-dish 40 miles long by 20 wide, the gas is on top, the oil in the middle, and salt water underneath. When the oil comes up the gas is extracted from it, condensed, and pushed back down again. Eventually the gas will be brought up for the last time and piped southward.

To maximize the efficiency of unitization, the producing wells will be clustered in small areas, with the holes themselves extending down and bent outward in different directions in order to cover a large underground area from one spot on the surface. In short, there won't be oil wells sticking up all over the Slope, but instead clusters of wells several miles apart. In the Lower 48 there are oil wells in towns, golf courses, at resort areas, and you have to know where they are to find them. With careful housekeeping practiced by the operators and drilling companies —and from my own observations they do practice good housekeeping—there is no reason to believe that oil will change the North Slope into a polluted area desolate of wildlife. The caribou, and the moose and the grizzlies and the foxes, and all those birds, should live very comfortably with man.

But just as there were basic elements of truth in the wolf uproar, so do those worried about preserving loveliness of the North Slope have some legitimate beef. Ugly marks of erosion do exist. The one agent assigned to the area couldn't possibly protect all the wildlife.

Although many a Hercules has gone back to Fairbanks with a load of empty oil drums—not one of 6000 drums remains on BP's tracts—it will be a long time before clumps of Alaska State Flowers no longer speckle the Slope. Years ago in his official reevaluation of Pet 4, consultant Jim Dalton put forward a plan to remove the jumbled mass of some 10,000 oil drums left by the Navy and its contractors. They are still there. Much of the North Slope area has yet to be explored geophysically, and as I pointed out, the seismic crews have been the worst offenders on the Slope.

Nor do the Alaskans really care that much. In general, they're pretty messy people. They say they have gone to Alaska to get away from the pollution of the Lower 48, but they also made an escape from the fastidiousness of suburbia, where a blade of crabgrass on the lawn provides grounds for ostracism. Alaskans live close to nature and nature stinks. A bear gorged on fish and berries does not dig a slit trench and cover up his offal; he spreads it around. If you too like to fish and eat berries, sooner or later you're going to step in it. So what?

Native villages are pretty and picturesque in the winter under the snow, but in the summer, with fish drying on the roofs and the litter uncovered, they can offend an eye and nostril sensitized by civilization as we know it in the Lower 48. The small, crowded shacks are not equipped with running water, either hot or cold, and neither the people nor their caribou garments would provide a good testimonial for a deodorant. But whether they're dirty or different is a matter of definition.

Alaskans, therefore, living with reality, not prudery, are not the best of naturekeepers. They throw beer cans in the rivers and leave their plastic-coated plates at picnic sites just as everybody else does. Visitors to the North Slope use the tundra as a wastebasket for their discarded yellow film packages; Tom Brennan, the Arco public relations man, goes around picking them up. The little oil company town of Prudhoe Bay is probably the neatest place in Alaska. The other major community on the North Slope, the native village of Barrow, is shocking by contrast.

Both Fairbanks and Anchorage have some lovely homes, but downtown Fairbanks is grubby. Anchorage, thanks partly to the earthquake that destroyed one of the worst areas, and also to a more sophisticated populace, has a well-tended downtown area, but, like Fairbanks, its outskirts represent too-rapid growth. The oil boom, added to a general carelessness on the part of people who live in the last frontier, has definitely increased the messiness of the urban areas as well as the popular tourist spots and the areas of early exploration.

As for the pipeline, even its bitterest critics have to date somehow overlooked the fact that on the Slope itself it is not just one pipeline, but a complex of pipelines feeding from the clusters of wells into the big one. Some of these must be above ground and visible to both man and caribou. But I don't think the caribou will mind crossing over them on ramps, or walking under them.

One of the bitter remarks that I have heard over and over in Alaska goes something like this: "They used to call it a hostile wilderness. Now all of a sudden it's a fragile ecology." The Alaskans fail to see that these two terms are not necessarily contradictory. The North Slope *is* a hostile wilderness; if you don't believe it, just start walking across it in a whiteout at 50 below zero. Somebody may find you next spring. But while it is indeed hostile to man, the tundra is in itself held in delicate balance. Push your arm down through the muck on a hot day in August, and you'll bang your knuckles on the rock-hard frozen permafrost beneath the surface. When the myriads of flowers are in profuse and colorful bloom it is the world's most beautiful layer of insulation, but that is nevertheless what it is: insulation. Scrape off what nature has taken 10,000 years to put on, and the permafrost will melt right on down. But after poking around in it and grinding it up with Caterpillars since 1943, surely by now people know what not to do. Most of them are not doing it any more.

It is perhaps a little sad to contemplate man's bursting his way through the Brooks Range with massive pipe-laying machinery. But a look at the map of Alaska is somewhat reassuring. Between Point Lay on the west coast and the Canadian border lie some 650 miles of mountains, in some areas extending for more than 100 miles north and south. Counting both the existing winter road through Anaktuvuk Pass and the projected pipeline through Dietrich Pass, that adds up to just two breaks throughout the entire mountain wilderness. In the entire state there are 4500 miles of highway, 7000 including local roads and streets. In Virginia, a fraction the size, we have a total of 60,000.

Still, anyone who has ever traveled on what roads there are, or on the Alaskan railway, knows the price the wildlife pay in death and injury. Somebody is always running into a caribou or moose; despite the vigilance of the locomotive engineers, the

Alaskan railway kills hundreds a year. More roads will kill more animals—and more people, too.

But as in most subheads of the progress vs. conservation debate, the argument runs around in a circle. These deaths are accidental; they will not noticeably affect the total number of animals. Meat for the roadbuilders is flown in from the Outside, not furnished by hired hunters like Buffalo Bill Cody as in the days of the building of the transcontinental railroads. The Alaskans think that no matter how many roads and pipelines are built they'll continue to have their caribou, and eat them, too.

RETURN OF THE NATIVES

As concern for the conservation of the wildlife and the wilderness increased, so did the original settlers of the Great Land begin to take a greater interest in their own personal ecology. The natives were getting restless, and in the efficient, productive ways they had learned from the white man. It took something as overwhelming as oil to unite the different native groups for the first time against their common enemy, the greatest predator of all, the white man. Oil made the white man himself, especially in the Lower 48, increasingly concerned about the native; the sympathy was tied in with the exploding involvement with world environment.

As we noted, when Alaska became a state a part of the deal was its right to select 103 million acres of the 375 million total, though years went by while the state only nibbled at its birthright. With the production of oil in the Kenai Peninsula the state began stepping up the selection process. The natives, who had in a century of American ownership lost only isolated tracts of land, now saw the danger of losing huge chunks of it. Only a tiny percentage of the natives—primarily members of the Tlingit and Haida tribes in the southeast—had gotten a white man's education, but there were nevertheless enough articulate natives scattered throughout the state to realize the need for uniting their forces, and to accomplish it.

In 1966, the Alaskan Native Brotherhood, composed of Indians in the southeast, joined forces with the other native groups to form the Alaska Federation of Natives. Its leaders were Emil Notti, with Italian, Aleut, and Athapascan ancestors; John Borbridge, Jr., outspoken and sideburned, of white and Indian parentage, and Eben Hobson, descendant of a Yankee whaler and a North Slope Eskimo, a former state senator and a captain in the Alaskan National Guard. The villages and regional councils making up the federation were already represented by several attorneys, but a new Alaskan, Anchorage attorney Robert Goldberg, helped the native organization secure the services of his father, former Supreme Court Justice Arthur Goldberg, and former Attorney General Ramsey Clark.

It was a perfect *pro bono publico* case. The sad plight of the Alaskan native is on record. The Alaskan aborigine is worse off than any other group in America. He has more unemployment, less income, greater health problems, poorer housing, and he lives in the harshest climate. He has to spend up to twice as much for the comforts we take for granted; flour for his bread is flown in by bush plane. He can expect to die at the age of thirty-five.

But he had a weapon, one made more powerful by the discovery of oil. He had a legal claim to land. Though the native had not staked out either the land around his dwelling place or his fishing or hunting grounds, a Governmental fact-finding commission unearthed exhaustive proof that the natives themselves recognize the occupancy of the individual's abode, the tribe's hunting and fishing areas.

Through its attorneys, the Alaska Federation of Natives demanded from the Federal Government legal title to some 40 million acres of land around their villages, $500 million in cash for land already taken, and a two percent royalty on all minerals produced in the state. Senator Henry M. Jackson, chairman of the Interior and Insular Affairs Committee, promised that the Senate would act on their demands. Pending the resolution of their claim, Stewart Udall, who was then Secretary of the Interior, froze all Federal land transactions in Alaska.

Udall's action put an end to the Alaskan state pastime, filing oil leases. Many hardy gamblers went ahead with what are known as priority filings, but there was no guarantee that the priorities would be recognized. As for the state, though it chose several million acres in 1968, bringing the total acreage of selected land to some 26 million, it could not take title. Everybody was stymied.

The land freeze became a vital issue in the confirmation of Wally Hickel as Secretary of the Interior. He had said, "what Secretary Udall can do by executive order, I can undo." At the hearing, however, he said he didn't know about the legality of the natives' claim, "but I firmly believe in my heart they have a moral claim." He promised to continue the land freeze until the issue was settled by Congress.

That settlement would be a long time coming. Four separate proposals were made, with wide variations on each of the issues—land, cash, and royalties. The proposals came from the AFN, the Department of the Interior, the Federal fact-finding commission, and from the State of Alaska. The two Alaska Senators, Ted Stevens and Mike Gravel, both members of Senator Jackson's committee, agreed to put up a united front but their togetherness could hardly be expected to last. Stevens was a Republican appointee filling the unexpired term of the late Senator Bob Bartlett, while Gravel was an elected Democrat. Stevens represented the establishment, which was inclined to the minimums in the native demands, while Gravel had bucked not only the conservatives, but the esteemed liberal incumbent, Ernest Gruening, in his successful campaign.

If Gravel owed his election to any bloc, it was to the natives. He had visited practically every village in Alaska by bush plane, meeting the natives, pressing the flesh. The pleasure was mutual. Having long admired Senator Gruening, who was an outstanding journalist before I was born, I was surprised to find such bitterness against him on the part of the natives. The most charitable consensus of my native friends was that Gruening, born in 1887, looked upon them with benign condescension. Mike Gravel, still in his 30s and blessed with an engaging personality, went to them as an equal with concern for their problems and a frank appeal for their votes.

Gravel's main difference with Stevens was in the provision pertaining to royalties. Both agreed to the demand of two percent, but Stevens wanted to put a shorter time limit on it.

Many people in Alaska were horrified by the idea of giving the natives any royalty at all. It was the Federal Government that had bought Alaska in the first place, and it was the Federal Government that should pay off the descendants of the real owners. But the royalty, no matter how the provision was worded, would come from the state.

"It's illegal as hell," Joe Keenan, director of the Division of Lands, said. Governor Miller's administration considered the royalty an unconstitutional infringement on the state itself. He wondered audibly whether any other state would stand still while the Federal Government dipped into its income to pay a Federal obligation.

A few Alaskans saw no reason to give the natives any land at all, saying they'd had 100 years to claim it. (Actually, it was difficult, if not impossible, during that period for a native to get title to a 160-acre homestead, much less enough land to track down a caribou.) Most Alaskans I've talked with could understand the natives' claim to land, even millions of acres, but some of these gave the native no credit whatsoever for the discovery and the development of the oil that would pay the royalty. "They lived on it for ten thousand years and never looked under the surface once," an irate banker said.

As the Senate committee deliberated, or squabbled, the animosity in Alaska grew stronger. Most of my Alaskan friends told me that there has never been any discrimination against the natives, but some of the natives said different. At an AFN convention I started talking with Frederick Paul of Seattle, attorney for the 4000 Eskimos living in eight villages on the North Slope. He estimated that he had spent thousands of hours and thousands of dollars of his own money representing his clients, with no compensation so far. He said that the case was challenging, that it was changing history.

I must have looked skeptical that a smart Seattle lawyer would gamble so much for a few natives, and he shouted at me, over the hubbub in the hall, "Look, I'm one-eighth Tlingit!"

"Well, you sure don't look it," I said, "and anyway that makes you a lot more white than Indian. Why fight yourself?"

"Well, I did do some soul searching before I decided that I'm a native, not a white man," he said. "But I'm glad I did. Years ago my grandmother was arrested and put in jail for trying to vote. I owe it to her memory to keep fighting."

Paul introduced me to his father, William F. Paul, Sr., one of the founders of the old Alaskan Brotherhood. He had had to leave the state in order to find clients for his corporate law practice. The elder Paul, who didn't look like an Indian either, said he remembered when natives had to sit in the balcony when they went to the movies, and when businesses put signs saying "No natives" in their windows.

The Pauls are not the only apparently white people who think of themselves as natives. A large number of AFN delegates in the crowded Odd Fellows Hall on the outskirts of Anchorage looked white. I thought a fat, fair-skinned, brown-haired woman sitting next to me, busily taking notes, was a reporter. Suddenly, however, she got up to discuss a motion on the floor. She was so incoherent with anger against the white man that I never did know exactly what she was complaining about, and I sure wasn't going to ask.

The white-appearing delegates resembled each other; the rest demonstrated the obvious differences between the three native races. There were skins of light tan and medium brown. There were Indians with long heads, Eskimos with round, Indians with aquiline noses, Eskimos with flat. Aleuts, comprising the minority, had faces like Easter Island statues. Some eyes were squinty, some round. I had the impression that most Eskimos wore glasses. Many looked bigger sitting down than standing up, for their legs were bowed from riding their mothers' backs when children, feet tied in front.

Whatever their differences, they were now united in their demands, they had a background of thousands of years of able politicking, and they were angry. As the months went by and the Senate still deliberated, they got angrier. Emil Notti, in a speech before a group of Washington State Indians, proposed that the Alaskan natives set up their own nation in western Alaska if the United States did not meet their demands. Frederick Paul protested the invasion of the North Slope by the State of Alaska and called upon Secretary Hickel to oust both the state and its lease holders.

It seemed that only the oil company executives were keeping their cool. Cliff Burglin, the lease broker, took a pragmatic attitude. Though it was his understanding that the land freeze was illegal and he considered the native demands excessive, he recognized that the situation existed and had to be resolved. "Let's settle the thing and get back to work," he said.

One dramatic piece of evidence to the effect that the thing can indeed be settled is the village of Tyonek, about 50 miles across Cook Inlet from Anchorage. Through some clever work on the part of their white attorneys, the 300 Indians of the Moquokee tribe in Tyonek arranged to make their own deal with the oil companies that wanted to drill there. They held out for a total of some $14 million. With that money Tyonek has constructed $30,000 homes, rent-free and tax-free, for its people. The village owns its own plane for direct transportation to Anchorage, an office building in Tyonek for which it receives $108,000 a year rent, five more buildings in Anchorage, a sawmill, and a fishery. Villagers who work for these enterprises get paid; those who don't, don't.

Like other villages in Alaska, Tyonek has an elementary school but no high school. Its secondary school students must leave home. For those who get over this hurdle, however, college education is on the village; the only criterion is getting admitted. Tyonek high school graduates have attended college with all expenses paid in the Lower 48; one girl went to the Lowest 50th, the University of Hawaii. All this turned out to be absolute altruism on the part of the oil companies. Their wells were dry.

The Alaska Federation of Natives planned a somewhat similar disposition for the income its demands would someday produce. Few doubted that the money would eventually be forthcoming; the big problem would be its distribution. Cash handouts to individual natives were never contemplated; native leaders are aware of the tendency toward alcoholism, and they don't want to provide their people with the opportunity to crawl further into the white man's bottle. They are also aware of the tendency of anyone with sudden cash to blow it—also to the benefit of the white slicker. The disposition proposed by the AFN was five percent to the statewide organization, 20 percent to each of 12 regional native corporations, and 75 percent to village corporations, each of which would become a small version of Tyonek.

In the spring of 1970 the Senate committee finally approved a billion-dollar settlement of the native claims. It provided up to ten million acres of land, a two percent royalty on oil and gas up to $500 million, and $500 million in cash spread over a 12-year period. The Senate passed it but the House didn't, and the bill died. Alaska sent a new representative, Nick Begich of Anchorage, to the ninety-second Congress in 1971, and the hardworking Democrat hoped to influence its passage. Even if he were successful, months would elapse before the full Senate and the House of Representatives would work out a compromise suitable to both—and then the State of Alaska, the natives, or both, might well run screaming to court. The natives weren't holding their breath for an immediate settlement, and the speculators and oil company explorationists interested in Federal land in Alaska were hibernating.

In the meantime the acquisitions department of the Trans-

Alaska Pipeline System was attempting to get a right-of-way through land the great proportion of which the ownership was still in doubt. Armand C. Spielman, who had done such a good job in Alaska as landman for the old Richfield Company, became acquisition manager for TAPS. When I talked to him he was having little difficulty securing right-of-way through land that was privately owned. Cliff Burglin, who considered Armand's appointment one of TAPS's smartest moves, asked Armand as a special favor to let him be the first in Fairbanks to sign the papers formally granting the right-of-way; Cliff owned land on the pipeline's route. He figured that the sooner the pipeline would be laid the sooner his oil would be coursing through it, and that the project would be good for the city of Fairbanks where he and his family intend to stay.

Dealing with the native councils through whose ancient hunting grounds the pipeline would pass was the job of Thomas W. diZerega, Jr., assigned to TAPS by Arco for that purpose. Tom's chief selling point was employment for the natives through whose territory the line would run. Construction of access roads and of the line itself would provide employment for thousands, with basic hourly rates of up to $10 an hour. With fringe benefits and bonuses a man working at common labor could make $28,000 a year. Skilled operators—and training programs would be set up—could add $10,000 to that income. It was up to Tom diZerega to convince the native leaders that their people would get their share of these jobs. He found the task easy.

"Once they believe you're honest," he said, "they're fine to do business with."

The councils and their attorneys had held preliminary conferences. Clifford T. Groh, an Anchorage attorney for two of the native councils, told me that he had had the normal difficulty convincing his clients that they could trust the white man. But then once, when he was out in the bush talking with the elders of a council, he received word by radio that his father had died. He couldn't stop the tears that came to his eyes, and he put his face in his hands. The Indians were silent, resp/ his grief.

After the first shock, Cliff found himself talking about his father. He told his Indian friends how his father had come from Poland as a poor immigrant, and had found happiness and opportunity in America. He poured out the whole story. The Indians gathered around and listened, and suddenly they all, original Americans and the son of an immigrant, were caught up in a powerful emotion of understanding.

After that they trusted him fully. The groups he represented released their protests to the pipeline's traversing their ancestral land in exchange for a letter of intent from TAPS promising employment.

"They've got the edge on the jobs," Cliff said. "They'll have the contractors lining up to get them."

Following the exchange of similar letters between TAPS and native councils through whose territory the pipeline would run, Secretary Hickel lifted the land freeze on the route as it pertained to the access roads. The freeze was still on as far as the land itself was involved, pending the settlement of the native claims, and the permit for the construction of the pipeline was yet to be issued. But at least one of the priorities of the line, the right-of-way through land subject to native claim, seemed to have been settled. Then another legal group came in, and on behalf of the five native villages sought an injunction against TAPS to prevent the construction of the access road. It was granted in a Federal court in Washington, D.C., in April, 1970. About the same time another injunction against the access road, sought by three conservation groups, was granted by the same court.

The pipeline had never begun. The road was blocked. And now, finally, the people of Alaska came to the full realization that the whole complex was as dormant as a grizzly in January.

One Saturday in late April Joe LaRocca called me at home in Virginia from Washington. The next night Governor Miller was bringing in a chartered 707 full of Alaskans to storm the nation's capital. Senator Stevens and Congressman Pollock were

paving the way from within. I sniffed some local politicking—
Miller, Stevens, and Pollock are Republicans, and this was an
election year—and Joe confirmed it. The Democrats—Senator
Gravel in Washington, gubernatorial candidate Larry Carr in
Anchorage—were very much uninvolved. Joe suggested I come
up and see the fun, but I'd seen people punch political pillows
in Washington before and begged off. Monday night Ed Merdes
called. He, and other Democrats including former Governor Bill
Egan, who was running again, had come along to make the
junket bi-partisan.

"You better get your ass up here," Ed said. "You've never
seen anything like this before. These guys are mad."

"What about?" I asked.

"What about, for Christ's sake," Ed hollered. "About the
runaround we're getting. The Federal Government's going to
lock up the whole North Slope for fifty years and save it for the
bird watchers!"

I felt the intensity the minute I walked into the breakfast
meeting in Washington the next morning. I sat down next to
Mayor Red Boucher of Fairbanks, and although we hadn't seen
each other for a couple of months he only gave me a nod. M. A.
Wright, chairman of the board of Humble, was speaking. His
talk was low key and conversational but he had the complete
attention of every man in the room. He explained the unitization
of the Prudhoe field, the alternate routes of getting the oil and
subsequently gas to market, and then went on to discuss with
surprising candor the pipeline situation.

The day before the chief of the U.S. Geological Service, William T. Pecora, had bluntly told the delegation that his organization had not been given sufficient data by TAPS. Until it was
forthcoming, no approval. Now Mike Wright was admitting
that communications between TAPS and the USGS "were not
as good as they should have been—there should have been more
sitting around the table and discussing this thing." He explained
that TAPS had drilled 250 corings in the Copper River Valley
but that in this area, and in the area north of the Yukon, it had

not furnished the USGS as much data as had been promised. They were going to have to do the whole thing over.

The next meeting was at 8:30 with Russell Train of the Environmental Control Commission in the new Senate office building. The Alaskans burst out of the hotel dining room like a college football team and headed for Capitol Hill. I walked up with Keith Miller and Ed Merdes. Ed, the liberal Democrat, was shouting in one of my ears; Keith, the conservative Republican, latched on to the other. I told Keith that I didn't envy him at all for the tremendous responsibility that was placed on his shoulders.

"Well," he said, "it could be easier, but I'm still running for reelection." He said that there was no doubt in his mind that the pipeline would eventually be built, possibly by 1974, and that the situation was urgent but not desperate. As pipeline construction could not begin immediately, it became obvious that his secret weapon was the construction of the haul road from Livengood north. Here was an area the size of California; was it unreasonable to build one gravel road into that area?

"I'm a liberal Democrat and I think the ecologists are performing a valid service in general," I said, "but I'll go along with you on the road."

"I'm gonna quote *you* on that," Keith said, and, as it turned out later, he did.

Ed broke in. "Keith, I hope you send your proposal into the Senate. You can count on my support. We're together on this."

Carried away by this togetherness, the three of us walked right past our destination, got lost on Capitol Hill, and held up the meeting.

Train, facing a hostile audience, did pretty well. He said that the Government was not against the pipeline but wanted to ensure that it would not proceed until all the questions had been answered. "This has been a long hard job," he said, "a frustrating job. I don't know of any problem on which so much time has been spent continuously . . . When I first heard of this project it was to be a cold oil line, and as such would present no problems.

But when it turned out that the oil would be hot, it changed the
rules of the game. We don't have designs or specifications for a
hot oil line from TAPS *yet*. We believe the pipeline can be built,
and we want to approve it, but we're still in a dilemma as to
how it can be done."

He pointed out forcefully that his commission was charged
with the responsibility for any decision affecting the environment.

Ed Merdes nudged me. "That's like putting a fox in the
chicken coop," he said bitterly.

"Sometimes you sound like you want to put the chicken in
with the foxes," I said.

Ed glared at me and whispered so loud that several people
went shhh. "Listen, if anybody doesn't want to see that place torn
up it's us, the people who live there."

When Train finished and turned the meeting over to discussion from the floor, the fox and chicken analogy went out the
window and it was more like a pack of wolves closing in on a
lone caribou. A contractor with millions of dollars of equipment
sitting idle turned the conversation to the road. Senator Bob
Blodgett of Nome, a burr-headed man so angry that the veins
stood out in his temples, stood up and said that he had lived in
the Arctic for 25 years, had built roads out from Nome under
the same conditions as the pipeline haul road, and demanded to
know why men with his experience had never been consulted.
"We've been told," he said, "never asked."

Train maintained that the road was tied in with the pipeline,
and that neither could be built without the other. Next to me
Merdes stiffened as though he'd been hit by a jolt of electricity.
"Whoever heard of forbidding a sovereign state of the union to
build a road!"

In that big room there were Republicans, Democrats, business-
men, contractors, union leaders, native leaders—full represen-
tation across the board. Regardless of their differences on other
matters, they were welded together on this one issue. Their unity
and determination were so strong they sent out shock waves.

The meeting broke up and small groups of two and three went to keep previously made appointments with various Senators and legislators.

I knew where I was going, to see my buddy Mike Gravel. This may have been a Republican-organized junket, but now it was one big snowball that was rolling downhill. Mike couldn't afford to stay out of this, and I set out for his office to tell him so.

Mike was out of town, but he was coming back that afternoon. I talked with Chuck Hamel, his executive assistant, and the rest of the staff for an hour and they agreed that Mike ought to get with it. I ran back to Republicans Miller, Stevens, and Pollock with the news.

I carried reports back and forth all day, as a matter of fact, caught in a typically Alaskan situation. Pollock and Miller were both Republicans, but Pollock was bucking Miller for the gubernatorial nomination. Gravel and Egan were both Democrats, but Mike was backing Larry Carr, back in Anchorage, for the Democratic nomination. There were cliques all over the place, and that left me as official errand boy, without portfolio.

All the Alaskans came back together again, physically and emotionally, at luncheon. Keith Miller climbed on the snowball and rode it. The pipeline decision, he said, was up to TAPS. Building the road to the North Slope was up to the State of Alaska. He therefore officially announced that he was going to request the legislature to appropriate $120 million for the road. There was silence for a moment, then a splattering of hand claps, and then Ed Merdes yelled, "Hey, stand up!" Up we got, clapping and shouting approval.

It was like spring break-up. Everybody figuratively ran outside without their parkas on and with something to say. Red Boucher proposed that Alaskans themselves develop a positive ecological program "to get these people off our backs." Bill Egan, climbing on the bandwagon with the incumbent governor whose job he wanted back, released a little pent-up steam. TAPS tells us one thing, he said, the Interior Department people tell us another. TAPS says they've given the information to Interior, Interior says they haven't. TAPS has refused to listen when Alaskans suggested building a plant to build the pipe; now the Japanese pipe was sitting in Alaska getting rusty.

Jules Wright seized the opportunity to ask his fellow contractors to remember to work with his fellow natives.

But most of the talk was on the road. Fantastic! Terrific! It would tie in the parks, the wildlife preserve, open up the area to tourism and the conservationists who might like to see what they were trying to conserve. Miller stood up again to remind everybody that they were no longer talking about a haul road for the pipeline, but a state highway.

This was a sobering thought. The gravel road could not meet Federal specifications; it would have to be built completely with state funds. The estimate of $120 million would approach the entire 1969 Alaskan state budget of $153 million.

But the people got the message. Later that afternoon, at an open hearing of the Senate Interior and Insular Committee presided over by Senator Jackson, with Senators Stevens and Gravel in attendance, the new state highway was thrown into the discussion. I looked at my watch; it was 4:10 P.M. At 8:10 that morning Keith and I had been talking about a haul road for the pipeline. In one day it had become a state highway.

It would be nice to report that the happy Alaskans went back home, put up the money, and started building the road, thus putting equipment, money, and people to work. It didn't work out that way. The longest legislative session in Alaska's short history was already bogged down on what to do with the $900 million proceeds from the lease sale. Now here came the proposal to spend an enormous amount of money to build one road from one unpopulated spot to another for the direct benefit, in effect, of the oil interests. The squabble in the legislature reached incredible extremes even for Alaska. The president of the Senate, Brad Phillips of Anchorage, got so mad at the chairman of the Finance Committee, Vance Phillips of Anchorage, that he disbanded the whole committee in order to fire him.

The State of Alaska, of course, didn't have the equipment to build the road; TAPS did. TAPS agreed to construct the road, but it had to be done for the state as contractor as TAPS itself was enjoined from building it by court order. TAPS also agreed to reimburse the state for the construction costs—when and if it started using it for the pipeline. That would overcome the objections from areas the road would not benefit—but suppose the pipeline never got started and the state was stuck with the road?

After weeks of discussion, and in the final hour of the session early one Sunday morning, the legislature agreed on a bill. The state would put up the money for the road with the provision that TAPS would pay it back at 7.5 percent interest whether or not the pipeline was ever built. Coincidentally, the legislature also doubled the severance tax on oil and gas to eight percent.

After the session had finally ended and everybody had gone home, TAPS officials dragged poor Keith Miller down to a meeting in Seattle and reluctantly told him they couldn't accept the proposition. They believed the project "to be of utmost importance to the economy of Alaska and the national security," they said, but they didn't want to buy a road without a pipeline. Further, by insisting that the pipeline reimburse the state for the road—TAPS had originally promised to turn the road over to the state gratis after the pipe was laid—the legislature had effectively made the proposed state highway a pipeline haul road. And that was already under injunction.

Keith had to cancel his trip to Expo 70 in Tokyo—it was Alaska day at the Fair—and start all over again. Only now it was June, the gravel pits were thawing out, and there wasn't much time left.

While the attention of Alaska was fastened on the road, progress was being made on the pipeline. The $25,000 junket to Washington had at least served to open up lines of communication and clarify some issues.

The traditional philosophy of the pipeliner is to sit on the front of a ditch-digging machine and solve each problem as he gets to it. The amount of advance planning that went into TAPS was revolutionary, but in the fragile environment of Alaska in the opening years of the ecological crusade it just wasn't enough. Ed Merdes's fox—the USGS—was under surveillance of the Federal Government and conservation groups over much of the world. He had to guard those chickens as they had never been guarded before.

TAPS agreed to restudy the terrain and submit to the USGS, early in 1971, detailed engineering plans for the pipeline. By that time the estimate for the total cost of the project had climbed to $1.5 billion.

Mike Gravel, in the meantime, had revealed a plan of his own. Through his unique relationship with Canada, he had learned of a pilot project in Inuvik, in the Mackenzie delta, where hot oil was being pumped through a line laid in permafrost. He had learned during a visit to Russia of hot oil lines in actual operation in the Siberian Arctic. He proposed an exchange of information between the three countries. Thanks in part to his interest in Russia-American relations, Alaska Airlines had begun flying excursions to Siberia and polar charter flights between Anchorage and Moscow. The information-sharing project did not seem impossible.

But there the matter rested. The oil had been sealed in the Prudhoe Bay anticline for hundreds of millions of years; it would keep. Technological expertise had been increasing over the past half-century; it might well prove compatible with man in his environment.

Just before the lease sale in 1969 my consultant friend, Jim Dalton, musing over a martini, said, "Sometimes I wish they'd take it all back and give us five years to get ready." Oil men with an impartial interest in Alaska and the Trans-Alaska Pipeline as compared to their companies' holdings in other parts of the world estimate that the pipeline will be built, according to the most stringent ecological standards, and in operation by 1974. Jim Dalton may have hit it right on the nose.

Chapter V

THE CHALLENGE OF BEING RICH

AS Fat Albert, stuffed with hairy and horny oil workers from the Slope, approached Fairbanks, a feminine voice with a pleasant but unfamiliar accent told us to fasten seat belts and observe the no-smoking sign. I tried to visualize the stewardess from her accent and decided she'd be a tall, willowy, blonde Scandinavian.

Well, that's what I know about accents. This one belonged to a pretty moon-faced girl with jet black hair named Linda Gologergeren. She comes from St. Lawrence Island in the Bering Sea. Linda's people, the Eiwhuelit Eskimos, are close to their Siberian cousins geographically, ethnically, and linguistically.

How in the world, I asked Linda, did a girl from that stormy, far-off island—you can see Siberia on the few occasions when the weather is clear—ever come to be a stewardess for Wien Consolidated Airlines? She laughed and told me. Her father, a GI during World War II, had picked up the equivalent of a high school diploma in the service, and had gone back home to become a schoolteacher. Linda pursued the quest for education two steps further. At 15 she'd taken the long trip to the Bureau of Indian Affairs school at Chemawa, Oregon, then had gone on to college in the Lower 48.

"I was so homesick and miserable," she said. "I was the only Eskimo girl in the college. I was scared and they thought I was dumb. I came back to Alaska and went with my girl friend when she applied for a job as stewardess. They hired me!"

I said I thought both she and the airlines seemed pretty smart to me.

"But I'm still homesick," she said. "I go home whenever I can, and it's so much fun. We get in our umiaks and go on picnics and we have dances and most of all we just gossip. But when I'm home I miss Anchorage, getting dressed up and going out, and my job. I love my job. I'm caught between home and here. All I can do is just keep trying to be happy wherever I am, and learn to accept it if I can't."

Sometime later I was talking with Ronald Senungetuk, a young artist and professor at the University of Alaska. Ron, from the Eskimo village of Wales on the Seward Peninsula, had also attended college Outside, and abroad as a Fulbright scholar. He had started out, he admitted with a little sneer, using the hand-and-eye coordination with which so many of his people are gifted to fashion "cute little Eskimos" for the tourist trade. But then he'd decided to hell with it. Art is art, and he was going to do what he wanted to do.

"I want to be proud, to have an identity," he said. He was intense, almost belligerent. "This is what I want my people to have—not the white man's cars and beer and TV."

The Eskimos have been described as a race in transition. Living their lives, simultaneously, today, are the walrus hunter back on St. Lawrence, Linda in her stewardess's cap, dreaming of gossip and giggles at seal-skinning time, Ron, who thinks he has found himself through art, and Willie Hensley, whom we met earlier, with his political office, his business connections, his blonde wife, and a growing dissatisfaction with the remoteness and squalor in his native Kotzebue. A race in transition . . .

The Great Land is itself in transition, and so are *all* its people. Governor Miller, in opening the $900 million lease sale, remarked that no matter what happened, the state "would never be the same." Dr. Frank Fraser Darling, the eminent English scholar, told the Alaska Science Conference, "you Alaskans are faced with the important task of learning to be rich."

For even if no icebreaking tankers, underwater tankers, or pipeline would ever deliver North Slope oil to the consumer, even if the land freeze would continue and prevent further exploration of potential fields, the Great Land already had its $900 million and the Alaskans had to decide what to do with it. That decision would be made in quiet, scenic little Juneau by the 60 elected legislators—lawyers and bankers, fishermen and bush pilots—in the 1970 legislative session beginning January 15. I didn't envy them their responsibility, but I looked forward to the session. Sixty people arguing about what to do with a billion dollars—what a bowl game!

The buildup had begun before the lease sale itself. On internal issues concerning the 300,000 people of the state you can get 300,000 viewpoints. On the disposition of the $900 million opinions ranged from shooting the works to not spending a penny, not even the interest. In my own private poll, education was the commodity most Alaskans were willing to buy. Even those who agreed on that priority didn't all agree on who should benefit: The kids from native villages being shipped out of the state to Indian schools, or the kids in sophisticated Anchorage going to school in double shifts.

Different groups called in different experts from the Outside for advice. The state was crawling with men wearing dark suits with narrow lapels and carrying briefcases. The Department of Natural Resources had already entrusted the Bank of America with the initial safekeeping of the lease sale funds, paying the bank its normal fees for transactions made. For further advice Governor Miller brought in Blyth & Company, a national investment firm, at $8333 a month. The legislative council, composed of members of both the Alaska Senate and House, hired Walter J. Levy of New York, the oil economist, for a two-year period at about $50,000 a year.

Governor Miller then invited the Stanford Research Institute to come in and, for a fee of $179,700, give advice on what to do with the money the other advisers were advising on. The legislative council brought in the Brookings Institution for $60,000 for the same purpose. "We are being asked to create a new civilization," was the way one of the Brookings people put it.

The Outside experts brought in more Outside experts, held lengthy conferences and seminars and released their findings in lengthy reports that occasioned many lengthy comments. I'll give you a condensation: The state ought to spend its money wisely for good things.

Some of the most intriguing proposals came from forthright individuals speaking for themselves. On the one extreme Cliff Burglin, the Fairbanks lease broker, said that the $900 million nest egg, plus additional money from future lease sales and royalties, should be entrusted to the local banks to finance business projects in the state until a total of $3 billion was invested. Then and only then should Alaska start buying yummy things for its people.

On the other end, Mike Gravel, as befitted a young man who took a dream to the Great Land and brought it back to the U.S. Senate a reality, proposed bold new concepts.

"We've got monumental problems in Alaska—education, unemployment, basic community services. We're not the only state in the union with problems, but we're the only state with money in the bank to solve those problems. We're the richest state in the nation; our people are the richest in the world. Our biggest problem isn't how much to stash away, how much interest to bargain for, but to get going on developing programs for our people, today. We ought to get started right now on making Alaska a model society."

Mike's ten-year program covered the board, from sewage disposal in Seward to telephones for Tuntatuliak. What I found most dramatic and imaginative, however, was his educational program. What Mike wants to do, and he has assembled the facts and figures to prove it can be done, is educate the kids of Alaska by television bounced off a satellite. As long as Alaska has only scratched the surface of communications anyway, why not plunge directly into televised contact?

The same leap-frogging idea should be applied to transportation, Mike said. The Great Land has already progressed directly from the sled runner to the airfoil. Why regress to the wheel? A truly modern system of air transportation covering the state would cost far less and be far more efficient than a ground transportation system. You could pour a billion dollars into highways through the hills and muskeg west and north of Anchorage-Fairbanks and still not have anything. Jumping directly from bush plane to cargo plane is really the only intelligent way to transport consumer goods to the outlying reaches of Alaska and to return the produce of its land and water. They've been flying fish back from the Bristol Bay region for years.

Mike has talked to me for hours about his ideas for jumping Alaska into the eighth decade of the twentieth century, and he convinced me that with both the technological expertise and the money available these bold, science-fiction sounding proposals were really more practical than gradual and traditional methods.

Many Alaskans agreed with him in principle. Ed Merdes, for example, though not prepared to hoist a satellite immediately, spoke of the $900 million nest egg in terms of creativity and advanced thinking. "I'm elated and excited over it. Think of the challenges! Think of the rewards!"

Even spokesmen of the opposite extreme, men like the conservative-and-proud-of-it delegate from Anchorage, Tom Finks, were in favor of holding onto the major part of the nest egg for meaningful purposes rather than nickeling it away in piecemeal projects.

Listening to talk like this I was getting carried away with rosy dreams of great new happenings in the Great Land. A couple of attractive females, even before the 1970 legislature convened, burst my bubble. First was Brideen Milner, the lady banker. "Don't expect great forward steps immediately," she said. "No businessman in the state truly comprehends what all this means to us. They're all in a state of shock. Until they wake up, and God knows how long that will be, Alaska is going to go forward like walking on thin ice."

Delegate Genie Chance, an exquisitely groomed blonde who achieved international fame during the earthquake by single-handedly holding down Anchorage's short-wave communications with the outside world for 59 hours, predicted the pragmatic politics of the forthcoming legislative session. She was already sad about what she knew was going to happen, but resigned and understanding.

"Listen," she said, "I don't know any member of the legislature who is not aware of the great opportunity we have to make our state a utopia. I think what most of us would like to do is to invest the entire sum and use the proceeds for the generations of Alaskans—*all* Alaskans—to come. But do you realize the political situation here this year? For half of the senators, who serve a four-year term, and for all of the delegates, whose term is two years, this is an election year. Can you imagine the pressures that will be brought to bear on us? Every community in this state is in dire need of basic community services. The property taxpayer is already burdened beyond his capacity to pay, even without the demands of the rapid growth we are experiencing. Our constituents have every justification in pressuring us for local relief, things as basic as law enforcement and schools. Most if not all of us agree that we must do something about education. But if we lift the lid off this steaming pot to pull out one chunk of meat, how are we going to put it back on again? We don't want to pass pork-barrel legislation, but as the pressures build up we're going to find ourselves rationalizing that if we don't our constituents will replace us with people who will. They're already talking about the forthcoming session as the $900 million legislature—it couldn't come at a worse possible time."

And it was quite a legislature. At first glance the Democrats had a majority in the House, 22-18—but seven of them had joined with the Republicans to keep their own majority leader from being elected speaker. In the Senate the Republicans had a one-man majority, but its 11 members could hardly be counted on to vote together on anything. Added to the political mish-mash was the geographic makeup of the legislature. Thirty-one members came from Anchorage and Fairbanks: that left just exactly nine to represent the rest of the state.

It was also a gubernatorial election year in 1970, and Keith Miller was running scared. When the session began, on January 15, Howard Pollock, Alaska's only Congressman, had not for-mally declared, but it was an open secret that he was going to run in the Republican primary for the gubernatorial nomination. "I'm not only going to run," he told me, "I'm going to win."

With Howard's hot breath on his neck, Keith Miller had to play it safe. His budget proposal to the $900 million legislature was a cautious casserole of a little something for everybody. He would set up a $500 million untouchable fund, deposit $100 million in state banks for home and development loans in Alaska, and hold $300 million in surplus. But at the same time he proposed increasing the operating budget from $153 mil-lion to $242 million, and it seemed unlikely that the money could be raised without dipping into the lease sale fund.

Having chosen this course, he could hardly go along with Mike Gravel's ten-year program for Utopia, when Mike pre-sented his plan for a model society to a joint session of the legis-lature. Miller dismissed it as being straight out of Alice in Won-derland.

The legislative council made its proposal, too. It was based partially on the Brookings recommendations, with anti-execu-tive partisanship thrown in. Both Senate and House set up spe-cial committees to study both programs all over again. Ron Rettig, the Anchorage banker, attended 40 meetings of the House committee in ten weeks "and we didn't accomplish a thing until the last three or four meetings." Senators and delegates alike were flopping around aimlessly like dying fish.

They were also marooned in Juneau. An Alaskan legislator's salary when the session began was $6000 and the price of one round-trip ticket to the capital. There is no ground transporta-tion to Juneau from anywhere, and, what with the fog and the rain that swooshes across the airport, sometimes you can't get there, or leave there, at all. The sleepy, by-passed little town is a lovely and picturesque place to visit by tourist boat or airline tour for about two days in the spring and summer, but longer than that—well, there must be a reason why the bars stay open until 5 A.M. To move the capital away from Juneau is one of the perennial Alaskan proposals.

As the deliberations droned on, past the estimated three months' duration, past four months, almost five, no one had to look for an argument. In the closing days the debates came close to being brawls. Finally, at 3:35 A.M. Sunday, June 7, the 147th day, the last bill was passed. The final budget was $316.8 million, but, what with money being appropriated for agencies that were not set up, and the governor's vetoes over other expenditures, it would take a computer to figure out exactly what the money went for. Certainly many features of the grand design of the Brookings seminars got lost in the pork barrel. When the ten Fairbanks legislators returned home, for example, one chortled, "We didn't bring home the bacon, we brought back the whole hog."

The 21 Anchorage members could have said the same thing. Even the nine remaining legislators, representing all the rest of the Great Land, carried back a pork chop or two to their constituents.

Several bond issues were authorized. The state went a long way toward improving education, both in the urban communities and in the bush; a teacher fresh out of college could start at $10,-000 a year. Steps were taken to make it easier to get home mortgages. In spite of the screams against the ecologists, the legislature passed a bill restricting oil activity in the Bristol Bay area, the Great Land's great fishery, although Miller vetoed it after everybody had gone home. An environmental quality control commission was set up. Ed Merdes sent me a copy of the bill proposing it and scribbled in the margin: "Boo—this is the most stringent purported regulation and state control of proposed development anywhere in the free world let alone in the entire U.S.A."

Conservation groups had one lobbyist in Juneau; the oil industry sent in 17 to pick up the legislators' bar checks. Still the legislature raised the severance tax to a maximum of four percent on natural gas and 8 percent on oil, figures generally in keeping with other oil-producing states. As one legislator explained, "the oil people are going to control the legislature in the future and if we don't raise the tax now we'll never get it."

The Alaska legislature, like the state itself, would never be the same again. The 1970 session, in effect, drove several legislators from office. Even with the new $9000 salary, they were crippled financially to the point that they had to get out of politics to make up for the five months they had lost. It would be some time before history would decide whether their contribution was worth the sacrifice.

HAPPY ENDING?

Jerome Weidman once published a collection of short stories called *The Captain's Tiger*. The tiger was an English Army orderly who liked stories to come out happily in the end, and Weidman obliged him. I go along with that; I like happy endings, too. I also like Alaska and Alaskans, every damn one of them, petroleum products and the men who provide them, clear streams and clean air and wildlife and the people who fight for them.

I also like you, the readers who have stuck with me this far. You are entitled to the truth. Can I provide a happy ending to all these conflicts raging in the Great Land and still play fair with you? I may be blinded by the beauty of the aurora-illuminated snows of the North Slope, but I honestly think I can.

Because I believe that the great Alaska oil rush has marked a turning point in the history of our planet, a point where mankind, in the words of Wally Hickel, begins using without abusing.

Wally Hickel himself is a good starting point for a happy ending. During the most frantic period of oil exploration in Alaska, the stocky, strong-jawed ex-fighter burst on the national scene like a wolverine. To many Americans he epitomized the human predator, the voracious entrepreneur who would despoil the country for private gain. Two years later he had become, to many of those who originally opposed him, the Polaris of the Nixon cabinet. As Secretary of the Interior, he was the chief architect of the environmental program first revealed in the President's 1970 State of the Union message; it was referred to as the Hickel plan. He stopped work on the Miami jet airport that many conservationists figured would cause extreme damage to the Florida Everglades. He brought punitive action against operators of offshore drilling platforms in the Gulf of Mexico on grounds that negligence had led to the big oil spill that caused extreme damage to aquatic life in the spring of 1970. He took steps against the developers in the Santa Barbara channel. He delayed the Trans-Alaska Pipeline. He was supposed to be in the hip pocket of the oil industry; gradually it developed that it was Wally's pocket that was stuffed with people dedicated to conserving our natural resources.

Then, following the Cambodian incursion and the clamor of dissent that mushroomed from young Americans, came his famous letter to President Nixon in which he begged the President to establish better communications with the young people of the country. He admitted on national television that his own warm relationship and open communication with his two oldest sons had strong influence on both his thinking and his actions.

In November the President demanded Hickel's resignation. Back in Anchorage for Christmas, Wally told his friends, "I don't know what I'll get for Christmas, but I got a goose for Thanksgiving." In the meantime he and Mayor John Lindsay of New York City had gotten together. There's a combination for you.

Some of my Hickel-hating friends in both Alaska and the oil

industry told me that Wally's actions were insincere and ex-
pedient, that he was out to win public support for a big political
future. Even if they were right, isn't it a healthy indication when
a man as smart as Hickel chooses as campaign planks conservation and communication with young people? It took Alaska to
develop Wally Hickel.

And though concerned individuals have been fighting against
the depredations of mankind for a long long time, it took the
State of Alaska to provide the great battlefield that may well
become the turning point of the war. When, in the history of
mankind, has a project of such magnitude as the Trans-Alaska
Pipeline been delayed by concern for the environment? I feel
for those friends of mine who have suffered financially because
of the delay in getting the Great Land's great resource to market,
but even they must admit that the confrontation was long over-
due.

It could not have occurred at a more dramatic time and place.
Despite the wails of frustration from many Alaskans, few would
actually submit to the plunder of their state. You have to be an
Alaskan, or travel extensively throughout the state's vastness,
to realize the insignificance of the 15 square miles the pipeline
represents; it's a piece of string on a golf course. Alaska has
been through this battle before, with timber, with salmon, with
gold, and the Great Land has swallowed up its plunderers.

The story of Alaskan salmon alone has been one of greed
conquered, however slowly and unsteadily, by conservation.
The proliferation of cruelly efficient nets that extended far out
from the beaches and prevented almost every fish from its desperate instinct-driven attempt to reach the spawning beds almost doomed both species and industry. But finally the fish were
given a chance, and in the summer of 1970 the greatest salmon
run ever recorded brought the strange hardship of overabundance
to many Alaskan fishermen. In the Bristol Bay area, in late
June, overstocked canneries had to turn away fishermen with
their catch. With hungry people all over the world, men had to

dump the results of their investment and labor on the beach to rot. The fish permitted to proceed unmolested to spawn future crops were so numerous that to observers from planes overhead they formed long dark ribbons in the rivers.

The balance of resources in this big and bountiful region tends to check selfish excess. Alaska is fully aware of the monetary value of her aquatic resources, and its fish and game department has developed the expertise to preserve it. Its multimillion-dollar cash crop depends upon unpolluted streams in which fish can spawn. What other state legislature would pass legislation restricting oil exploration in as huge an area as that surrounding Bristol Bay? Even though the governor vetoed the bill, the fact that it was passed is an indication that future exploration and development will be under strict scrutiny to preserve the purity of Alaskan streams, for salmon if not for man.

Conservationist pressure came as a shock to the first wave of pipeliners, who have been generally accustomed to buying their way across the countryside. To their credit, however, most oil executives have accepted the invitation to be good citizens. They have contributed to the development of concepts and hardware of strikingly innovative nature, many of which may be put to good use in other parts of the world.

One small example is a new method of sewage treatment. With all the animals running around loose in Alaska, and with its very immensity and sparse population, little thought was given in the past to the disposal of human waste. What's one more dung heap? But as TAPS management foresaw large construction camps dotted along the route, it encouraged University of Alaska engineers to develop a simple and ingenious system. They came up with a circular trough, several hundred feet in circumference, in which raw sewage flows round and round under pressure, bubbling and churning and turning and aerating itself. With this continuing supply of oxygen the happy little bacteria can gorge themselves to bursting on the plentiful food, breaking it down and purifying it in nature's own way. The runoff is cleaner than state standards require. The simple process will doubtless be used on other jobs in other areas. Some people in the Lower 48 probably wish the community upstream used it.

This is but one minor example of the new thinking in Alaska, in the oil company board rooms, in Wall Street: expenditures of time, money, and expertise not grudgingly approved but actively fostered in the new era of ecology. In the plunder of the planet man has been the enemy. In Alaska in 1970 the capped wells, the idle construction equipment, the silent rusting piles of pipe gave proof that we're beginning to hold the line against ourselves. The next step is cooperation: the use of our resources coupled with the conservation of the land, air, water, and life that provide them all in the first place.

So many projects and studies to this end are underway in Alaska that the scientific journals are having difficulty keeping up with them. The Great Land has become the Arctic laboratory of the world. (Oh, to be a young scientist or engineer; Alaska is where the action is!) One application of recent and current studies could be to provide a new home for the expanding population of the world. As a scientist at the University of Alaska said, "Man has only two places left to go, the sea and the northlands, and we haven't got gills."

A glance at a map shows vast, unpopulated, undeveloped reaches not only throughout the whole of Alaska, but across Canada and Siberia as well. The development of the oil fields in Alaska has proved to many newcomers what the people of Fairbanks have known for years: Life under the northern lights can be rich, rewarding, and beautiful. A third of the way around the top of the world and 300 miles to the north, almost on the same latitude as Prudhoe Bay, 125,000 people live in comparative comfort in the Siberian city of Norilsk. They move about town in underground passageways; they have an Olympic-size swimming pool. If you think that people would never live that far north and under such conditions, just remember that 2000 years ago the Roman historian Tacitus said the same thing about France.

By the time surplus population spills into the sub-Arctic, there'll be plenty of food available for them. Many vegetables grow beautifully in the long days of summer; the 70-pound cabbages in the Matanuska Valley just north of Anchorage are legendary.

Grain has been another matter; Alaska grows only about a tenth of what its few humans and livestock consume. But serendipity, and an agronomist named James A. Harding, are changing that. Jim knew very well that the lack of adequate rainfall in central Alaska made annual barley crops uncertain at best. By the time the snow melted and the soil could be plowed and planted the dry season was on. But he kept poking around and one day, just outside of Fairbanks, he noticed some healthy sprouts sticking their heads out of an abandoned field.

What had happened? Well, it turned out that the previous year the owner of the field had been so disgusted with the crop that he made only a half-hearted attempt to harvest it. A lot of grains were left. That winter dogsled races were held on the field, and the spectators milled around, stomping the grains down into the ground. That spring as the sun moved northward the snows melted and the grain germinated in the warming, still-moist ground. Up popped the barley shoots.

Jim ran to his friend Ed Merdes with his discovery, and Ed, who can get enthusiastic about the sun coming up in the morning, nearly went out of his mind. He interested Arco (fertilizer) and John Deere (farm equipment) in his new project. Under recent and more practical legislation providing for land development, he and Jim acquired some thousands of acres on the Tanana River and began clearing. They sowed their barley in the fall and sure enough, next spring green shoots replaced the white snow.

Much as Ed and Jim like barley, pigs like it better. They eat it, grow, and produce more pigs—up to 15 per litter. It's more efficient to raise pigs indoors anyway, so they don't care whether they're close to the Arctic Circle; they probably don't even know it as they chomp away. Ed and Jim see a great new market for their snow-planted barley and juicy pork at much cheaper prices for their fellow Alaskans. From barley for pigs they can go in several directions, perhaps other grains for cattle (ah, fresh milk!) or for humans.

The new interest in Alaska has had an influence on rapport and cooperation between the people in the outlying areas of the two great competing powers, the U.S.A. and the U.S.S.R. While Washington and Moscow have been spending trillions of dollars and rubles in sophisticated weapons of attack and defense, in Alaska and Siberia people have been waving at each other across the 2-mile strait that separates them. America's defense on Little Diomede Island, across the international dateline from the Soviet Union's Big Diomede, consists of a half-dozen Eskimo National Guardsmen armed with three M-14 rifles.

From Anchorage non-stop flights of a dozen airlines reach out to cities both in Europe and the Orient. It's ironic that not until after the oil rush could travelers between Anchorage and Fairbanks and New York (and Honolulu) enjoy the same non-stop service as that between Anchorage and a dozen European cities, and Tokyo.

Tourists were all over the place, drawn by the fervor of interest in Alaska. Television specials and newspaper and magazine stories on the Great Land came pouring out. During the period the plots of two comic strips—Mark Trail and Steve Canyon—were based on Alaska happenings. More cars and campers bored holes through the dust of the Alaska highway. Other cruise ships joined the Alaska state ferries. Anchorage became a convention city.

Beginning in the summer of 1970, if you wanted to visit the North Slope all you needed was the money for a round-trip ticket; Fat Albert was open to the public. There were even tourist accommodations available. Wien had to add another flight.

But what about all that oil? Leaving aside for the moment

the problem of transporting it to market, let's consider its impact on that market. During the Seventies more oil will be consumed in the world than in all the years since the Civil War. In 1980 the world—and America is by far the largest consumer—will be using twice as much oil as in 1970.

All this oil has got to come from somewhere. Since the Alaska discovery, other potential fields have been explored, but the Alaskan field is rich, ready, and right now. It is in America. We don't have to fight for it, intrigue for it, or line foreign pockets for it. It has a vital bearing on national security: directly, because it can be used by and for our armed forces; indirectly, because it can relieve the dependence of the free world on the oil-rich hot spots of the world like the Middle East.

Whether Alaskan oil can overcome the intricate price-fixing stratagems of the industry and Government and reduce the current cost to the consumer is dubious. But it's positive that without it, as other reserves decrease, the price will go up.

Though oil has been the central character of the Alaskan drama, natural gas is waiting to come on stage. The shortage of natural gas is crucial. You have no trouble buying gasoline for your car, but as the Seventies began large consumers of natural gas, especially the power companies in the Eastern industrial corridor, were beginning to get panicky. Hold on, fellows, relief is on the way. Alaska has plenty of natural gas. As with oil, the problem is getting it to market. Several transmission companies have begun working on gas pipeline projects across Canada from the producing regions of the Mackenzie delta in Canada and the North Slope of Alaska to markets in southern Canada and the United States. Earliest predictions for Arctic gas in midcontinent furnaces are for the year 1975.

With these impending crises in energy, it seems incomprehensible that North America will continue to be deprived of the Arctic portion of its life force, oil and gas. Senator Henry Jackson of Washington, a friend of Alaska since territorial days and a reasonable, well-informed, and responsible citizen, told me with confidence, "I have such faith in both American technology and American concern for our environment that I know a mutually satisfactory solution will be worked out." In short, Alaskan oil will reach the Lower 48.

On the assumption that in the mid-1970s North Slope oil will be reaching its market, whether by pipeline, icebreaking tanker, submarine tanker, or all three, let's postulate now on what this will mean to the Great Land itself.

In money alone, the maximum capacity of the pipeline, two million barrels a day, could bring in close to a half-billion dollars a year to the state treasury.

"What we have here in Alaska," said Cliff Burglin, the Fairbanks lease broker who knows the petroleum resources as well as any man, "is infinite money. We have enough resources here to take care of everybody's pet project. The problem will be to spend it all. It's like me trying to drink up the Cheena River. We've got enough to support the nation, not just Alaska. Hell, here we are worrying about native claims and how to spend a billion dollars when we've got enough oil to pay the national debt."

Big oil resources provide a two-stage paradoxical bonanza. The development stage is an employment boom, with riggers and equipment operators and pipeline welders receiving salaries of $20,000 a year and more. According to guarantees already made, many of the recipients of these salaries will be the Alaskan natives.

On the completion of the big construction projects, employment dries up, but money continues to pour in in the form of royalties and taxes. What formerly benefited several thousand individuals directly, and many more indirectly, now benefits the entire citizenry through the state.

Bruce Kendall, a former state representative and owner of the Roosevelt Hotel in Anchorage, collared me one morning and started spouting figures on the advantages of oil to Alaska. The economics of oil in Alaska meant a great deal more coming from

Bruce. He, and the Roosevelt, are so typically Alaskan; that's why I stay there. The hotel's checkroom, for example, has no key; when you go off on a trip you simply put your stuff in there and when you get back you walk in and take it out. The checkroom—I don't know why it's called a checkroom, there are no checks—is customarily filled with duffel bags, tool kits, surveying equipment, cardboard suitcases tied with cord. One day I noticed a pair of binoculars, a rifle, a motorcycle wheel, and, all by itself on a shelf, one toothbrush.

Bruce set out to prove that Alaska could be oil rich and still be the same. He noted the other major Alaskan sources of income and the number of employees: Federal projects, 17,000; military, 25,000; fishing, 23,000. None come close in capital investment to the amount spent by the oil industry: including the pipeline, three and a half billion dollars. Yet, with production in full swing, the oil industry would employ at most 6000 people. Those 6000 people would generate many times the income of mass industry, such as steel or automotive manufacture.

"That's why," he said, "we can have our bonanza without crowding. We'll never have a Lake Erie in Alaska. We'll be rich, but we'll still be a wilderness, a wilderness with all its open spaces and rugged beauty."

With oil on stream, it will not take Alaska long to build its nest egg back to a billion dollars and have another half billion coming in yearly—without necessarily increasing its population beyond natural growth.

Comparative figures for the nation's most populous state, California, with 70 times as many people, would be $70 billion on hand, and a yearly income of $35 billion from oil alone. Ask the governor, or the mayor of Los Angeles, how he'd like to have that kind of budget to play with.

And Alaska has the equivalent. This is not an oversimplification; it's an understatement. We are talking here only about the North Slope. Geologists say that Alaska has 14 other areas with a petroleum potential, not including the proved Cook Inlet field. "There'll be land opportunities in Alaska for the next 3000 years," Cliff Burglin says. (Tip: he's looking toward Crystal Bay and the Gulf of Alaska, and the western part of the North Slope.) Nor does this include the locatable minerals. Cliff casually tossed out the idea that digging the pipeline would discover enough mineral deposits to pay for itself.

With all the wealth in hand, let alone that in geological speculation, the ideas of practical dreamers like Senator Mike Gravel don't seem so much out of Alice in Wonderland after all. Educating youngsters in one-room schools in the bush by satellite television is still on the horizon, but Mike has influenced the commercial application of satellite TV to the point that Alaskans now see the major events—Superbowl, Apollo 14—along with the rest of the country.

And the state has already begun a major overhaul of primary education along conventional lines. It is increasing the number of secondary schools, for example. Kids in their early teens from tiny native villages will still have to leave home for a high school education, but at least the time will soon come when they will be able to stay in Alaska rather than be herded off to Oklahoma.

Another result of Gravel's Washington muscle was a $40 million Federal project to build a mile of road in every native village. If you have ever seen or walked on a road that may not seem such a big deal; to people who have never traveled on anything but packed snow, mud, or perhaps a boardwalk, a road is a luxury. One mile connects the heart of a village with its landing strip.

The 1970 elections may have hastened the settlement of the native land claims. I was surprised that Keith Miller, having served during Alaska's most eventful year and beaten off Pollock's challenge for the Republican nomination, was defeated. ("I was a little surprised myself," Mike Gravel admitted.) It may have been that Keith had played it too safe.

Bill Egan, Alaska's first governor who returned to Juneau after a four-year Hickel-caused hiatus, had the solid core of the

Democratic party behind him; of the four gubernatorial elections in Alaska's short state history, he has won three. He also had the ebullient newcomer, Red Boucher, with him as secretary of state (lieutenant governor). They had promised a "flexible" attitude toward native claims and piled up a big majority in the bush.

"The native land claims should be viewed not as an obstacle, but as an opportunity," Egan said in his inaugural address. "It will open the door to full participation by all of us in the economic, political and social life of the state. For this state cannot survive with half of its people enslaved by poverty."

Whatever the details of the settlements of the native claims, today's native children can look forward to longer and healthier lives of greater opportunity on land that is their own. They'll still have their wilderness to hunt and fish in, but won't it be nice to come back to a well-built house, toast their toes by an oil-burning stove, and watch the big dogsled race on color TV?

The curtain is rising on the third act of the Alaskan drama. On the immense stage we see the Alaskans still stumbling around in the shock of sudden wealth. Further development of the action is up to the characters themselves. Will the Great Land remain only the Great Land, which in itself is plenty good enough for many of its people, or will there be a smashing ending—Utopia?

Either way, huge chunks of the land itself will remain the same. Even if and when small cities develop over the state in the next century or two, enough land has already been locked up in the form of natural parks and ranges to ensure a continuing population of wildlife and a wilderness haven for the civilization-sated segment of the human population to visit for temporary peace in a world that has not changed and never will. From the national parks and monuments in the south and southeast to the wildlife range on the Arctic Ocean, the State of Alaska already contains a total of areas comprising 190,000 square miles. That's a combined area equal in size to the states of New York, Illinois, and Idaho for animals and people to roam around in. The Chugach State Park just outside Anchorage contains 800 square miles. Don't worry about the land and its creatures.

But what about the people? If, as is quite possible, the population of Alaska multiplies several times over the next thousand years or so, will the new breed of Alaskans lose their warm characteristics of enthusiastic love of life, absence of pretense and sham, and open friendliness? Will there come a time when an Alaskan will not stop on a road to help his fellow man? I don't believe it. Even during the period of xenophobia that ushered in the 1970s, when Alaskans felt everybody from the Outside was against them, I had trouble repressing a smile at their warm perversity. I bet a hundred Alaskans have grabbed my arm and bitched to me about the damn Outsiders—but it never seemed to occur to them that I was one myself. Finally I came to realize that to them I was *not* an Outsider, that I had been accepted in the club. For this is the world's most nonexclusive organization. All it takes to belong is an open-minded visit, a handshake, and willingness to be friends. That's all I had to offer, and I don't think I've got an enemy in the whole state.

Lowell Thomas, Jr., possessor of a famous name and a good income from photographing and producing nature films, could afford to live anywhere. He took his family to Alaska through choice, for the enjoyment of life. What triggered the decision was the air traffic and polluted air of the New York area; he had a single-engine Cessna and loved to fly it.

Lowell and his wife, Tay, and their two children have a big rambling log house on the outskirts of Anchorage. Ski trails wander through the backyard. If there's an idyllic existence this side of Bali Hai, the Thomases have it. The whole family loves to ski, and Lowell extends the season through the summer, landing on glaciers high in the nearby mountains for a day's run. The kids skate in the winter, not only on the neighborhood rinks, but on the icy streets to and from them. In the summer the family piles into their camper and takes off, today stretching their sleeping bags out at the foot of a glacier, tomorrow sharing the choice fishing spots with the big black bears. Both Thomases and bears maintain a live and let live policy that neither extends to the leaping salmon, grayling, or rainbow trout.

Like most of the Alaskans we met, however, the Thomases do not merely take from the land they love; they contribute. Lowell is a state senator and concerned with the affairs of both city and state. In addition to keeping house, which includes waxing the floors, Tay writes books, is an elected member of the city school board, and is most active in a dozen civic organizations. Anchorage is a buzzing center for social life and cultural activities. After listening to Tay talk about life in Alaska, Bonnie was ready to move to Anchorage.

Alaskans take themselves as they are, and they offer themselves to you in the same way. One Saturday afternoon I dropped in on Mike Gravel for a long chat in his Washington office, and my wife, Bonnie, went out to see his wife, Rita, in their new home.

Naturally Rita offered Bonnie coffee—every Alaskan offers you coffee. The senator's wife served it in mismatched brown mugs on a silver tray. "That's Alaska," Rita laughed.

In Anchorage, on nights when I didn't have anything planned, I usually stopped by the Anchorage Westward's Bar, always picking up an interesting conversation, then went over to the Rice Bowl. For a time the bartender at the Rice Bowl was Walter Woo, an American-educated chemical engineer who had a prosperous import-export business in Hong Kong. When he visited his brother George, who owned the Rice Bowl, he helped out behind the bar as a matter of course.

The Rice Bowl is a friendly and popular place and I met half of Anchorage there, as well as travelers from most of the world. One of my Rice Bowl friends was Ron Van Sickle, a slender man with a trim mustache whose specialty as a realtor was in arranging for people coming to or leaving Alaska to trade homes with people Outside with the same problem. Ron had an Appaloosa horse named Thunderchief, and he liked to take off with Thunderchief for days at a time, riding up into the lush valleys of the Chugach Range, where the grass reached up to the stirrups. Just 20 miles from bustling Anchorage he would be in another world, a world filled with the song of countless birds, populated with moose, bears, wolves, foxes, marmots, porcupines, beavers. Ron and Thunderchief lived with all of them in peace. Ron carried a rifle along with his bedroll, but he'd never fired it.

When the Atomic Energy Commission announced plans to detonate a device on Amchitka Island in the Aleutians, many of us, including geologists, were concerned over the possibility that it would trigger another earthquake in this unstable region. A lot of people, remembering the 1964 earthquake, made plans to get out of the city on the day of the blast. I sure did. Ron planned to take Thunderchief and his Japanese girl friend and ride up in the hills. When the day came, however, he couldn't do it.

"Suppose we were on a mountain and looked down and saw the city disappear," he said. "It would hurt too much. Thunderchief and I decided to stay with our friends."

Another of my Alaskan friends is Ky Kozinsky, a crusty old foreman for the state school system. I hadn't made hotel reservations for the week of the lease sale and Ed Merdes asked Ky to put me up in his little bachelor apartment. The man had never seen me before but he gave me a home for a week. He never smiled and talked in curt gruff grunts. One night I came in before he did and saw, on the kitchen table, a bowl of peaches. I ate two and drank a glass of milk. When Ky came in I told him, with some embarrassment, that I had helped myself to his peaches. He glowered at me. He looked furious. I began wondering where I would go that night.

"You don't have to tell me what you eat in my house," Ky finally growled. "You're my brother."

I'd never had a brother before, and suddenly, there in Ky Kozinsky's little kitchen, there in Alaska, I realized I had not just one, not just Ky, but many brothers. In the Great Land, where the aurora lights up the sky and the snow beneath, where the temperatures drop to the minus 60s and a minor mishap

—a sprained ankle, a flat tire—can mean slow death in the howling snow-filled wind, where earthquakes rock the land and floods wash it away; where even the tide of riches brings problems that tax human ingenuity, intelligence, and tolerance, man is reduced to a puny animal indeed, and only through cooperation and concern can he survive, much less enjoy the bounties of this rich and beautiful, still wild frontier. In the Great Land all men are brothers.

Index

ACV, Air-cushioned vehicle: *See* Hovercraft.

235